ost Gonzo Band / Jerry Jeff Walker • Willie Nelson / Tracy Nelson • Amazing Rhythm Aces / Gove Scrivenor • Earl Scruggs
e Dirt Band / Kiwi • Larry Gatlin / Alex Harvey • Willis Alan Ramsey / Roy Buchanan • Michael Murphey • Steve Goodman
/ Gove • Johnny Rodriguez / Linda Hargrove • John Hartford / The Dillards • Jesse Win
ost Gonzo Band • Norton Buffalo • John McEuen with Vassar Clements, Byron Berline, a
bone / Steve Fromholz • Tom Waits • Delbert McClinton / Cate Brothers • Pure Prairie League / Bobby Bare
h Brown • Don Williams / Janie Fricke • Songwriters' Special with Willie Nelson, Floyd Tillman, Red Lane, Hank Cochran,
ountain Boys / Uncle Walt's Band • Joe Ely / Jerry Jeff Walker • Hank Williams Jr. / Shake Russell Band • Johnny Gimble
Marty Robbins • Carl Perkins / Joe Sun • Mel Tillis / Gail Davies • The Charlie Daniels Band • Bobby Bare / Lacy J. Dalton
a • David Grisman Quintet / "Mandolin Special" with Tiny Moore, Jethro Burns, and Johnny Gimble • Bill Monroe and the
e, Hank Cochran, Don Gant, Rock Killough, Sonny Throckmorton, and Whitey Shafer • Charley Pride / Razzy Bailey • Michael
ell • Kris Kristofferson • Jerry Reed / Chet Atkins • Johnny Lee / Charly McClain • Willie Nelson / Guy Clark • Merle
rs / George Strait • Don McLean / Terri Gibbs • Roy Clark / The Geezinslaws • Pete Fountain / Jazzmanian Devil • George
ers' Special with Butch Hancock, Townes Van Zandt, David Halley and Jimmie Dale Gilmore • Roy Orbison • Songwriters'
ie Fricke / B.J. Thomas • Frizzell and West / Con Hunley • Michael Murphey / Gary P. Nunn • Rosanne Cash / Steve Wariner
les / Lee Greenwood • Jerry Lee Lewis • Freddie Powers with Willie Nelson and Merle Haggard • Gary Morris / Gail Davies
itt / The Le Roi Brothers with Ray Campi and Sleepy La Beef • John Anderson / Eliza Gilkyson • George Strait / The Kendalls
s Playboys • Neil Young and the International Harvesters • Exile / The Maines Brothers with Terry Allen • Waylon Jennings
ohnson • The Dirt Band / Steve Goodman Tribute • Juice Newton / Mark Gray • Larry Gatlin / Nanci Griffith • Freddie
is / The Geezinslaws • George Jones / Vern Gosdin • John Schneider / Southern Pacific • Tanya Tucker / Sawyer Brown
te Wolf • Louise Mandrell / Mel McDaniel • George Strait / Dwight Yoakam • Legends of Bluegrass with Jim & Jesse and
' Special with Emmylou Harris, Rosanne Cash, Gail Davies, Lacy J. Dalton, Mary Ann Kennedy, and Pam Rose • Austin City
y Jeff Walker, Gary P. Nunn, and The Lost Gonzo Band • Ronnie Milsap • Steve Wariner / Restless Heart • Brenda Lee
nny Gimble, Butch Thompson, and Peter Ostroushko • Randy Travis / Kathy Mattea • Johnny Cash with June Carter and The
d the Howlers • Lyle Lovett / Judy Rodman • Riders in the Sky / Hot Rize • Michael Martin Murphey / Marty Stuart • The
• Larry Gatlin and The Gatlin Brothers / Holly Dunn • John Prine / Asleep at the Wheel • k.d. lang and the reclines / Foster
Smith • Ricky Skaggs / The Whites • The Dirt Band / New Grass Revival • Gene Watson / Moe Bandy • Bellamy Brothers
Emmylou Harris / Nanci Griffith and The Blue Moon Orchestra • Delbert McClinton / The Crickets • Dwight Yoakam / Patty
owcase with Robert Earl Keen Jr., Rosie Flores, Tony Perez, and Jimmie Dale Gilmore • Leonard Cohen • Keith Whitley / Skip
eil • Gary Morris / Mary Chapin Carpenter • Kathy Mattea / Tish Hinojosa • Waylon Jennings / Marty Stuart • Stevie Ray
Freeman, Angela Strehli, John Mills, Jon Blondell, and Will Sexton • "Will the Circle Be Unbroken" with The Nitty Gritty Dirt
Carlson, Vassar Clements, and Jimmy Martin • Lyle Lovett and His Large Band • Michelle Shocked / Strength in Numbers
Wariner • Ricky Van Shelton / Kelly Willis • Sara Hickman / Kennedy-Rose • Shelby Lynne / Willie Nelson • Alan Jackson
net Atkins with Johnny Gimble and The Cluster Pluckers • The Robert Cray Band / Buddy Guy • Shawn Colvin / John Hammond
ll, Don Edwards, and Sons of the San Joaquin • Songwriters' Special with Nanci Griffith, Indigo Girls, Mary Chapin Carpenter,
ss and Union Station • Albert Collins / Danny Gatton • K.T. Oslin • Travis Tritt / Holly Dunn • The Subdudes / Bela Fleck
• Kevin Welch / Will T. Massey • Doug Stone / Maura O'Connell • John Prine / Jimmie Dale Gilmore • Michael Nesmith
id • Lyle Lovett and His Large Band / Dr. John • Delbert McClinton / Lee Roy Parnell • Mary Chapin Carpenter • Garrison
at Plains • John Gorka / Steve Forbert • Taj Mahal / Tish Hinojosa • Rosanne Cash / Carlene Carter • Hal Ketchum / Kelly
Dean • Patty Loveless / Monte Warden • The Best of Merle Haggard: A Retrospective • Songwriters' Special with Willie
arden Smith • Leonard Cohen / Christine Albert with Paul Glasse • John Hiatt and the Guilty Dogs / Radney Foster • Vince
Jackson • The Neville Brothers / Jimmie Vaughan and the Tilt-A-Whirl Band • The Mavericks / Robert Earl Keen • Tejano
Chesnutt / Tracy Byrd • Shawn Colvin / Bill Miller • David Ball / Gary P. Nunn with special guests Jim Henson's Muppets
Strangers • John Prine / Todd Snider and The Nervous Wrecks • Asleep at the Wheel's 25th Anniversary with Willie Nelson,
d, Iris DeMent, and Freddie Powers • Lee Roy Parnell / A.J. Croce • The Allman Brothers Band • Roger Miller / Marty Robbins
hony" with Michael Martin Murphey & Friends with The Oklahoma City Philharmonic • Wynonna • Songwriters' Special with Willie
Walter Hyatt with Lyle Lovett, David Ball, Champ Hood, Willis Alan Ramsey, Marcia Ball, Shawn Colvin, Jimmie Dale Gilmore
rs, Wayne Hancock, Mary Cutrufello, and Don Walser • Mary Chapin Carpenter / BR5-49 • Travis Tritt / Wade Hayes • Eric
n / Jack Ingram • Sheryl Crow • Blues Night with Delbert McClinton and Miss Lavelle White • Junior Brown / Robbie Fulks
and Asleep at the Wheel • The Indigo Girls with special guests Vonda Shepard, Freedy Johnston, and Mark Eitzel / Kim Richey
mmylou Harris, Willie Nelson, Steve Earle, Rodney Crowell, Nanci Griffith, John T. Van Zandt, and Jack Clement • Boz Scaggs
Matraca Berg • Dixie Chicks / Charlie Robison • Ruth Brown / Lionel Hampton and His Orchestra • Billy Bragg sings Woody
Vaughan • Mexican Roots Music: A Celebration with Los Lobos, Freddy Fender, Flaco Jimenez, Ruben Ramos, Rick Trevino
/ Monte Montgomery • Hootie & The Blowfish with Nanci Griffith and Peter Holsapple • Bobby Blue Bland / Susan Tedeschi

AUSTIN CITY LIMITS ®

25 YEARS OF AMERICAN MUSIC

AUSTIN CITY LIMITS ®

John T. Davis
Photography by Scott Newton

Timeline by Dan Forte

Foreword by Lyle Lovett

BILLBOARD BOOKS
An imprint of Watson-Guptill Publications/New York

This book is dedicated to two KLRU-TV employees
who symbolized the dedication, hard work, and
creative spirit of the hundreds of people who bring
Austin City Limits to music fans all over the world,
the late Rebekah K. Morris and the late Barbara Hood.

Copyright ©2000 by Austin City Limits
First published in 2000 in the United States by Billboard Books
an imprint of Watson-Guptill Publications
a division of BPI Communications, Inc.
1515 Broadway, New York, New York 10036

Library of Congress Cataloging-in-Publication Data

Davis, John T. (John Terry,) 1955-
    Austin city limits : 25 years of American music / John T. Davis ;
Photography by Scott Newton ; timeline by Dan Forte ; foreword by
Lyle Lovett.
        p.   cm.
    Includes index.
    ISBN 0-8230-8303-9
    1. Austin city limits (Television program) 2. Country music—
History and criticism. I. Newton, Scott. II. Title.
ML3524.D38 1999
791.45'72-dc21   99-36010
                                        CIP

Printed in the United States of America

First printing, 2000

1 2 3 4 5 6 7 8 9 / 08 07 06 05 04 03 02 01 00

All references to dates (for example, "five years ago I...,") are drawn
from the time of the book's writing, November-December 1998.

All dates appearing in parentheses after artists' photos indicate the date
of the show's taping (shows usually aired one year later).

Senior Editor: Bob Nirkind
Editor: Victoria Craven
Designer: Jay Anning, Thumb Print
Production Manager: Ellen Greene

ACKNOWLEDGMENTS

From KLRU-TV and the Producers

This book represents the culmination of twenty-five years of individual and institutional teamwork almost unprecedented on the television landscape.

From the original creators through the producers and directors, the people who point the cameras, aim the lights, mix the music, and assemble the millions of electronic bits that translate into magic on your home TV, it has taken hundreds of folks working together to keep this Texas home-grown musical treasure thriving for a quarter of a century. It's impossible to do justice in this space alone to everybody who has contributed to *Austin City Limits,* but here goes:

To the original team of producers, directors, and talent coordinators, including Bill Arhos, Paul Bosner, Bruce Scafe, Mike Tolleson, Joe Gracey, Craig Hillis, Van Keller, Charles Vaughan, and Howard Chalmers, who turned a flight of fantasy into an actual television program. To Allan Muir, whose personality, style, and instincts shaped the look and direction of the show for years to come. KLRU wishes to acknowledge the photographers from the first three seasons—Gary Bishop, Janet Bandy, Carlos Guerra, and David Eberhard—whose photographs could not be credited individually in this book.

To the many executives and programmers with the Public Broadcasting Service, and to the hundreds of individual stations that brought *Austin City Limits* into the households of America, as well as to the corporate donors and underwriters—both large and small—whose generosity provided the fuel to keep the production humming over the years. To the University of Texas at Austin—the "home" of *Austin City Limits*—for its support and for its state-of-the-art facilities.

To the hard-working staff, many of whom went on to pursue other endeavors, but many of whom have stayed on to dedicate their life's work to this single effort. Likewise, to an incredibly loyal corps of volunteers who have manned the barricades (and beer lines) to serve and protect the public and the talent.

To our agent, Jim Hornfischer, whose tireless efforts found a home for this book, and to our editors at Billboard Books, Bob Nirkind and Victoria Craven, and Art Director Jay Anning.

And, yes indeed, to the hundreds of artists and thousands of musicians whose collective voice and art leave an enduring legacy, and to the millions of viewers and listeners who each week "go home with the armadillo."

And to Willie . . .

From the Author

I would like to thank the staff, crew, and volunteers of *Austin City Limits,* whose tireless friendship, professionalism, and enthusiasm have enabled me to experience priceless musical moments over the years, and who proved invaluable in this book's production. Special thanks are also due to Mary Beth Rogers, Terry Lickona, and Ed Bailey, who were instrumental in the preparation of this book.

Thanks, too, to all the musicians who lent their time and stories to this volume, especially Lucinda Williams and Bruce Hornsby, who permitted me to have an unfettered look at "a day in the life." Finally, thanks to the coaches and trainers at the Dog & Duck Pub, whose protein shakes and smart drinks inspired most, if not all, of the literary sagacity that permeates this tome.

On a personal note, this book is for Betty and Johnny, who always believed, and for Jan, who talks the talk and walks the walk.

From the Photographer

When I took ancient Greek as a foreign language in college, I learned that when a performer turned in a particularly good performance and was congratulated for it, the performer's attitude was that it wasn't really him who had done well, it was the Muse flowing through him. He was just a channel—it was the Muse that had done well.

That's how I see today's performers, as channels for the Muse. So when I'm looking through the camera, trying to slice out an instant in time that encapsulates that person, I'm always asking myself, "Can you see the Muse?" When I can, I push the button.

That keeps it interesting—the thought that I'm not really photographing a particular performer, but trying to capture that creative, divine spirit that motivates all performers. When I succeed, people say, "Hey, that's a good picture." I try to be a channel for the Muse myself. That keeps it fresh.

CONTENTS

PREFACE **8**

FOREWORD BY LYLE LOVETT **10**

INTRODUCTION *A Short History of Austin City Limits* **12**

SETTING THE STAGE
THE AUSTIN SCENE *Groover's Paradise* **20**

THE SHOW *Austin Unlimited* **26**

TIMELINE
1975 – 1999 . . . . **36**

THE STARS
LEGENDS *Pancho Was a Bandit, Boys . . .* **46**

COUNTRY *If You Don't Think I Love You, Ask My Wife* **58**

BLUES *There's the Blues and There's Zip-A-Dee-Do-Dah* **80**

TEJANO AND CONJUNTO *"Chulas Fronteras"* **92**

SINGER-SONGWRITERS *You Got to Sing Like You Don't Need the Money* **100**

WOMEN IN SONG *Grrrls with Guitars* **110**

LONE STARS *Texas Is a State of Mind* **122**

RISING STARS *Garth Who?* **132**

NONE OF THE ABOVE *It Was Never Just About Cowboys* **142**

BACKSTAGE
A DAY IN THE LIFE OF *AUSTIN CITY LIMITS* *December 5, 1998* **164**

FREQUENTLY ASKED QUESTIONS *How, What, Where, When* **172**

AFTERWORD *Austin City Limits Forever* **175**

CHRONOLOGY OF PROGRAMS AND SONGS **176**

INDEX **190**

PREFACE

THIS BOOK COMMEMORATES the twenty-fifth anniversary of *Austin City Limits,* a PBS television series that has reflected music *as it is performed* in concert, the way that performers are seen and heard live. The program is and always has been a musicians' showcase, offering them the opportunity to rise or fall based on the fans' acceptance of their performances. Today it is most gratifying, but a little startling, to hear a young star announce to an audience that, as a child, he or she had either dreamed of performing or vowed to perform on *Austin City Limits.*

The musicians have welcomed this opportunity, and a mix of established stars, rising stars, and virtual unknowns—armed mostly with stringed instruments and potential, and playing for musician's scale wages—have graced the *Austin City Limits* stage. The series and this book are a tribute to those musicians.

To help set the stage for the rest of the book, a bit of history is in order. In 1974 PBS affiliate KLRU-TV in Austin, Texas, having recently moved into an excellent new production facility on the campus of the University of Texas, was looking for a way to break into the national production picture for public television. Fortuitously, a year earlier, PBS, a membership organization whose stations produce most of their programs, began a "program fair," which allowed PBS stations to vote on programs to be distributed by PBS.

Paul Bosner, the first producer of the series; Bruce Scafe, the first director; and I decided that an economical and relatively easy way to break into the new PBS scheme would be to exploit a burgeoning local music scene that boasted at least sixty-five bands that called Austin home, and seemed to represent "country gone awry." The leaders of this group of "Redneck Rockers," as they were often called, were the late B. W. Stevenson and Jerry Jeff Walker. Willie Nelson was the local guru who had returned to Austin to play music and golf. I wrote a proposal to the Corporation for Public Broadcasting seeking money for a pilot and got all of $13,000 to do one.

I'm not sure where Jerry Jeff was, but Mike Tolleson, then affiliated with the famous local club Armadillo World Headquarters, booked B. W. Stevenson and Willie Nelson to play for the pilot on successive evenings. B. W. was great, but not enough people were invited, and it looked like we had a party where half the guests had failed to show up.

Willie's house was full, however, and he played some licks not even his band had heard before. At one point during "Bloody Mary Morning," Jody Payne, the lead guitarist, stopped playing and walked over to look at Willie's

LONDON HOMESICK BLUES

When you're down on your luck and you ain't got a buck
In London you're a goner
Even London Bridge has fallen down
And moved to Arizona, now I know why
And I'll substantiate the rumor that the English sense of humor
Is drier than the Texas sand
You can put up your dukes or you can bet your boots
That I'm leaving just as fast as I can.

> I wanna go home with the armadillo
> Good country music from Amarillo to Abilene
> The friendliest people
> And the prettiest women you've ever seen.

Well, it's cold over here, and I swear
I wished they would turn the heat on
And where in the world is that English girl
I promised I would meet on the third floor?
And of the whole damned lot, the only friend I've got
Is a smoke and a cheap guitar
And my mind keeps roaming and my heart keeps longing
To be home in a Texas bar.

(Repeat chorus)

Well, I decided that I'd get my cowboy hat
And go down to Marble Arch Station
'Cause when a Texan fancies that he'll take his chances
Fancy chances will be taken, that's for sure
And them limey eyes, they were eyeing the prize
Some people call manly footwear. And they said,
"You're from down South and when you open your mouth
You always seem to put your foot there."

(Repeat chorus)

hands in wonderment. Not having heard any of these artists live before, I myself was stunned at what I was hearing and seeing.

Armed with a classic Willie Nelson and Family performance for a series with no title, we were on our way to selling something in the PBS program cooperative. I got the idea for a title while sitting in a park taking a break during a PBS conference, from a movie marquee showing *Macon County Line.* I told Bosner that *Travis County Line* had a "good ring" to it but was certainly a rip-off of the other title.

"How about *Austin City Limits*?" Bosner asked.

"Fine with me," I told him. "It ain't like we're making history here."

Well, in twenty-five years we've made a little music history. *Austin City Limits,* probably for the first time, chronicled a new form of music on videotape.

I personally think it had a profound influence and effect on the "Nashville Sound," because this music, this "progressive country" was, indeed, progressive; the star shone no brighter than the lead guitar or the bass or the drums, because the sidemen were liberated to play as they knew how to play, and it didn't much matter what their discipline was. It was blues, bluegrass, country, and more rolled into one, and as distinctive as the emergence of rap. Traditional Nashville was quick to change their formula, luckily for us.

Most of the original Austin bands vaporized within *ACL*'s first two years, but Nashville and the rest of the country came to the rescue, and *Austin City Limits* survived. In the third year, Chet Atkins called and was booked on the series, and U.T. football's Coach Darrell Royal prevailed on his buddy Merle Haggard to perform. Those two appearances gave us more national impetus, and less dependency on what had became known as "the Austin sound" before it abruptly went away.

The list of artists from that point on is legendary: Ray Charles, Roy Orbison, Garth Brooks, Emmylou Harris, the Judds, Pure Prairie League, Nanci Griffith, Fats Domino, Lyle Lovett, Vince Gill, the Dixie Chicks, John Mayall, B.B. King, Jerry Lee Lewis, virtually ad infinitum. (The list is in the back of the book!)

And the bands have returned, to the tune of about a hundred club concerts a week, prompting the city to lay claim to being "The Live Music Capital of the World."

The audio has been impeccable from day one, which (I am told) led Willie Nelson to remark that our version of his *Stardust* performance sounded better than the album audio.

Chet Atkins paid yet another ultimate compliment to the quality of the audio. Due to mix with us during a time when his daughter was ill, he said, "Oh, go ahead. I've talked to your audio people and they know what they're doing."

For a television series to continue for twenty-five years is pretty remarkable, and it takes a lot of luck, skill, and perseverance to make that happen. Most of it we owe to the PBS stations who have supported it with their dollars for so long, as well as to the musicians, the viewing fans, and a very capable staff of people, some of whom have been with the series since its inception.

I am also grateful to the songwriters who can't sing and the singers who can't write who somehow found each other.

Gary P. Nunn can both sing and write, and since the second season his "London Homesick Blues" has been the perfect theme song for *Austin City Limits.*

BILL ARHOS, *Austin City Limits*
Founder and Executive Producer

FOREWORD

TURNING THE KNOB, changing the channels the old-fashioned way one evening in 1976, I landed on KUHT, Houston's PBS station—the country's first PBS station—and saw a band on a stage in front of an enthusiastic audience.

Two tall, skinny men with long, blond hair, one on each end of the stage, stood playing acoustic guitars as a beautiful dark-haired girl sat on a stool between them in the center of the stage, singing, "The lady has no heart. . . ."

"What *is* this?" I thought. I sat down, mesmerized, arm's length from the television, and didn't touch the knob again until after Gary P. Nunn's "London Homesick Blues" played and the credits for the show ran.

The band was Wheatfield. The tall, skinny men were Craig Calvert and Chris (Ezra) Idlet, the dark-haired girl was Connie Mims, and what it was, was *Austin City Limits* in its first season.

I was captivated seeing *Austin City Limits* for the first time. This was a show that spoke to me. I was eighteen years old and 1976 was the year I had begun performing. I'd seen Wheatfield's name in club advertisements in the Houston papers and had wanted to see them perform; I'd played a whole summer in restaurants ending *my* shows with "London Homesick Blues."

Watching *Austin City Limits* on Friday nights became a ritual for me. In many cases, it was my first chance to see artists whose music I was listening to and whose songs I was singing. I'd seen Willie Nelson at the Armadillo World Headquarters, Willis Alan Ramsey at Austin's Paramount Theatre, and Michael Murphey at G. Rollie White Coliseum in College Station, but *Austin City Limits* was the first place I ever saw Townes Van Zandt, Steven Fromholz, Jerry Jeff Walker, and Asleep at the Wheel. *Austin City Limits* turned these Texas music legends into flesh and blood.

And it wasn't only Texas music I saw in those first seasons. There were performances by Ry Cooder, John Prine, Tom Waits, Taj Mahal, Doc Watson, the Neville Brothers, and Ray Charles.

Austin City Limits was a coveted venue. Because the one-hour program usually featured two artists, thirty minutes each, and often paired nationally known performers with lesser-known regional or local performers, it gave the lesser-knowns a chance to be seen by the whole country.

By 1981 I was playing Austin regularly. My friend Wayne Miller had gone to film school at the University of Texas and had spent many hours at the KLRU studios on campus where the show is produced; he knew everyone who worked on the show. Wayne was invited to all the tapings, and when I was in town to play emmajoe's or the Cactus Cafe or the Waterloo Ice House, he'd take me with him.

He introduced me to Bill Arhos, the show's executive producer, to Terry Lickona, the producer, and to Gary Menotti, the director. Sometimes Wayne and I would sit in the audience, and sometimes we'd sit in the control room and watch Gary direct.

Gary's directing style belied his usual jovial, nonchalant manner. As music blasted through the speakers at full volume, he'd pace wildly back and forth across the control room, waving his arms and shouting at video monitors, calling shots with precision. The shows were great.

It all made sense to me. The people who worked on the show loved music; some of them were musicians themselves. They cared about the show. It was no accident that *Austin City Limits* was a thoughtful, honest presentation of singers, songwriters, and musicians.

My first time onstage was to sing with Nanci Griffith in her first performance on the show in 1984. It was exciting to go from watching on television, to sitting in the audience, to standing onstage.

I taped my first show in January 1987 for Season 12, and I've been lucky enough to do several others since. The shows that stand out for me are the special event shows I was invited to do with other performers. Sitting onstage with Willie Nelson and Rodney Crowell, taping our songwriter-in-the-round show, and hanging out with old friends while taping the Walter Hyatt and Townes Van Zandt tribute shows are among my fondest memories.

Every time I'm on the show, I'm thankful for the opportunity. Because the performer gets to play a real concert, the viewer gets to see a real concert. *Austin City Limits* lets a performer be himself, and do a show from beginning to end without interruption. Nobody yells "Action" or "Cut." Terry Lickona introduces you, and you start playing. It's as simple as that.

I feel honored to have stood on the same stage as the performers in this book, and I feel honored to be included with them among its pages.

Thanks to Bill Arhos, Terry Lickona, Gary Menotti, and the *Austin City Limits* crew for their dedication and hard work, and for giving all of us the opportunity to watch and listen.

LYLE LOVETT
January 1999

From Season 14, 1989

INTRODUCTION

A Short History Of Austin City Limits

TO THIS DAY, some people still think it is taped outdoors. That is not an unreasonable supposition. There is the city skyline in the distance, with the granite dome of the Capitol glowing pink and the white limestone shaft of the University Tower. There are hanging limbs of verdant greenery, and the suggestion of stars overhead. All of it is meant to conjure up an idyllic outdoor venue deep in the heart of Texas, under a Lone Star moon.

And all of it is false. Only the music is real.

"Everywhere I went, people asked me, 'When are you going to be on *Austin City Limits*?'" recalls singer-songwriter Jimmy LaFave (who did, in fact, appear in 1996). "People in Belgium and Holland . . . they think it's outside and want to know why it's never raining."

The students, business people, skateboard punks, and winos who pass by its nearly windowless facade probably don't give much thought to the olive-green building on the corner of 26th Street and Guadalupe, at the edge of the University of Texas campus. It blends into the urban scenery, another anonymous box in the cityscape.

STEVIE RAY VAUGHAN (1983)
Stevie Ray Vaughan's first appearance on the show was fraught with nervous energy, insecurity, and, yes, too much cocaine. Yet the muse cooperated and Stevie gave a landmark performance at the beginning of a brilliant, all-too-short career.

BILL MONROE (1986)
He created a music style and called it bluegrass.

But inside that box, in KLRU-TV's Studio 6-A on the sixth floor, the alternative reality of *Austin City Limits* holds dominion.

The sun in that world is a bewildering array of spotlights with multicolored gels. The foliage is artificial—leafy fakery wired to the backs of the bleachers surrounding the stage and the rear of the stage itself.

The backdrop is plywood and paint and Christmas lights and it looks, in person and up close, like something a particularly ambitious drama class might assemble for a high school play. But it is more than convincing when viewed through a TV screen. Each year letters arrive at KLRU, asking where visitors can pitch a tent next to the *ACL* stage.

And no, it never rains.

LORETTA LYNN (1997)
"The Queen of Country Music," a title that fits this gracious lady who is one of country's pioneering female performers and songwriters.

SHERYL CROW (1997)
Sheryl Crow is the real deal. She's a top-notch, solid rock performer.

MERLE HAGGARD (1981)
The "Okie from Muskogee," ex-con and friend of the working man, never pulls punches in his songs. He also put together one of the best bands (The Strangers) this side of Bob Wills and His Texas Playboys.

Showtime: Home with the Armadillo

On show nights, ticketholders begin queueing up early in the evening, the lines winding across the patio between the buildings of the U.T. journalism department. Upstairs, on the sixth floor, lights are being adjusted, cameras are being tested, and microphones and musical equipment are subjected to last-minute checks. In the video and audio control rooms behind the audience bleachers, technicians are running down the same checklists they have annotated hundreds of times before.

The director double-checks a number on a stopwatch, makes a note on a shot sheet, and hands the page off to an aide to be copied and distributed to the cameramen on the floor. He rolls his shoulders to loosen up, runs his fingers through his hair, bounces lightly on the balls of his feet.

The producer talks to the featured artist's manager, spreading some last-minute oil on troubled waters. The chilled Gewürztraminer, the Mongolian yak paté, and the personal astrologer clearly called for in the artist's contract rider are nowhere in evidence. The producer sighs inwardly and begins, once more, to explain the nature of the PBS/*Austin City Limits* fly-by-wire essence.

Down in the artists' dressing room on the fifth floor, the night's headliner double-checks her set list for the last time and munches contentedly on a deli sandwich and sips from a bottle of water. The lack of couture snacks and designer goodies appears to bother her not a whit.

Someone gives the word, someone else flips a switch, and the big three-sided backdrop behind the stage blazes forth with hundreds of tiny multicolored lights. The city skyline blazes forth in sharp relief.

The band is downstairs, gathering by the freight elevator for the ride to the sixth floor, and the fans outside on line are humming with anticipation as the doors open. But for the moment, in Studio 6-A, things seem tranquil and time has crystallized. Like a conductor with his raised baton, the room seems pregnant with possibility. . . .

TAMMY WYNETTE (1983)

"I've done so many TV shows and it's always 'hurry up' and 'stop,' hurry-stop, hurry-stop," Tammy Wynette explained. "Austin City Limits is wonderful because I don't notice the cameras and can really play to the audience."

GEORGE STRAIT (1981)

Country superstar George Strait in his first Austin City Limits *appearance. Good looks and a back-to-the-basics style have kept him at the forefront of today's country singers.*

Step Inside This House: The Faces of Austin City Limits

Austin City Limits was the brainchild of Bill Arhos, a cigar-smoking Public Broadcasting System veteran, and a few other kindred spirits, among them producer Paul Bosner. (Arhos and Bosner appropriated a Dixie-fried B-movie title, *Macon County Line,* for their baby.) The idea was originally to create a series that showcased the eclectic country-rock musical scene that coalesced around Austin in the early 1970s. Simple, huh?

Today that function has been eclipsed by several others. Each week *Austin City Limits* presents another of its faces to its viewers:

A Musical Crossroads: The show has demonstrated an ongoing willingness to showcase musicians and musical genres from myriad skeins of the American tapestry. Few other programs would showcase Leonard Cohen, the Neville Brothers, Tom Waits, the Nitty Gritty Dirt Band, Flaco Jimenez, and original members of Bob Wills' Texas Playboys western swing band with equal fervor.

An American Music Archive: In its vaults, *Austin City Limits* preserves signature performances by a host of musicians who have since slipped beyond the pale. In some cases, these performances were taken near the end of the artists' lives and sum up a lifetime of musical achievement. In other cases an *ACL* segment may mark their only prolonged television appearance. A representative sampling includes shows by Roy Orbison, Ernest Tubb, Tammy Wynette, Bill Monroe, Stevie Ray Vaughan, Marty Robbins, Townes Van Zandt, Lightnin' Hopkins, Carl Perkins, and others.

ALAN JACKSON (1994)
"Years ago, back in Georgia before a lot of country videos were on TV, the show we used to catch on Saturday night was Austin City Limits. *This show inspired me and helped me make a decision to try and make a living in this business."*

DWIGHT YOAKAM WITH BUCK OWENS (1988)
Dwight Yoakam teamed with the legendary Buck Owens (right) for an incredible duet of "The Streets of Bakersfield."

JOHNNY GIMBLE (1979)

Johnny Gimble may be the heart and soul of western swing. As a former Texas Playboy he's living historical proof, but also proof that the joy of music supercedes everything else.

A Stars' Showcase: Despite paying only union scale, *ACL* has been remarkably lucky in capturing some of the biggest names in rock and country music over the years. Some artists, such as Garth Brooks, were snagged on the way up, while others appeared at the peak of their careers. Besides Brooks, headliners who have appeared include B.B. King, Merle Haggard, Loretta Lynn, the Allman Brothers Band, Willie Nelson, Reba McEntire, Bonnie Raitt, George Jones, Manhattan Transfer, Johnny Cash, Sheryl Crow, Trisha Yearwood, Alan Jackson, George Strait, Lionel Hampton, Dwight Yoakam, and others.

A Cutting-Edge Forum: The producers of the show keep as close to the edge of the envelope as circumstances permit. Early appearances by Keb' Mo', Hal Ketchum, Shawn Colvin, Alison Krauss, Mary Chapin Carpenter, Nanci Griffith, Junior Brown, Stevie Ray Vaughan, Susan Tedeschi, Rick Treviño, Steve Earle, Allison Moorer, k.d. lang, Cowboy Junkies, Whiskeytown, Rosanne Cash, Kenny Wayne Shepherd, Old 97's, Gillian Welch, Fastball, the Mavericks, Jonny Lang, and more attest to this.

A Home on the Video Range for Texas Music: From the beginning the series has existed in large part to showcase the sprawling, joyous, multicultural, many-faceted, even the downright messy mosaic that is indigenous Texas music: western swing, zydeco, homegrown singer-songwriters, jazz and blues, Tejano, mainstream country, rock, border-country conjunto . . . well, you get the idea. Native and adopted musicians from the city and the state who have been featured on the program include artists from a host of different genres, from the brothers Flaco and Santiago Jimenez, Delbert McClinton, Gatemouth Brown, Nanci Griffith, Eric Johnson, Johnny Gimble, Marcia Ball, Asleep at the Wheel, and the Fabulous Thunderbirds, to Waylon Jennings, Jerry Jeff Walker, the Dixie Chicks, Jimmie and Stevie Ray Vaughan, Robert Earl Keen, Albert Collins, Kelly Willis, Fastball, and Mary Cutrufello.

A Backdrop for Musical Magic: As far back as 1979 *Austin City Limits* has demonstrated a commitment to presenting musicians in unique configurations, resulting in a mosaic of unpredictable and irreplaceable moments.

JOHNNY CASH (1987)

Johnny Cash paid ACL the ultimate compliment: after fifty years in the music business, he said his 1987 Austin City Limits show was the best performance he had ever done on television.

From that first special ("John McEuen and Friends," featuring the Dirt Band veteran with his guests, the late folklorist Elizabeth Cotten, fiddlers Byron Berline and Vassar Clements, and others), to Season 24's star-studded "Mexican Roots Music Celebration," the show's most consistently memorable hours have been those in which disparate musicians combine their talents onstage in one-time-only combinations. In other words, where else can you see Manhattan Transfer performing with Asleep at the Wheel and Ricky Skaggs? Or Nanci Griffith sitting in as "a chick singer" (her words) with Hootie & the Blowfish?

To date there have been a host of Songwriters' Specials, starring Willie Nelson, Merle Haggard, Kris Kristofferson, Nanci Griffith, Waylon Jennings, the Indigo Girls, Lyle Lovett, Mary Chapin Carpenter, Rosanne Cash, John Prine, Emmylou Harris, and others.

There have been tributes to the mandolin and the accordion, starring virtuosos of each instrument. Other showcases have feted Tejano music, western swing, and traditional cowboy music. Earlier shows have honored songwriter Steve Goodman and bluegrass patriarch Bill Monroe.

Members of Bob Wills' Original Texas Playboys reunited for only the second time in forty years for *ACL*'s cameras; their musical heirs, Asleep at the Wheel, celebrated their twenty-fifth anniversary on the show.

On a more solemn note, performers (including Lyle Lovett, Shawn Colvin, David Ball, Jimmie Dale Gilmore, Allison Moorer, Guy Clark, Emmylou Harris, Willie Nelson, Steve Earle, Nanci Griffith, and Rodney Crowell) reunited on the *ACL* stage in Seasons 22 and 23 for celebrations of two fallen comrades, Walter Hyatt and Townes Van Zandt.

Again and again, moments that are as unique as they are timeless have been captured by the cameras of *Austin City Limits.*

JOHN PRINE (1977)
The former mailman-from-Chicago-turned-songwriter has always charmed his fans with his appeal to the everyman in all of us.

SONGWRITERS' SPECIAL (1986)
Gail Davies, Rosanne Cash, Emmylou Harris, and Lacy J. Dalton (left to right) took the Songwriters' Specials in a new direction.

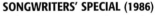

SETTING THE STAGE

"It's a matter of geography. Half a dozen cultures collide here; Mexican and Anglo, German and Native American, Caribbean and African. Austin is where all the Texas kids who grow up in towns where being different could get you maimed or killed, come and get to be themselves. Which results in a lot of notes and ideas and energies, all mingling and sparkling, like metaphysical bumper cars, or stars in a spectacular, unstable Milky Way. Yep, you can feel it all right. It's all around. It's in the swing music, and the funny songs played well ('I Bought the Shoes That Just Walked Out On Me') and in the weird, barbecue-smelling air, and the Christmas lights that drape the bungalows all year long."

—Austin musician and artist JO CAROL PIERCE,
quoted in the *Washington Post*

THE CITY OF AUSTIN SEES ITSELF reflected in the millions of eyes of a nationwide television audience. People know Austin, Texas—or think they do—because of the picture *Austin City Limits* has painted. The show's special genius has been to take the city of its origins and reflect it to the world at large in an idealized form. Even the local Chamber of Commerce recognizes that nothing the city has ever generated, promoted, or exported has come close to creating the indelible civic identity that *Austin City Limits* has conferred upon its hometown.

GROOVER'S PARADISE

Thanks to *ACL,* when people around the country think of the Texas capital, they don't necessarily envision billionaire moguls like Michael Dell, or pontificating state politicians. They think instead of Stevie Ray Vaughan or the Neville Brothers or Emmylou Harris playing on a hillside above a glittering skyline.

Willie Nelson was celebrated as a songwriter in Nashville in the sixties, but his own albums sold poorly. He sang all around the beat, and his guitar playing owed as much to gypsy jazz guitarist Django Reinhardt as it did to Merle Travis. He smoked way too much dope and hung out with way too many guitar-pulling malcontents ever to be embraced to Nashville's starched bosom.

At Christmastime in 1969, as the story goes, Willie had just finished recording a song called "What Can You Do To Me Now?" when the phone rang; his house was burning down. He dashed into the smoking ruins to rescue his guitar and a stash of marijuana. Somebody, he decided, was trying to tell him something. He returned home to Texas, to a little town called Bandera, and the faithful audiences in the Texas Hill Country.

Nelson was no black-leather-clad desperado like his buddy Waylon Jennings. He wrote hardscrabble songs of anguish and loss with the deceptive simplicity of haikus. When he swung for the fences artistically, it was with an album that followed a man into hell and back out again—1975's *Red-Headed Stranger.* When Willie migrated from Bandera to Austin in the early seventies, he found something akin to the Promised Land.

DOUG SAHM (1990)

Doug has been around since before day one. This San Antonio kid cut his first single at the age of twelve. His musical style melds blues, rock, country, and Tex-Mex with plenty of attitude. Since he founded the Texas Tornados in 1990, he and bandmates Freddy Fender, Flaco Jimenez, and Augie Meyers have reigned supreme over Tex-Mex.

Austin, Texas, in the mid-seventies. Doug Sahm, in a 1974 album of the same name, dubbed it "Groover's Paradise." (Ah, how times change. Twenty-five years later, Sir Doug, observing the narrow-eyed, success-besotted yuppies who invaded the city in the nineties, wrote another civic anthem entitled "Get A Life." Way to surf that old gestalt, Doug.)

Jerry Jeff Walker, who skidded into town in 1971, used to clarify his address: "Hell, I don't live in Texas; I live in Austin."

Texas musician Steve Earle knew better than to try to headquarter in the city. There was, he once remarked, way too much cheap dope and way too many pretty girls to get any serious work done.

Nanci Griffith grew up in Austin in what might best be described as a libertarian household, especially for conservative Texas in the early sixties. "I thought every place was like Austin, just like any other child thinks their hometown is just like everyone's hometown," she recollected. "My parents were beatniks, and they knew such incredible people. As a child, having known [Thirteenth Floor Elevators' acid-rocker] Roky Erickson as a person, because my parents were friends with his parents . . . hearing the music that I've heard in Austin all my life, I feel very fortunate to have that as a background."

In *The Gay Place,* his definitive 1962 novel of hormone-drunk state politicians at play in the carnal fields of Austin, Billy Lee Brammer summed up a central appeal of the town. There was, he wrote, "room enough to caper." And for many years, at least in golden-tinged retrospect, there was.

Quite deliberately, *Austin City Limits* still capitalizes on the legacy of those freewheeling times. To understand its appeal, it helps to understand what made Austin itself such a desirable place when the show was conceived.

There is no law that said Austin was destined to emerge as a fermenting hotbed of live music. It wasn't as though the Muses did a high-five over the Texas Hill Country one day and said, "Strike up the band, by Zeus!"

JIMMIE DALE GILMORE (1991)
To call it new age country is a disservice. Texan Jimmie Dale Gilmore's songs transcend the clichés.

WAYLON JENNINGS (1989)

As a one-time bass player for Buddy Holly, Waylon Jennings predates almost everyone else in popular music. He's certainly carved out a large chunk of the country audience as his own. This shot captures the feel of his "outlaw country" image.

Austin has the usual cultural trappings for a city its size. Other cities also have big universities and thriving industries. Forty-nine other cities can even lay claim to being state capitals. But Austin's central and enduring cultural artifact has always been music.

The modern musical tradition might be said to stretch back to two men, Kenneth Threadgill and Johnny Holmes. The day after the demise of Prohibition, Kenneth Threadgill obtained the first beer license in Travis County, the better to serve the patrons who stopped by his gas station/beer joint out on the old Dallas Highway. Years later Janis Joplin became the most famous musical alumnus of Threadgill's regular folk music hoots.

And not long after World War II ended, Johnny Holmes opened the Victory Grill on the city's East Side to provide a home to local and touring blues and R&B musicians. Between them Holmes and Threadgill helped to incubate the contemporary music scene in Austin.

In the Lone Star capital, home to the University of Texas and the Texas Legislature (and an accompanying bohemian mindset that embodied elements of both), music, politics, upheavals along social, sexual, and cultural fault lines, and a certain summertime-and-the-livin'-is-easy laissez faire attitude combined to create an oasis in the heart of conservative, post-LBJ Texas.

In the late sixties and early seventies, clubs sprouted like magic mushrooms, epitomized by the city's premiere psychedelic nightclub, the Vulcan Gas Company, and its successor, a cavernous National Guard armory rechristened the Armadillo World Headquarters.

In addition, there were R&B joints like the IL Club, Ernie's Chicken Shack, and Charlie's Playhouse over on the East Side; campus-area hangouts with names like the One Knite, the Jade Room, and the Old New Orleans Room; folkie havens like the Chequered Flag and Threadgill's; and neon-lit honky-tonk beer joints such as Big G's and the Broken Spoke, the latter of which advertised as its primary attractions, "Dine, Dance and Beer."

Downtown, on a then-moribund strip of pavement called Sixth Street, friendly little Mexican cervecerias like the Green Spot and La Perla jostled amiably alongside one another. And there were neon-glowing roadhouses out past the lights on the edge of town—Soap Creek Saloon, the Skyline Club, and Dessau Hall.

The artistic freedom was breathtaking. "Audiences actually encouraged performers to show them something new and completely different," Joe Nick Patoski wrote of the era in his biography of Stevie Ray Vaughan. "The only price was the absence of all the material trappings associated with success."

The music itself was a yeasty blend of country, rock, pop, folk, jazz, and blues. Or, as veteran Austin tunesmith Steven Fromholz describes it, "Freeform-country-folk-rock-science-fiction-gospel-gum-bluegrass-opera-cowjazz music."

Gary P. Nunn, who authored "London Homesick Blues," which went on to become the *Austin City Limits* theme song, could play a Ray Price country shuffle with the best of them, but he drew just as much musical inspiration from Ray Charles. Lubbock singer-songwriter Jimmie Dale Gilmore venerated Hank Williams as a master musician, but he gave just as much weight to the legacy of the Beatles.

"I am a traditionalist," Gilmore has said. "But the 'folk' music that I'm a product of is everything from Hank Williams and Elvis and Little Richard and the Beatles, to Joan Baez, Chuck Berry, and Brenda Lee. That, to me, is folk music." Austin has long been a haven for musicians with those sorts of elastic boundaries.

Writing of Joe Ely, a West Texas contemporary of Gilmore's, writer John Morthland described the best of his music thus: "Ely's breed of country comes straight from the bars and dance halls, and is somehow both lyrical and rugged. Bluesman Elmore James' signature electric guitar riff turns up in the middle of a traditional country blues number; a jarring hard-rock guitar solo shatters a country ballad, an accordion fits into a waltz or a rocker that may be influenced equally by both Mexican border music and Cajun music. The open rhythms of West Texas rockabilly blend with the harder Memphis stuff of Carl Perkins. . . ." Morthland might almost have been describing the city's music aesthetic as a whole.

That same liberating musical abandon, the appropriation of whatever joyous influences lay at hand or came to mind, the airy disregard for the commercial conventions of the day, all have characterized the best of Austin's music over the years.

Austin was a smaller and saner place in the mid-seventies, a different world in many respects. There were no fax machines, no personal computers, no cell phones, no crackheads, no Internet, no cable TV, no Thai restaurants, no double mochachinos, no kickboxing classes, no "relationship issues," no AIDS. There was maybe one mall. No Gaps.

Then, as now, Austin served as an incubator for budding talent. Stars-to-be spent their daylight hours slinging hash, bagging groceries, or fixing cars. Grammy-winning songwriter Lucinda Williams once toiled as a receptionist for a local law firm. She didn't last long. "They said I wasn't *perky* enough," she recounted, in her characteristic deadpan drawl.

George Strait used to play at the Broken Spoke for anyone with three bucks in their pocket. Stevie Ray Vaughan once struggled to draw a weekly crowd at the Rome Inn. Shawn Colvin came to town as part of a country-rock band called the Dixie Diesels and gigged for whomever would have her. Nanci Griffith and Lyle Lovett used to share duet bills and happy hour gigs at emmajoe's. There was no cover charge; emmajoe's owners circulated a battered metal pitcher to solicit contributions for the future Grammy winners.

Then there was Willie Nelson, who came down out of the Texas Hill Country like Moses. After his retreat from Nashville, Nelson came home, grew his hair, fired up a joint, and started a dance that featured a pas de deux between two improbable and seemingly irreconcilable figures, the redneck cowboy and the long-haired rocker. No one had ever seen anything quite like it.

As Fromholz, who was an integral part of the scene, explained to the *Austin Chronicle*, "What happened was, all these guys who were drinking tequila and all these guys who were smoking pot said, 'Here,' and they swapped. And it took. You had rednecks and you had hippies, and they were all there for one reason: They loved to get loaded and listen to music and we were doing something they all liked. It was kind of crazy."

Willie played the Armadillo World Headquarters for the first time one hot August night in 1972, and everyone held their breath. Willie knew better. "I knew all along that the kids would respond to what we were doing, and my band knew that I knew, so they weren't worried," Nelson recalled years later. "But my booking agent thought I was crazy, and so did the industry people in the offices in New York and Nashville and L.A. But they didn't know what we did, they never got out of their offices to check out what was happening."

ONE KNITE
One of the original live music dives that ignited the Austin scene in the 1970s.

Scott Newton recalls celebrating Austin's own W.C. Clark's fiftieth birthday with an extravaganza featuring Austin's burgeoning blues scene. Among the performers were (left to right) Angela Strehli, Lou Ann Barton, Stevie Ray and Jimmie Vaughan, W.C. Clark, Jon Blondell (obscured), and Kim Wilson. W.C. is Austin's blues inspiration. A native, he's done it all. He, Stevie, and Lou Ann Barton were the Triple Threat Review in the seventies. His pure singing voice and tasty guitar can still be heard nightly echoing down the streets and alleys of Austin.

Of course, not everyone fell in love with the idea of squeezing into a pair of shit-kicking Tony Lamas, jumping into a battered pickup truck, and bouncing down a Hill Country backroad, swigging Lone Star Beer and belting out another chorus of "Up Against the Wall, Redneck Mother."

The high-profile success of the progressive country boom skewed Austin's music scene and marginalized the East Side blues and rhythm and blues musicians who were truly responsible for much if not most of the city's musical vitality.

Veteran musicians like W.C. Clark, who mentored both of the Vaughan boys; Robert Shaw, Erbie Bowser, and Grey Ghost (three of the last of the prewar "piano professors"); master musician Gene Ramey; and more all watched the parade pass them by, flags flying. Similarly, great Chicano musicians such as Ruben Ramos, *orquesta* leader Nash Hernandez, and Little Joe Hernandez and Sunny Ozuna (both of whom played in town often enough to claim resident status) were also ignored by the media, who flocked to chronicle the city's newly hip ambiance.

You didn't have to be black or brown to feel excluded. Plenty of white players dissed the predominant scene. "It wasn't very popular, what we were doin'," guitarist Jimmie Vaughan told critic Ed Ward. "It's just what we liked. We didn't care. I was just playing Lazy Lester songs and having a good time."

Even some of the musicians who made hay off the sudden enthusiasm for All Things Bubba were wary of the sudden canonization of the hippie-cowboy hybrid. Doug Sahm, that prodigious encyclopedia of Texas music who has raced through a baker's dozen of musical incarnations in a long, strange road from the Sir Douglas Quintet to the Texas Tornados, was quoted as telling *Rolling Stone* in the late seventies, "People are tired of this cosmic cowboy shit. They're ready to rock and roll." With a long history of watching bubbles rise and burst, Sahm knew a transitory fad when he saw one.

Some Austin country-rockers such as Rusty Wier and Michael Martin Murphey were signed by major record labels. But without a subsequent string of breakout national hits, the redneck rock scene turned inbred and inconsequential. It didn't help any that a cocaine front moved in during the latter part of the seventies and raised everyone's aggravation level.

Down in Houston, in the meantime, Mickey Gilley and John Travolta hijacked the country-rock express with the contrived phenomenon of *Urban Cowboy*. Back in Austin, as the seventies turned to the eighties, the spark of musical vitality passed first to young punk and New Wave musicians, galvanized by the Sex Pistols' visit to San Antonio in 1977, and then to the blues and R&B musicians who oscillated around Clifford Antone's smoking new blues club down on Sixth Street.

In time, Stevie Vaughan and Double Trouble, the Fabulous Thunderbirds, Timbuk 3, Eric Johnson, the Butthole Surfers, Marcia Ball, Abra Moore, Fastball, and other musicians of varying stylistic hue would add more colors to the national perception of Austin's musical palette.

Reflecting the music business as a whole, the civic scene would devolve into a balkanized stew of micro-styles, including roots-rock, swing, coffeehouse spoken word, rap and hip-hop, funk, lounge, techno, trash disco, acid house, and whatever else caught the ear of the young aspiring musicians who continued to migrate to the city.

By the time the South by Southwest Music and Media Conference debuted in 1986, Austin's legacy as the mecca of the cosmic cowboys was a thing of distant legend.

The young shaven-head techno-wunderkinder would roll their eyes when some old fart with a graying ponytail would start waxing rhapsodic about the good ol' days of the 'Dillo and Willie 'n' Waylon and the boys. Home with the armadillo was a ranch-style three-bedroom tract house in a generic North Austin suburb with a fast-track job at Dell Computer or Motorola.

SXSW (South by Southwest Music and Media Conference) was the new, cosmopolitan, multifaceted, international face of Austin music. But *Austin City Limits* endured. And, to paraphrase William Faulkner, it found a way not only to endure but to prevail.

AUSTIN CITY LIMITS
REUNION SPECIAL (1986)
Many of the artists who launched the Austin music scene in the seventies (which in turn launched Austin City Limits*) returned in 1986 for a one-of-a-kind jam. Front row, left to right: John Inman (Lost Gonzo Band), Steve Fromholz, Tracy Nelson, Bob Livingston (Lost Gonzo Band), Gary P. Nunn (center), Marcia Ball, Ray Benson (Asleep at the Wheel), Jerry Jeff Walker. Back row, members of Austin's legendary Greezy Wheels.*

THE SHOW

T HE MAN WHO ENABLED *AUSTIN CITY LIMITS* to endure and prevail was Bill Arhos. He did have plenty of help, particularly in the form of producer Paul Bosner, director Bruce Scafe, executive producer Howard Chalmers, and the talent coordinator for Season 1, Joe Gracey. But Bill was front and center at the creation and, as surely as Faulkner created Yoknapatawpha County, Arhos was instrumental in conjuring up the parallel musical universe of *ACL*.

A Texas native, Arhos has worked at KLRU (and its predecessor, KLRN) since 1962. Over the years he has served as the station's program director, general manager, and president, as well as *ACL's* producer and, later, executive producer.

In a retrospective he penned after the show's tenth season, Arhos wrote, "Once the PBS Station Program Cooperative came into existence in 1974, we were anxious to submit an offering to the system. At some point Bosner and Scafe came to me with the idea of doing a music program of some kind. . . . I took [our] desire to hit the system with something of national significance to my station management, who received it with the same enthusiasm as they would if I had suggested we do Boccaccio's *Tales of the Decameron.* One of the quotes, I remember, was, 'Nobody likes that shit. . . .'"

Years later, it had been proven beyond dispute that millions of people did, in fact, like that shit.

In Clifford Endres's excellent history of the show's first decade, *Austin City Limits* (University of Texas Press), he quoted Arhos as citing the obvious incentive for a locally produced show based on Austin music: "What was the most visible cultural product of Austin?" Arhos asked rhetorically. "It'd be like ignoring a rhinoceros in your bathtub."

Arhos, Scafe, and Bosner taped two pilot programs in November 1974 for about $7000. The first featured the late country-rocker B. W. Stevenson, the second Willie Nelson. At the time, ironically, Stevenson had a higher national profile than Willie, thanks to hits such as "My Maria." But not enough people turned up to make a lively looking crowd on camera for Stevenson's episode (not an uncommon problem in the show's early days), so Nelson's taping became the show's official pilot, which sold the PBS brass on funding a first season.

Austin City Limits was a go for a first season of thirteen episodes, to be taped in 1975 and aired in 1976 (each season since has been mostly taped in one calendar year and aired the next).

"Set designer Augie Kymmel and Scafe scrounged material for the stage and bleachers from the basement and wherever else they could find them," Endres continued. "There were no tables or chairs on the floor. Instead, Scafe and

RAY CHARLES (1984)
The quintessential American pop star. He does it all, from blues, rock, and country to jazz and Broadway.

Kymmel put down an old carpet on which people sprawled pop-festival style, sometimes thronging the floor so that the cameras could hardly move."

The set evolved into a more traditional arrangement, with bleachers ringing the stage on three sides, and cabaret-style tables and chairs occupying the open floor space. The famous city mural backdrop (derived from an actual photo by staff photographer Scott Newton) was unveiled for Season 7 in 1982.

Arhos was a key figure in keeping the show going through lean economic times, years when public funding for the arts took a beating from conservatives, and still other years when the mercurial tastes of the public and the music industry threatened to leave the show behind. In addition, executive-in-charge Dick Peterson's tight-fisted control of the budget helped the station to squeeze twice the value of every dollar spent. Without his input and budget management to complement Arhos's vision, the show would have ceased production long ago.

THE SET FOR THE WILLIE NELSON PILOT

Willie's pilot: a simple set, a simple stage, a roomful of fans. Some things never change.

AUSTIN CITY LIMITS ORIGINAL STAGE

We don't know what the producers had in mind, but the similarities between the original Austin City Limits *stage (above) and that of the Armadillo World Headquarters (shown at left) were striking.*

The Armadillo World Headquarters was an Austin cultural institution. Though it closed in 1980, its legend and lore live on.

In 1976, when *ACL*'s first series of programs beamed across the PBS airwaves, there was no MTV or Country Music Television, no widespread cable, digital, HDTV, or satellite TV systems, no niche programming, no micro-targeted market research. As a commodity on television, country music for many years was barely a blip on the programming radar, although not wholly invisible on the tube. TV has been presenting country on the networks since 1955's *Ozark Jubilee,* which was hosted by Red Foley for ABC. In his wake, talents from Tennessee Ernie Ford to Jimmy Dean, Glen Campbell, and Buck Owens (via the corn-pone colossus *Hee-Haw*) all held varying tenures on network variety shows, most of which seemed to share an unfortunate fondness for straw, red-checked gingham, and yee-haw bucolic hokum.

RICK TREVIÑO (1994)
"I'm not a Tejano player, I'm a country singer," explained Rick Treviño. "But my country music is played on Tejano radio. That's my culture, but it's something I didn't do growing up. This is giving me a good chance to grow into my own culture."

MARTY STUART (1989)
"The thing I appreciate about Austin City Limits *so much is that it has never compromised its integrity, it's never compromised its dignity from its original vision," declared Marty Stuart. "To me it's done the ultimate in the field of entertainment—it's educated and entertained at the same time."*

THE MAVERICKS (1994)
Nashville meets Miami: The Mavericks are one of the most unique bands to hit the scene in the '90s.

Austin City Limits, airing as it did long before the advent of cable stations like The Nashville Network and CMT, or radio formats such as AAA and the country-based Americana model, was a window onto a strange and wonderful musical world for lots of folks out there in the hinterlands where the buses don't run. "Years ago, back in Georgia, before a lot of country videos—or any videos—were on TV, the show we used to catch on Saturday nights was *Austin City Limits,*" recalled Alan Jackson. "This show inspired me, and helped me make a decision to try and make a living in this business."

In truth, live music of any genre had little devoted television coverage beyond the lip-synched choreography of *American Bandstand* or *Soul Train.* In the seventies shows such as *Don Kirschner's Rock Concert* and *Midnight Special* held brief sway, with concert clips stitched together seemingly at random.

Except for the PBS series *Soundstage* and, much later, MTV's vastly hyped *Unplugged* series (seemingly an unvarnished effort to mimic *ACL*'s intimate ambiance), PBS's *Sessions at West 54th* and VH-1's *Storyteller* series, few sustained attempts have been made to present popular music on television in an uninterrupted fashion without the interposition of commercials and contrived showbiz touches geared toward notoriously short viewer attention spans. Or, as Willie Nelson told Asleep at the Wheel bandleader Ray Benson, "Every time I go on TV they make me do golf jokes with Bob Hope."

WILLIE NELSON (1974)

Willie Nelson was forty-one years old, burned out on Nashville and happy to call Austin, Texas, home. It was the original pilot episode for Austin City Limits, *a day real history was made (recorded October 17, 1974; broadcast in early 1975).*

EMMYLOU HARRIS (1992)

"If ever there was a woman who personifies the idea that performers are a channel for the muse, it is Emmylou Harris. Her crystalline soprano clearly emanates from a more ethereal place. She is grace and exquisite beauty all wrapped up into one person. It has been an honor having her grace our stage several times over the years," said Scott Newton.

Since 1976, *Austin City Limits* has stood largely apart and alone. It remains so twenty-five years after establishing what many viewers and musicians consider the gold standard for presenting live music on television.

Watching a conventional television musical performance being taped is something like enduring dentistry on the installment plan. Performers play a few bars and halt while cameras and lights are repositioned, play a few more bars and halt again at a whim of the director or a faceless gnome in the control room. It's a maddening, tedious process. Either that, or it's a speed-of-soundbite, one-shot deal on Leno or Letterman, without context or continuity.

On *Austin City Limits,* unless there is a snafu on the part of either the band or the technical people, the show just rolls. The studio is intimate enough, the lights are just dim enough, and the free beer and bonhomie flow just lively enough to create a real sense of an organic performance.

Artists typically play between sixty and ninety minutes, a fair simulacrum of a set they might deliver in a club or from a concert stage. There is enough time to create ebb and flow, momentum and creative tension. The difference shows up on the screen.

As for the audio mix, longtime audio director David Hough and audio supervisor Billy Lee Myers, Jr., mix the music itself separately after the taping on multi-track machines with analog and digital capabilities in Studio 6-A, giving the sound a depth and sheen and texture that no other show on television approaches. "We've been working together for so long that David can think of something and I'll reach for the button," said Myers with the justifiable pride that comes from working together for ten hours a day for twenty years.

With today's home-theater setups, viewers can appreciate the sterling sound quality of the show, but it has been a perk of inestimable value to the artists for a long time.

Perhaps Mary Chapin Carpenter put it best after her taping in 1993: "This is the only television show I've ever done that I don't even know a camera is going. All you have to do is watch one show and you can see how important the atmosphere is. There's a live audience that's there to hear the music . . . and the atmosphere that is created here is one of great comfort and respect for the music, and also a nice intimacy. I like to visually see people and make that connection somehow. And you can do that from here.

"To me, tonight's show had all the ingredients that one would ever want in it as a musician, in terms of everything that we get back from playing, from the audience to the sense of comfort, and also that sense of freewheeling, of being able to do whatever we felt like doing. Those are all the good things that you want to feel every gig."

Vince Gill has hosted the Country Music Association awards in front of a national television audience, has packed arenas from sea to shining sea, and has topped the charts and raked in millions seemingly at whim, but he always comes back to *Austin City Limits.* To hear him tell it, there's a reason for that. "It's hip for all the right reasons," Gill says. "*Austin City Limits* is hip because they let musicians be musicians."

It's hard to argue that *ACL* did not benefit from being far removed from the media hotbeds of New York and Los Angeles, left free to incubate its own distinctive style without slavishly aping the trends of commercial programming.

The same principle of isolation applied to protean Lone Star musicians like Bob Wills, Buddy Holly, and Waylon Jennings, who didn't know they couldn't mix elements of jazz,

MARY CHAPIN CARPENTER (1992)

"When you do television, there's a camera in your face and the red light goes on . . . it's kind of a freaky feeling. When there's no audience, it's an artificial atmosphere. Somehow, Austin City Limits *manages to bridge that ground where it's television but the audience is there and the energy is very important to the performance. Nothing gets in the way of that here."*

VINCE GILL (1994)

"Austin City Limits is the hippest show on television," according to Vince Gill.

rock, country, swing, and blues, simply because they were working in the wilds of Texas, and no big-city tastemaker ever bothered to tell them such things Simply Weren't Done.

Bonnie Raitt, who has an unfettered fondness for Austin and things Austinesque, appreciates the distinction between Texas and (from the Lone Star perspective) the Left and Right Coasts. "New York and L.A. are not Texas," Raitt said. "If something came out of New Orleans or Minneapolis, it would have a certain hometown-hero/underdog thing to it, where people are proud of their city and proud of what makes them different.

"The same thing that makes Austin great is what makes the show great. There's a certain pride in the maverick quality, the lack of homogeneity. Proud to be an outside viewpoint. It's not embarrassed, it's not second-rate, it's not also-ran, it's not trying to be L.A. or New York. It's not trying to be anything, it just *is* Texas."

Raitt, like other gifted performers who fall between the stylistic cracks of rigid radio formats, valued *ACL* as an invaluable forum for getting her music out to the public in the days of shrinking, restrictive radio programming.

Shawn Colvin is the proud possessor of three Grammy awards and a wall full of gold records today, but at the time of her first appearance in Season 16 in 1991, radio did not know what to make of her, nor she of it. "It was huge!" Colvin says today of her first appearance. "I don't think you can measure the value that it has for someone like me. In effect, *Austin City Limits* perfectly fit that area between the cracks that I fell into, that radio was not able to cover. What other programs were there?"

Canadian poet, icon, and songwriter Leonard Cohen was even more emphatic. "*Austin City Limits* has kept me alive in this country for the past five years," Cohen said in 1993. "It's the only place I've ever appeared on television. It's the only outlet for my songs, for my performances, that there is in this country, so I have a special affection for the program."

BONNIE RAITT (1983)

According to Bonnie Raitt, for the musicians "who care about reaching people and touching people and celebrating music . . . Austin City Limits is such an incalculable part of why we're still around, you couldn't put a price tag on it. I couldn't hold up any other cultural phenomenon as high as I would this."

LEONARD COHEN (1993)
"If I knew where a good song came from, I'd go there more often. . . . I don't know what inspires me. It's a vice. It's also a job. It's something you do every day. You find your self-respect in your work."

When *Austin City Limits* began, it showcased hometown and regional performers mostly out of necessity. Then as now the show paid only union scale, and most major stars' managers and booking agents back then sometimes wouldn't even deign to return the show's calls.

Unlike such graying country music eminences as Bill Monroe and Ray Price who graced the KLRU stage at the show's inception, the stars who appear today were weaned on *Austin City Limits* as children. For some, the introduction was damned near prenatal, since their parents watched the show before them.

Bluegrass prodigy Alison Krauss, who took home an armload of Country Music Association awards around the time of her 1995 taping, is only five years older than the show itself; two recently featured blues guitar prodigies, Kenny Wayne Shepherd and Jonny Lang, were not even born when the series premiered in 1976. "All the guys in the band, we grew up watching the show," said Shepherd after his inaugural appearance in 1996.

Again and again artists venturing into Studio 6-A, either for the first time or for a return visit, have commented on what a familiar feel the set, the show, and the staff impart. Some feel like they are making an infrequent visit to a far-removed branch of the family. Others feel like they are wandering into a half-remembered old house, a déjà vu sensation of having passed this way before:

"It's kind of mind-boggling that I've been part of their family for over sixteen years,"

STEVE GOODMAN (1977)

If you believe, as staff photographer Scott Newton does, that the eyes are the window to the soul, then you will understand that storyteller supreme Steve Goodman had the brightest eyes imaginable—eyes like diamonds. He also had the quickest wit, the readiest repartee this side of Robin Williams. As we all shrug off this mortal coil, it's nice to know that we'll be greeted and entertained by the likes of Steve.

Vince Gill reminisced in 1994. "Although the first two times I did it I was working with somebody else, it was still a big deal. I still have the tape of the Rosanne [Cash] show in '83. It's fun to pull out and watch. The only thing bad about that is the shirt I wore. How could you ever think that shirt was cool?"

"Everybody here at *Austin City Limits* has let me hang around for years," Lyle Lovett admitted. "I think I'd like to do a duet with Terry Lickona next, and then maybe Gary [Menotti]. Then Arhos."

Musicians returning to the *Austin City Limits* set for subsequent tapings are greeted by familiar faces. The core group of the *ACL* staff has remained consistent over the years, a remarkable feat in the mercurial world of broadcasting. Some, such as cameraman Michael Emery, are nearly through the second decade of their *ACL* tenure. Others, like associate director Mike Archenhold, have been at the station since before the show's inception.

Many of the staff have literally grown up with one another within the show's confines, and some have discovered within the show a sense of family and a commitment to an institution that has proven more durable—literally—than friendships, marriages, childbirth, love affairs, or even mortal illness.

Associate producer Susan Caldwell reminisced about the ties that have bound her to the *ACL* staff for much of her adult life. "There was a time in the eighties when these were the only people I was around. This was my family. I was fresh out of college, and the friends that I made at *ACL* were so great and so bright and loved music and were to the left on the political scale, and fresh and articulate, and things were kind of wild. It was right up my alley: Hey! This is great!"

Joe Cook, the loquacious sixty-two-year-old West Virginia native who has handled artist security for the show since 1981, said that musicians absorb the spirit of the close-knit staff. "We care about each other," said Cook. "We're a family centered around music. When artists come to us, it's like coming to the house, and they love it. It's like a family, and every one of the artists knows it."

It seems to be a given, in this bottom-line age, that people will strive relentlessly onward and upward, propelled by a tunnel-vision perspective that ruthlessly discards the present in favor of some future Type-A ideal of "success." Yet the staff and crew of *Austin City Limits,* most of whom could make much more elsewhere, remain with the show, season after season. Their lives, and the lives of the viewers with whom they commune, have been immersed in art and song beyond price.

Austin City Limits Staff for 1998–99/Season 24

BILL ARHOS . . . . *Executive Producer*

TERRY LICKONA . . . . *Producer*

GARY MENOTTI . . . . *Director*

MIKE ARCHENHOLD . . . . *Associate Director*

SUSAN CALDWELL . . . . *Associate Producer*

JEFF PETERSON . . . . *Associate Producer*

DICK PETERSON . . . . *Director of Production*

LINDA LEHMUSVIRTA . . . . *Production Manager*

RICARDO GARZA . . . . *Unit Manager*

DAVID HOUGH . . . . *Audio Director*

BILLY LEE MYERS JR. . . . . *Audio Supervisor*

SHARON CULLEN . . . . *Audio*

DAN MARTAUS . . . . *Video and Editor*

JACK WELLS . . . . *Engineering Director*

DAVE KUIPERS . . . . *Engineering Supervisor*

BOB SELBY . . . . *Lighting Director*

WALTER OLDEN . . . . *Lighting Technician*

ED FUENTES . . . . *Technical Director*

RAY LUCERO . . . . *Stage Manager*

DOUG ROBB, MICHAEL EMERY, VANCE HOLMES,
ROBERT MOORHEAD, MIKE ARCHENHOLD,
TODD PANKEY, DUSTY SEXTON . . . . *Camera Operators*

GENE HARRIS, JIMMY WEWER . . . . *Engineering*

TIFFANY TYSON/PAT COSGROVE,
STEPHANIE WRIGHT . . . . *Publicity*

EDWARD BAILEY . . . . *Director of Marketing*

SCOTT NEWTON . . . . *Photographer*

RANDIE FRASER . . . . *Volunteer Coordinator*

JOE COOK . . . . *Security*

GLENDA FACEMIRE . . . . *Makeup*

MARY BETH ROGERS . . . . *Executive in Charge*

TIMELINE

LIKE ANY GOOD STORY, the saga of *Austin City Limits* has a beginning, a middle . . . but, thank goodness, no end in sight. The following timeline adds some perspective as to what was going on in the rest of the music world and the world at large while home and studio audiences forgot their troubles for an hour and danced to Asleep at the Wheel or Clifton Chenier's Red Hot Louisiana Band, or collectively mourned the losses of friends like Walter Hyatt and Townes Van Zandt.

Rather than a laundry list of *ACL* shows and performers (you can find that in the Chronology of Programs and Songs at the back of this book on pages 176 through 189), the *Austin City Limits* timeline also includes milestones (some large, some not so large) in the lives and careers of the artists that have become members of the *Austin City Limits* family—many now members of the Rock and Roll or Country Music halls of fame.

DAN FORTE

1975

AUSTIN CITY LIMITS

WILLIE NELSON

Willie Nelson is the featured artist on the pilot episode of *Austin City Limits*; although most people in the music industry have scarcely heard of, let alone been to, Austin, Texas.

FREDDIE FENDER

In a year peppered with disco and soft rock, Freddy Fender reaches the #1 spot on *Billboard*'s Pop chart with "Before the Next Teardrop Falls" and is named Most Promising Male Vocalist by the Academy of Country Music.

The king of western swing Bob Wills (b. 1905) dies.

Canadian Kathy Dawn (k.d.) Lang, 14, writes her first song, "Hoping My Dreams Will Come True."

MUSIC

Bruce Springsteen graces the covers of *Time* and *Newsweek* in the same week.

Eight years after "Society's Child," Janis Ian scores a #3 hit with "At Seventeen."

The Grammy for Record of the Year goes to . . . "Love Will Keep Us Together" by The Captain and Tennille.

WORLD EVENTS

The U.S. launches an evacuation of Saigon one day before the South Vietnamese government surrenders to North Vietnam.

The average cost of a gallon of regular gasoline in the U.S. is 56.7 cents.

There are two separate attempts to assassinate President Ford in a single month.

The VHS video format is invented in Japan.

After her 1974 kidnapping by the Symbionese Liberation Army, Patty Hearst is arrested by the FBI for participating in a bank robbery with the SLA.

One Flew Over the Cuckoo's Nest nabs Oscars for Best Picture, Best Director (Milos Forman), Best Actor (Jack Nicholson), and Best Actress (Louise Fletcher).

1976

BOB WILLS' TEXAS PLAYBOYS

Original members of Bob Wills' Texas Playboys reunite for the first time in 30 years on *Austin City Limits*. Sadly, Jesse Ashlock, Keith Coleman, and Clifton "Sleepy" Johnson, all fiddlers in the group, die that same year.

Legendary Texas songwriter Townes Van Zandt's first and only full performance on *ACL*.

Bluegrass fiddler Alison Krauss enters kindergarten, and guitarist Kenny Wayne Shepherd is born.

Waylon Jennings, his wife Jessi Colter, Willie Nelson, and Tompall Glaser team up for *Wanted: The Outlaws;* which becomes country music's first platinum album.

The David Grisman Quintet plays its first gig, marking the dawn of "Dawg" music, a hybrid of bluegrass, jazz, and other styles.

WAYLON JENNINGS

The Beatles turn down a $30 million offer to reunite.

Frampton Comes Alive! does just that: it resuscitates Peter Frampton's stalled career, topping *Billboard*'s album chart for 10 weeks and selling 13 million copies.

Ragtime composer Scott Joplin posthumously receives a special Pulitzer Prize.

The Band says farewell at "The Last Waltz," in San Francisco's Winterland, where they are joined by friends such as Eric Clapton, Neil Young, Muddy Waters, Joni Mitchell, and Bob Dylan.

Memphis disc jockey Rick Dees satirizes the disco craze with "Disco Duck"–which climbs to #1.

The Ramones draft the blueprint for punk rock with their self-titled debut album.

America celebrates its Bicentennial.

In Montreal, Canada, Romanian gymnast Nadia Comeneci scores the first perfect 10 in Olympic history, on the uneven bars.

A mysterious illness dubbed "Legionnaire's disease" kills 29 people who attended an American Legion convention in Philadelphia.

Jimmy Carter is elected 39th president of the U.S.

Mao Zedong (b. 1893) dies.

The federal minimum wage in the U.S. is $2.30/hour.

1977

MARTY STUART

Gary P. Nunn's "London Homesick Blues" (with its familiar chorus, "I wanna go home with the armadillo . . . ") is used as *ACL* theme song for the first time—and has continued ever since.

Willie Nelson performs at Jimmy Carter's inaugural bash.

Multi-instrumentalist/vocalist Ricky Skaggs replaces Rodney Crowell in Emmylou Harris's Hot Band; Crowell releases solo debut, *I Ain't Livin' Long Like This.*

Banjo king Earl Scruggs (Flatt & Scruggs) appears with sons as part of the "Earl Scruggs Revue."

Lester Flatt's former guitar prodigy, Marty Stuart, releases his solo debut, *Marty, with a Little Help from His Friends.*

Jimmy Buffett's first appearance on *ACL*. Says he wrote "Margaritaville" about Austin.

Fleetwood Mac's *Rumours* owns the #1 spot for 31 weeks.

Seven years after his most recent Top 20 hit (as leader of the First Edition), Kenny Rogers rockets to #5 with "Lucille."

It's a tie! Grammy's Song of the Year honor is shared by "Evergreen" (co-written by its performer, Barbra Streisand) and "You Light Up My Life" (whose singer, Debby Boone, also wins Best New Artist).

Thomas Edison's invention, the phonograph, celebrates its hundredth anniversary.

The king is dead. Elvis Presley dies at the age of 42.

Roots, Part 8 becomes top-rated TV telecast of all time.

In the first exercise of capital punishment in the U.S. in ten years, convicted murderer Gary Gilmore is executed by a Utah firing squad.

The Nobel Peace Prize is awarded to Amnesty International.

George Lucas's *Star Wars* breaks all box office records and revolutionizes the role of special effects in motion pictures.

Groucho Marx (b. 1890) and Charlie Chaplin (b. 1889) both die.

1978

EARL SCRUGGS

CHET ATKINS

ACL showcases major Nashville country stars for the first time with the appearances of Chet Atkins and Merle Haggard.

Fiddler Johnny Gimble makes his first appearance on the show, with Bob Wills' Original Texas Playboys.

Asleep at the Wheel wins its first Grammy, for Best Country Instrumental Performance: "One O'Clock Jump."

Los Lobos, an East Los Angeles group playing traditional Mexican folk music, presses a few hundred copies of their debut album, *Just Another Band from East L.A.*

JOHNNY GIMBLE

Saturday Night Fever soundtrack occupies the #1 slot for 24 weeks and yields three #1 singles for the Bee Gees, yet it receives zero Oscar nominations.

Who drummer Keith Moon (b. 1947) dies.

John Travolta becomes as familiar a face in record racks as on the big screen, with the *Grease* soundtrack following in *Saturday Night Fever*'s footsteps–to #1.

Gary Busey portrays Lubbock, Texas's, favorite son in *The Buddy Holly Story.*

U.S. Congressman Leo Ryan and members of his entourage are murdered while investigating the Jonestown cult in Guyana. More than 900 members of the cult then commit mass suicide on orders from leader Jim Jones.

Muhammad Ali defeats Leon Spinks to become boxing's heavyweight champion for an unprecedented third time.

Polish Cardinal Karol Wojtyla is named Pope John Paul II, the first non-Italian pontiff in 456 years.

Boston Celtic John Havlicek retires as the NBA's all-time leader in games played (1,270).

Britain's Louise Brown, the world's first test tube baby, is born.

1979

With new producer Terry Lickona, *Austin City Limits* broadens its scope to include styles other than country and Texas. Artists as diverse as Tom Waits, Taj Mahal, Lightnin' Hopkins, and the Neville Brothers appear.

TAJ MAHAL

Willie Nelson co-stars with Robert Redford and Jane Fonda in *The Electric Horseman.*

Vince Gill makes his first *ACL* appearance, as singer-guitarist for Pure Prairie League.

Austin's progressive jazz group Passenger backs Canadian songwriter Leonard Cohen on his *Recent Songs* album and becomes his touring unit.

Ry Cooder records rock's first digital album, *Bop Till You Drop.*

PASSENGER

1980

Austin City Limits' first "Songwriters' Special" inaugurates a popular concept repeated many times through the years.

Notable performances on *ACL* this year include Roy Clark, Joe Ely, Jerry Jeff Walker, Hank Williams Jr., Marty Robbins, Carl Perkins, Mel Tillis, and Ray Charles, the first major black or pop artist to appear on the show.

Mickey Gilley's football field–sized Pasadena, Texas, club, Gilley's, is the setting for *Urban Cowboy,* starring John Travolta. Thousands of cowboy bars rear up like mechanical-bull phoenixes from the ashes of as many disco insurance fires.

Clarence "Gatemouth" Brown and Roy Clark meld blues and country on one of *ACL's* most unique collaborations.

Johnny Cash's daughter Rosanne releases her debut album, *Right or Wrong,* produced by then-husband Rodney Crowell.

The movie *Coal Miner's Daughter,* based on Loretta Lynn's autobiography, earns Sissy Spacek a Best Actress Oscar.

RAY CHARLES   GATEMOUTH BROWN

1981

GEORGE JONES

Kris Kristofferson plays the lead in *Heaven's Gate,* one of the biggest (and most expensive) flops in the history of cinema.

Rockabilly revivalist Robert Gordon plays a tiny California club, Berkeley Square, with Washington, D.C.'s, best-kept secret, Danny Gatton, on guitar. A bootleg tape of the show circulates among guitarists around the world and earns the name "The Humbler," to describe the effect Gatton's ability has on other pickers.

The Exchange Club Carl Perkins Center for the Prevention of Child Abuse opens in Jackson, Tennessee.

Blues guitarist Jonny Lang is born.

"The Voice," George Jones, appears and introduces legendary guest Hank Thompson as "the Queen of Country Music."

ACL's first "instrumental showcase" spotlights the mandolin, with Johnny Gimble, Tiny Moore, Jethro Burns, and David Grisman.

Bill Monroe, the "Father of Bluegrass," makes his first appearance on *ACL.*

BILL MONROE

Sony introduces the Walkman portable cassette player.

Eleven fans are trampled to death at a Who concert in Cincinnati.

The Anti-Defamation League issues a statement deploring Frank Zappa's song "Jewish Princess"; Zappa follows up with a song called "Catholic Girls."

The Y.M.C.A. unsuccessfully sues the Village People over the group's catchy ditty "Y.M.C.A."

Jazz bassist-composer Charles Mingus (b. 1922) dies of Lou Gehrig's Disease.

Cat Stevens becomes a devout Muslim and retires from the music business.

John Lennon (b. 1940) is assassinated by a deranged fan outside his apartment building.

Pink Floyd's *The Wall* holds on to #1 for 15 weeks on *Billboard's* album chart.

Former Fleetwood Mac roadie Christopher Cross sails away with five Grammy Awards.

Harry Chapin (b. 1942) dies in a car crash on his way to a benefit concert.

MTV, a 24-hour music video channel, debuts.

Bob Marley (b. 1945) and Bill Haley (b. 1925) both die.

Deborah Harry and Blondie release their album, *Compilations: The Best of Blondie.*

New wave meets country when Elvis Costello records *Almost Blue* in Nashville.

REO Speedwagon's album *Hi Infidelity* clings to #1 for 15 weeks. (Really. You can look it up.)

Tony awards go to *Amadeus* for Best Play and *42nd Street* for Best Musical.

The World Health Organization announces that smallpox is officially eradicated.

The worst commercial nuclear accident in U.S. history occurs at Three Mile Island, in Middletown, Pennsylvania.

John Wayne (b. 1907) dies.

Sixty-three Americans are among those taken hostage by militant followers of Ayatollah Khomeini in Tehran, Iran.

Iraq's Saddam Hussein launches an attack on Iran, beginning a decade-long war.

U.S. hockey team beats USSR, 4-3, and goes on to win gold at the Winter Olympics in Lake Placid, New York.

Eight Americans are killed in an ill-fated attempt to rescue hostages held in Iran.

The eruption of Washington State's Mount St. Helens, with an estimated force of 500 times the Hiroshima atomic bomb, leaves 60 dead.

The U.S. boycotts the Moscow Summer Olympics following the Soviet invasion of Afghanistan.

Ted Turner launches the first all-news network, CNN.

Ronald Reagan is elected 40th president of the U.S.

Minutes after Ronald Reagan's inauguration, Iran releases all remaining American hostages—held for a total of 444 days.

Egyptian president Anwar Sadat (b. 1918) is assassinated.

President Reagan and Pope John Paul II both survive assassination attempts.

Sandra Day O'Connor becomes the first woman appointed to the U.S. Supreme Court.

Prince Charles weds Lady Diana Spencer.

Pac-Man leads the video game craze.

The first cases of Acquired Immune Deficiency Syndrome (AIDS) are recognized.

1982

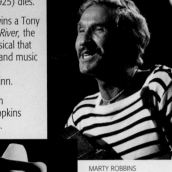

MARTY ROBBINS

Austin City Limits' familiar skyline backdrop is introduced. It has been in continuous use ever since.

Asleep at the Wheel logs its millionth road mile. "That's not counting air miles," points out leader Ray Benson.

Country singer Marty Robbins (b. 1925) dies.

Roger Miller wins a Tony award for *Big River,* the Broadway musical that set his words and music to the story of Huckleberry Finn.

Bluesman Sam "Lightnin'" Hopkins (b. 1912) dies.

An unknown Texas country singer named George Strait makes his first appearance on the show.

GEORGE STRAIT

Both the vocal and instrumental versions of Marvin Gaye's "Sexual Healing" win Grammys in the R & B category.

Jazz pianist/composer Thelonious Monk (b. 1917) dies.

The Go-Go's become the first "all-girl/play-their-own-instruments" group to reach #1, with their LP *Beauty and the Beat.*

Toto wins Grammys for Best Single, "Rosanna," and Best LP, *Toto IV.*

Comedian Bill Murray sings an impromptu (and energetic) rendition of Olivia Newton-John's "Physical" on the premiere installment of NBC's *Late Night with David Letterman.*

British troops attack Argentina, after it invades the Falkland Islands.

In December the unemployment rate in the U.S. hits 10.8 percent, its highest level since 1940.

Bill Bradley is inducted into the NBA Hall of Fame.

Doctors perform the first artificial heart transplant in America.

Alva Myrdal, Sweden, and Alfonso Garcia Robles, Mexico, win Nobel Peace Prizes.

The Equal Rights Amendment is defeated after a 10-year fight for ratification.

1983

ROY ORBISON

The reclusive Roy Orbison emerges from retirement for a spine-tingling performance, ranking as one of *ACL*'s best.

Los Lobos's "Anselma" garners a Grammy in a new category: Best Mexican-American Performance.

Merle Travis (b. 1917), the man for whom a whole school of traditional country guitar playing was named, dies.

MERLE TRAVIS

The Society for the Preservation of Bluegrass Music in America names 12-year-old Alison Krauss the Most Promising Fiddler in the Midwest.

The debut single by a retired nurse and her guitar-strumming daughter reaches country's Top 20–the Judds's "Had a Dream."

First appearances: B.B. King, Loretta Lynn, Tammy Wynette.

Willie Nelson and Roger Miller engage in an impromtu dance onstage during Miller's performance of "Milkcow Blues."

Only six albums reach the #1 spot in the entire year—because one of them, Michael Jackson's *Thriller,* monopolizes that seat for 37 weeks. The album nets the Gloved One three #1 singles and eight Grammys.

ZZ Top's *Eliminator* enters *Billboard*'s Top Pop Albums chart, where it will reside for the next 183 weeks.

The Everly Brothers reunite after a 10-year split.

Pop lyricist Ira Gershwin (b. 1896) and Chicago blues architect Muddy Waters (b. 1915) die.

Challenger crew member Sally Ride becomes the first woman to travel in space.

Seven percent of American households own a computer.

A truck bomb kills 241 at a U.S. Marine base in Beirut, Lebanon.

Soviets shoot down Korean Airlines flight 007, killing all 269 onboard.

Author Alice Walker wins the Pulitzer Prize for *The Color Purple.*

The 251st and final episode of TV's *M*A*S*H* airs.

1984

JERRY LEE LEWIS

Although best known for great country music, *ACL* brings a diverse array of talent and musical styles to TV, as evidenced by this year's lineup, which includes Ray Charles, Jerry Lee Lewis, Bonnie Raitt, and Stevie Ray Vaughan.

The Grammy for Best Ethnic or Traditional Folk Recording goes to 92-year-old Elizabeth Cotten.

STEVE GOODMAN

A country group called Sawyer Brown wins the $100,000 first prize on TV's *Star Search.*

Steve Goodman (b. 1948), composer of "A Dying Cub Fan's Last Request," succumbs to leukemia; days later the Chicago Cubs win their division.

Los Lobos is named Band of the Year in *Rolling Stone*'s Critics' Poll.

"E.T.," Ernest Tubb (b. 1914), dies.

ERNEST TUBB

Only *four* albums reach #1 spot, one being Prince's *Purple Rain,* which stays there 24 weeks.

Big band leader Count Basie (b. 1904) dies.

Tina Turner's triumphant comeback uncovers decades of spousal abuse at the hands of ex-husband Ike Turner.

During a domestic squabble Marvin Gaye (b. 1939) is shot and killed by his father.

Democratic presidential candidate Walter Mondale chooses Geraldine Ferraro as the first female vice-presidential candidate for a major party. Reagan is re-elected president, carrying 49 states.

Indian Prime Minister Indira Gandhi (b. 1917) is assassinated by two of her bodyguards, members of a minority Sikh sect.

Britain's Torvill and Dean win Olympic gold in Sarajevo, Yugoslavia, and the figure skating duo's fourth World Championship.

HIV is identified as causing AIDS.

Muhammad Ali is diagnosed with Parkinson's Disease.

1985

Austin City Limits

Austin City Limits celebrates its 10th anniversary with a special show in downtown Austin with Bob Wills' Original Texas Playboys; 5,000 fans turn out.

Nanci Griffith makes her first appearance on the show, with Lyle Lovett as guest backup singer.

Zydeco accordion king Clifton Chenier (b. 1925) dies, as does Texas blues piano pioneer Robert Shaw (b. 1908).

Willie Nelson transforms his annual Fourth of July Picnic into FarmAid.

Doc Watson's son and long-time picking partner, Merle Watson (b. 1949), dies in a tractor accident near his farm in North Carolina.

Neil Young goes country in first and only *ACL* appearance.

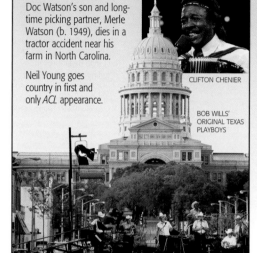

CLIFTON CHENIER

BOB WILLS' ORIGINAL TEXAS PLAYBOYS

Music

The album *Centerfield* marks the triumphant return of John Fogerty to Creedence Clearwater Revival.

"This is like treating dandruff by decapitation," Frank Zappa tells a Congressional panel debating the censorship of rock lyrics. He refers to the Parents Music Resource Center (PMRC, spearheaded by Tipper Gore) as "a bunch of bored housewives."

Initiated by Bob Geldof of the Boomtown Rats, the Live Aid concerts raise $70 million for African famine relief.

USA for Africa's "We Are the World"—written by Stevie Wonder and Lionel Ritchie, produced by Quincy Jones, and featuring a vast array of artists from all genres—similarly raises money to feed starving Africans.

World Events

Palestinian terrorists hijack the Italian cruise ship *Achille Lauro,* killing one American passenger.

Rock Hudson's (b. 1925) death from AIDS heightens public awareness of the disease.

The election of the charismatic Mikhail Gorbachev leads to more liberal reforms and the eventual breakup of the Soviet Union.

Michael Jordan is named NBA Rookie of the Year.

1986

Austin City Limits

AUSTIN CITY LIMITS REUNION SPECIAL

The *Austin City Limits* Reunion Special includes Marcia Ball, Asleep at the Wheel, Jerry Jeff Walker, and others from the show's first year.

Singer-songwriter Tom Waits co-stars (with John Lurie and Roberto Benigni) in the Jim Jarmusch film *Down by Law.*

After four less-than-gold albums, the Fabulous (but label-less) Thunderbirds gamble by going to London to record their self-financed LP, *Tuff Enuff.* It goes platinum.

Folk singer Kate Wolf dies (b. 1942), as does country picker Joe Maphis (b. 1921), and Texas Playboys "piano pounder" Al Strickland (b. 1908).

After 17 seasons Buck Owens leaves *Hee-Haw* in the hands of co-host Roy Clark, who stays on another eight years, until the show ends its 25-year reign as the longest-running syndicated program in TV history.

After a decade of neglect, *ACL* presents first all-women songwriters' showcase, with Emmylou Harris, Rosanne Cash, Gail Davies, and Lacy J. Dalton.

Music

Run-D.M.C.'s *Raising Hell* popularizes rap music.

Peter Gabriel's *So* spawns the hit singles "Sledgehammer," "In Your Eyes," "Red Rain," "Big Time," and "Don't Give Up" (with Kate Bush).

Paul Simon's *Graceland* wins Grammy for Best Album and helps popularize "world music."

The Rock and Roll Hall of Fame announces its first ten inductees: Fats Domino, Ray Charles, Buddy Holly, Little Richard, Chuck Berry, the Everly Brothers, Sam Cooke, Jerry Lee Lewis, James Brown, and Elvis Presley.

World Events

The brutal Vietnam War epic *Platoon* wins Academy Awards for Best Picture and Best Director (Oliver Stone).

Space shuttle Challenger explodes shortly after takeoff, killing everyone on board: six astronauts and school teacher Christa McAuliffe.

Phillipine President Ferdinand Marcos flees his country and seeks asylum in the U.S. Corazon Aquino, widow of his political opponent, takes office.

Martin Luther King Jr. Day is observed for the first time as a national holiday.

A nuclear accident at a power station in Chernobyl, Ukraine, kills 4,300 and affects the health of more than three million people.

1987

Austin City Limits

Lyle Lovett makes the first of many memorable appearances. Other firsts include Leon Russell, Randy Travis, Kathy Mattea, and Johnny Cash with June Carter and the Carter Family.

Fats Domino brings a touch of Mardi Gras to the *ACL* stage in his only appearance.

Los Lobos provide the music (and Ritchie Valens's singing voice) for the movie *La Bamba.*

LYLE LOVETT

Ray Charles, Fats Domino, and B.B. King are given Lifetime Achievement Awards by the National Academy of Recorded Arts and Sciences.

Electric mandolinist Tiny Moore (b. 1920), an alumnus of the Texas Playboys and Merle Haggard's band, dies.

Roy Orbison, Carl Perkins, and B.B. King are inducted into the Rock and Roll Hall of Fame.

Folk-blues singer Elizabeth Cotten (b. 1892) dies.

Reba McEntire wins CMA's Female Vocalist of the Year award for the fourth straight year.

Eric Johnson wins *Guitar Player* magazine's Readers' Poll for New Talent.

FATS DOMINO

Music

Fred Astaire (b. 1899) dies.

Singer-songwriter John Hiatt substantially enlarges his cult following with the release of *Bring the Family,* on which he is backed by Ry Cooder, Nick Lowe, and Jim Keltner. The four briefly regroup in 1992 as Little Village.

Classical guitarist Andrés Segovia (b. 1893) dies.

At a "Welcome Home" concert for Vietnam vets, John Fogerty performs Creedence Clearwater Revival songs publicly for the first time since the band's breakup in 1972.

World Events

President Reagan submits first-ever trillion-dollar budget to Congress.

Cher wins Best Actress Oscar for *Moonstruck.*

The Dow Jones tops 2,000 for the first time ever.

Lt. Col. Oliver North testifies before the televised Iran-Contra hearings. A year later he is convicted of conspiring to defraud the United States government.

On October 19, "Black Monday," the stock market crashes; Dow plummets a record 508 points.

1988

Austin City Limits is at the helm for the PBS special "Buddy Holly and the Crickets—A Tribute," featuring, among others, Brian Setzer, Duane Eddy, Bobby Vee, Marshall Crenshaw, John Fogerty, and Don "American Pie" McLean, along with the Crickets themselves.

"Take it away, Leon!" Texas Playboys steel guitarist Leon McAuliffe dies.

REBA McENTIRE

After coaxing Buck Owens out of retirement, Dwight Yoakam and the country legend record a duet version of Owens's 1972 recording, "Streets of Bakersfield."

Guitarist Roy Buchanan (b. 1939) dies under mysterious circumstances in a Virginia jail cell.

Roy Orbison (b. 1936) dies, but not before the debut release of the super incognito group the Traveling Wilburys teams the singer with Bob Dylan, George Harrison, Jeff Lynne, and Tom Petty.

Reba McEntire appears on ACL for the first time; her manager insists that the Austin skyline backdrop be "turned off."

Loretta Lynn is inducted into the Country Music Hall of Fame, and after winning the Readers' Poll blues category five times, Stevie Ray Vaughan is inducted into Guitar Player magazine's Gallery of Greats.

Singer-songwriter B.W. Stevenson (b. 1949) dies during heart surgery.

Hard rockers dominate Billboard's album chart, with #1 efforts by Van Halen, Def Leppard, Guns N' Roses, and Bon Jovi. But the Grammy in the new Hard Rock/Heavy Metal category goes to . . . Jethro Tull?

Spurred on by concerts in shopping malls (featured in her videos) 16-year-old Tiffany's self-titled debut album dances its way to #1.

Sonny Bono is elected mayor of Palm Springs.

In the U.S. vice-presidential debate Lloyd Bentsen informs Dan Quayle, "You're no Jack Kennedy."

Pan Am Flight 103 explodes over Lockerbie, Scotland, killing 259 onboard and 11 on the ground. Investigations lead to Libyan terrorists.

Drexel Burnham Lambert agrees to pay a 650 million-dollar settlement for insider trading and other federal violations.

George Bush is elected 41st president of the U.S.

America endures its worst drought in 50 years.

1989

On Los Lobos's first ACL appearance they are joined by their mentor, accordionist Flaco Jimenez.

Delbert McClinton's 1989 ACL appearance is released as an Alligator Records CD, Live from Austin.

Traditional country artist Keith Whitley (b. 1955) dies of alcohol poisoning.

Canadian Leonard Cohen brings his iconoclastic folk to ACL, garnering the biggest response in ACL history.

LEONARD COHEN

After eight albums spanning 17 years, Bonnie Raitt's Nick of Time wins her her first three Grammys, including Album of the Year.

Mandolinist Kenneth "Jethro" Burns (b. 1920) dies.

Garth Brooks releases his self-titled debut album.

Fiddler Martie Seidel and banjo-playing sister Emily Erwin form a group in Dallas with bassist Laura Lynch and guitarist Robin Lynn Macy, calling themselves the "Dixie Chicks," inspired by the Little Feat song "Dixie Chickens."

FLACO JIMENEZ

The duo Milli Vanilli wins the Grammy for New Artist, but when it's later discovered that they didn't actually sing on their album, they're asked to give back the award.

Irving Berlin (b. 1888) dies at the age of 101.

Bruce Springsteen splits with the E Street Band.

The Beastie Boys release Paul's Boutique.

East and West Germans tear down the Berlin Wall.

At least 700 are massacred when Chinese troops crush a nonviolent pro-democracy demonstration in Beijing's Tiananmen Square.

An earthquake registering 7.1 on the Richter scale interrupts the Oakland-San Francisco World Series. Sixty-two die, many when an elevated freeway collapses.

The Exxon Valdez grounds off Prince William Sound, Alaska, spilling 10,000,000 gallons of oil.

Pete Rose is banished from baseball for betting on games.

Serbian president Slobodan Milosevic revokes Kosovo's autonomy in the former Yugoslavia. Kosovo is 90 percent ethnic Albanians.

1990

ACL's 50th birthday salute to the "Godfather of Austin Blues," W.C. Clark, brings out Austin's blues elite and marks Stevie Ray Vaughan's last appearance on the show.

GARTH BROOKS

Garth Brooks approaches megastar status and marks his first ACL appearance; he compares it to "playing in the World Series."

Nitty Gritty Dirt Band assembles all-star country and bluegrass cast for "Will the Circle Be Unbroken," including John Denver.

STEVIE RAY VAUGHAN

Following a triumphant concert at Wisconsin's Alpine Valley amphitheater, Stevie Ray Vaughan (b. 1954) dies in a helicopter crash near Troy, Wisconsin.

B.B. King receives a star on Hollywood's Walk of Fame.

Family Style by Vaughan Brothers Jimmie and Stevie Ray wins Grammys for Contemporary Blues Recording and Rock Instrumental ("D/FW").

B.B. KING

Former Oakland A's batboy Stanley Kirk Burrell dubs himself M.C. Hammer and dances his way to the top of the charts with Please Hammer Don't Hurt 'Em—the #1 album for 21 weeks.

The Rome performance of opera's "Three Tenors," Placido Domingo, Luciano Pavarotti, and José Carreras, is viewed by a television audience of 1.5 billion.

Following Iraq's invasion of the tiny but oil-rich Kuwait, a U.S.-led coalition of two dozen countries unleashes Desert Storm, soon defeating Iraq in the Persian Gulf War.

Tennis's Martina Navratilova wins her ninth Wimbledon championship.

Previously an animated short on The Tracy Ullman Show, The Simpsons premiers on the Fox network.

Muppets creator Jim Henson (b. 1936) dies.

In a South African prison since 1964, Nelson Mandela is released. He becomes the nation's president in 1994 and signs the post-apartheid constitution into law in 1996.

1991

Austin City Limits' "Salute to the Cowboy" features Michael Martin Murphey, Riders in the Sky, and others.

Grammy winner and Austin resident Shawn Colvin's first appearance.

SHAWN COLVIN

DOTTIE WEST

Garth Brooks wins an unprecedented six Academy of Country Music awards.

Willie Nelson releases *The IRS Tapes,* profits from which go to Uncle Sam to defray the singer's multi-million dollar tax debt.

Country singer Dottie West (b. 1932) and zydeco rubboard player Cleveland Chenier both die.

Manhattan Transfer collects its eighth Grammy, for Best Contemporary Jazz Performance.

Guitarist Jimmie Vaughan sings in public for the first time–at Royal Albert Hall in London, performing with Eric Clapton.

1992

INDIGO GIRLS

The Austin reunion of Dan Hicks (who hadn't released a record in 14 years) and his Hot Licks (who broke up 16 years ago) draws 1,000-plus and prompts producer Terry Lickona to have them re-reunite for *ACL*'s 17th season.

This season begins with an extremely popular all-female Songwriters' Special featuring Indigo Girls, Nanci Griffith, Mary Chapin Carpenter, and Julie Gold.

Vince Gill plays *ACL* a second time (as a solo artist), and Travis Tritt, Hal Ketchum, and Trisha Yearwood give show-stopping first-time performances.

While acting in the Robert Altman movie *The Player,* Lyle Lovett meets future ex-wife Julia Roberts.

JOHNNY CASH

Roger Miller (b. 1936) dies.

George Strait stars as (what else?) a country singer in the movie *Pure Country.*

Johnny Cash and Bobby Blue Bland are inducted into the Rock and Roll Hall of Fame.

1993

WILLIE NELSON

ALBERT COLLINS

Happy birthday, Willie! For his 60th birthday, the Redheaded Stranger is inducted into the Country Music Hall of Fame and paid tribute on the CBS special "The Big Six-O."

Performances by Asleep at the Wheel, Lyle Lovett, Dr. John, Garrison Keillor and the Hopeful Gospel Quartet, Chet Atkins, Johnny Gimble, and Suzy Bogguss show *ACL* has something for everyone.

"The Master of the Telecaster," blues great Albert Collins (b. 1932) dies.

In the same year that Garth Brooks is made a member of the Grand Ole Opry, 21-year-old Alison Krauss becomes the first bluegrass artist to be inducted into the Opry in 29 years.

The tongue-in-cheek country group the Geezinslaws win the National Association of Record Merchandisers' Independent Country Album of the Year award for *Feelin' Good, Gittin' Up, Gittin' Down.*

Rap star M.C. Hammer drops the "M.C." from his name.

For the first time *Billboard*'s album charts are based on actual sales, recorded by UPC bar codes via SoundScan. Soon after, Garth Brooks's *Ropin' the Wind* becomes the first album to debut at #1 on both the Pop and Country charts.

Bob Dylan turns 50. His 30 years in the music business are saluted at a Madison Square Garden concert featuring George Harrison, Roger McGuinn, Sinead O'Connor, and Bob himself.

Concert promoter Bill Graham (b. 1931) dies.

Natalie Cole duets with her deceased father (on *Unforgettable with Love*), Harry Connick Jr.'s soundtrack to the movie *When Harry Met Sally . . .*, and Tony Bennett bills with rock acts helping to usher in a swing revival.

Grand Ole Opry star Roy Acuff (b. 1903) dies, as does blues guitar master Albert King (b. 1923).

Seattle bands like Pearl Jam and Nirvana, whose *Nevermind* shoots to #1, announce the arrival of grunge.

Country hunk Billy Ray Cyrus's "Achy Breaky Heart" introduces the dance the "Achy Breaky."

The tragic death of Eric Clapton's son Conor in 1991 halts his career briefly, but inspires the Grammy-winning "Tears in Heaven," from the album *Unplugged,* also Grammy winning.

Cream reunites to perform at its induction into the Rock and Roll Hall of Fame–John Fogerty fronts a super group to play (fellow inductees) Creedence Clearwater Revival songs while former bandmates Doug Clifford and Stu Cook sit in the audience and eventually walk out.

Frank Zappa (b. 1940) and Dizzy Gillespie (b. 1917) die.

Variety is the spice of life. Barbra Streisand, Aerosmith, Garth Brooks, Pearl Jam, and an "unplugged" Eric Clapton all place albums at #1.

By now most major record labels no longer press vinyl LPs, having replaced them with compact discs.

A Hard Day's Night is available on CD-ROM.

Whitney Houston wins Grammys for "I Will Always Love You" and *The Bodyguard.*

Magic Johnson retires from basketball after he tests positive for HIV.

Dr. Seuss (Theodor Seuss Geisel, b. 1904) dies.

Mt. Pinitubo erupts in the Philipines.

Nolan Ryan tosses a record seventh no-hitter for Houston.

A cyclone in Bangladesh claims 139,000 lives.

Riots erupt in Los Angeles after four L.A. police officers who were videotaped beating Rodney King are acquitted by an all-white jury.

Johnny Carson retires after 30 years as host of the *Tonight Show.*

Bill Clinton defeats incumbent George Bush to become 42nd president of the U.S.

Jackie Joyner-Kersee, sister of 1984 triple-jump champion Al Joyner, takes the gold in the heptathlon in Barcelona. (Her sister-in-law, Florence Griffith Joyner, won three golds in the '88 games.)

Ex-heavyweight champ Mike Tyson is convicted of rape.

An earthquake centered near Los Angeles sets off fires, floods, and mudslides. Sixty-one die as a result.

The Nobel Peace Prize is given jointly to South Africans F.W. de Klerk and Nelson Mandela.

Nolan Ryan strikes out career-record 5,714th batter before retiring from baseball.

Michael Jordan retires from basketball.

Terrorists' bomb kills six at NYC's World Trade Center.

Nancy Kerrigan, figure skating's front-runner for the upcoming Olympics in Lillehammer, Norway, is clubbed in the knee by two attackers hired by the husband of skating rival Tonya Harding. Kerrigan goes on to Olympic silver.

After a 51-day standoff with the Branch Davidian cult in Waco, Texas, Federal agents storm the compound. Seventeen children are among the 75 who die.

1994

This star-studded season includes appearances by Willie Nelson, Lyle Lovett, Rodney Crowell, Rosanne Cash and Carlene Carter, Bruce Hornsby, and Suzanne Vega.

JOAN BAEZ

Folk legend Joan Baez wows audience in first and only *ACL* appearance.

Johnny Cash's pared down *American Recordings* cops a Grammy for Best Contemporary Folk Album.

At age 60 the "Pavarotti of the Plains," Austin yodeler Don Walser, quits his day job after 45 years of service with the Texas National Guard.

52-year-old Doug Sahm's CD *The Last Real Texas Blues Band* marks his 39th year as a recording artist. He cut his first disc, a 78, at age 13.

Guitarist Danny Gatton (b. 1945) commits suicide.

Sheryl Crow dominates the 37th annual Grammy Awards, winning Best New Artist, Female Pop Vocal, and Record of the Year, for "All I Wanna Do."

DOUG SAHM

The independent film *Pulp Fiction* ushers in a mini-revival of instrumental surf music.

Composer Henry Mancini (b. 1924) dies.

The Rolling Stones play 60 shows in 43 cities for a none-too-shabby paycheck of $121.2 million. But on a per-show basis, Barbra Streisand fares better, grossing $58.9 mil for only 22 shows (in only six cities).

Nirvana leader Kurt Cobain (b. 1967) commits suicide.

Eric Clapton returns to his blues roots with *From the Cradle,* which becomes the first blues album to reach #1 on the Pop chart in . . . since . . . well, ever.

In Rwanda, Hutu extremists massacre hundreds of thousands of Tutsis and Hutu moderates.

Former U.S. president Richard Nixon (b. 1913) dies.

Tom Hanks wins his second consecutive Best Actor Oscar for *Forrest Gump;* in 1993 he won for *Philadelphia.*

Jacqueline Kennedy Onassis (b. 1929) dies.

Paula Jones files a sexual harassment suit against President Clinton over an incident that allegedly took place in Arkansas in '91, while he was governor. It is settled is 1998 for a reported $850,000.

1995

NEIL YOUNG

Austin City Limits' 20th anniversary.

"Stevie Ray Vaughan: A Retrospective" becomes most popular *ACL* show of all time and is released commercially by Epic Music Video.

Neil Young and the Allman Brothers Band are among those inducted into the Rock and Roll Hall of Fame.

The Muppets make a surprise appearance with Gary P. Nunn to join in the *ACL* theme song, "London Homesick Blues."

Buck Owens flies to Austin to attend his annual birthday tribute at the Continental Club for the first time. The 66-year-old legend is so moved he takes the stage and sings a few of his hits.

Highlights this year include special shows on Bluegrass (Ricky Skaggs, Ralph Stanley, and Larry Sparks) and first-ever Tejano Music (Freddy Fender, Flaco Jimenez, La Diferenzia, Rick Orozco, Joel Nava).

BUCK OWENS

Twenty-five years after their breakup, the Beatles are back! *Anthology I* returns them to familiar territory: #1.

Hammer adds "M.C." back to his name. Fans can only speculate as to why.

Tejano star Selena (b. 1971) is shot and murdered by the founder of her fan club.

Capitalizing on the fact that she's the oldest person alive, 120-year-old Jeanne Calment of France releases a rap album entitled *The March of Time.*

Grateful Dead guitarist Jerry Garcia (b. 1942) dies.

Rykodisc simultaneously re-releases 53 albums by Frank Zappa and/or the Mothers of Invention.

The average cost of a gallon of unleaded regular gasoline in the U.S. is $1.14 (point 7).

In baseball, Cal Ripkin Jr.'s 2,131st game for the Baltimore Orioles breaks Lou Gehrig's 56-year record for most consecutive games played.

O.J. Simpson is acquitted of the murders of ex-wife Nicole Brown and Ronald Goldman.

Israeli Prime Minister Yitzak Rabin (b. 1922) is assassinated.

In the deadliest terrorist attack in U.S. history, 168 die, including 19 children, while another 500-plus are wounded after a bomb blows up the Alfred P. Murrah Federal Building in Oklahoma City. Timothy McVeigh is later convicted for the murders.

1996

SAGEBRUSH SYMPHONY

The first and only *Austin City Limits*-on-the-road, "Sagebrush Symphony," features Michael Martin Murphey and the Oklahoma City Symphony.

Johnny Gimble's second cousin, 18-year-old fiddler Jason Roberts, becomes the 81st band member to join Asleep at the Wheel. The band celebrates its 25th Anniversary on the *ACL* stage, reuniting alumni and friends such as Charlie Daniels, Wade Hayes, and Gimble (marking the fiddler's 21st *ACL* appearance).

The king (some would say inventor) of bluegrass, Bill Monroe, dies, as does country singer Faron Young.

Junior Brown's "My Wife Thinks You're Dead" wins CMA award for Video of the Year.

Austin songwriting scene fixture Walter Hyatt (b. 1949) dies in the crash of a ValuJet DC-9 in Florida.

WALTER HYATT

"Big Daddy," the late Tom Donahue, who invented free-form "underground" radio in San Francisco in the late '60s, is given a spot in the Rock and Roll Hall of Fame's "Non-Performer" category.

Jazz singer Ella Fitzgerald (b. 1917) dies.

Only a few years after a slew of million sellers, rapper M.C. "Can't Touch This" Hammer (formerly Hammer; formerly M.C. Hammer; formerly Stanley Kirk Burrell) files for bankruptcy.

Rap star Tupac Shakur (b. 1971) is murdered.

Two years after their first trials ended in hung juries, Lyle and Erik Menendez are convicted of murdering their wealthy parents and are sentenced to life without parole.

Forty percent of American households own a computer.

Suspected Unabomber Theodore Kaczynski is officially charged with a series of bombings committed over a period of 17 years.

Bill Clinton is re-elected president, defeating Bob Dole.

Muhammad Ali lights the torch at the Summer Olympics in Atlanta. The games are marred when a bomb goes off in Olympic Village, killing two and injuring 111.

Prince Charles and Princess Diana divorce.

1997

PBS airs *ACL*'s first Christmas Special, "A Nitty Gritty Christmas," with Nanci Griffith, Kathy Mattea, and Aaron Neville joining the NGDB.

Original country "outlaws" Willie Nelson, Waylon Jennings, and Kris Kristofferson make first appearance together on *ACL* stage.

ACL stretches limits to present rock diva Sheryl Crow, stirring controversy.

JOHN DENVER

John Denver (b. 1943) dies when his light plane crashes in Monterey Bay, California.

Bluegrass legend Bill Monroe is named to the Rock and Roll Hall of Fame's roster of Early Influences.

Singer-songwriter Townes Van Zandt (b. 1944) dies, as does Nashville pianist Floyd Cramer (b. 1933), and bassist Keith Ferguson (b. 1946), formerly of the Fabulous Thunderbirds.

TOWNES VAN ZANDT

Shawn Colvin's "Sunny Came Home" wins Song of the Year and Record of the Year Grammys.

Austin City Limits' website is launched in January.

Polka-meister Jimmy Sturr finds room on his mantel for his eighth Grammy, for *Living on Polka Time*.

Paul McCartney is knighted.

Musicals opening on Broadway include *The Lion King, The Scarlet Pimpernel, Ragtime,* and revivals of *The Sound of Music,* and *Cabaret.*

Wynton Marsalis wins Pulitzer Prize in music for *Blood on the Fields.*

Temperature increases, flooding, and droughts across several continents are blamed on a South American ocean current known as El Niño.

Jimmy Stewart (b. 1908) dies.

TV comedienne Ellen DeGeneres comes out, onscreen and off, becoming the first gay lead character in prime time.

Great Britain returns control of Hong Kong to China after 150 years.

The federal minimum wage is raised to $5.15/hour.

Princess Diana (b. 1961) is killed in an automobile accident in Paris.

Mother Teresa (b. 1910) dies.

1998

Manhattan Transfer brings New York to Texas—*Austin*, Texas, specifically, where the vocal group is joined on the *ACL* stage by Ricky Skaggs and Asleep at the Wheel.

MANHATTAN TRANSFER

One of *ACL*'s most emotional hours celebrates the music and memory of songwriter Townes Van Zandt with a tribute to him.

The guitar world mourns the losses of rockabilly legend Carl Perkins (b. 1928) and Texas Playboy Eldon Shamblin (b. 1916).

The Allman Brothers Band celebrates its 30th rockin' year.

Tammy Wynette (b. 1942) and Eddie Rabbitt (b. 1941) both die, as does Helen Carter (b. 1927) of the Carter Family.

At year's end Garth Brooks's U.S. record sales reach 89 million, making him the all-time biggest selling solo artist in America.

TAMMY WYNETTE

Dixie Chicks, without Lynch and Macy and with Natalie Maines, win Grammys for Best Country Album, *Wide Open Spaces,* and Best Country Vocal Performance (Group), "There's Your Trouble," as well as the American Music Award for Favorite New Country Artist.

Aretha Franklin floors the Radio City Music Hall audience at the 40th annual Grammy Awards broadcast when she substitutes for an ailing Luciano Pavarotti, singing opera with uncanny skill and of course soul.

MTV Awards go to Madonna's "Ray of Light," for Best Video of the Year, Will Smith's "Just the Two of Us," for Best Male Video, and Natalie Imbruglia's "Torn," for Best New Artist.

Frank Sinatra (b. 1915) dies.

Sonny Bono (b. 1935) dies in tragic skiing accident.

Puff Daddy and the Family win Grammy for Best Rap Album, *No Way Out.*

St. Louis Cardinal Mark McGwire hits 70 home runs, breaking Roger Maris's 37-year-record. Chicago Cub Sammy Sosa places second with 64.

Released in December of '97, *Titanic* tallies $500 million in box office receipts by the end of March, making it the largest- (and fastest-) grossing movie of all time.

Bill Clinton tells the world, "I did not have sexual relations with that woman, Miss Lewinsky."

Viagra, which treats male impotence, goes on the market.

The Dow Jones Industrial Average tops 9,000.

Former White House intern Monica Lewinsky testifies that she and President Clinton had a sexual affair.

Singing cowboy Roy Rogers (b. 1911) dies.

1999

Bill Arhos, founder of *Austin City Limits*, retires.

Bob Wills and his Texas Playboys are collectively honored as Early Influences by the Rock and Roll Hall of Fame.

Anita Carter of the Carter Family (b. 1933) dies.

The W.C. Handy Awards bestow upon bluesman W.C. Clark the distinction of Artist Most Deserving of Wider Recognition.

Asleep at the Wheel releases its 21st album on its 15th label: *Ride with Bob—Celebrating the Music of Bob Wills.*

Texas Playboys' bassist Joe Frank Furgeson (b. 1914) dies.

ASLEEP AT THE WHEEL

Lauryn Hill wins 5 Grammys, the most ever for a woman in one year.

Cher tops the charts with "Believe," the most successful single of her decades-long career.

Shania Twain becomes the only female artist in history to have two albums—*The Woman in Me* and *Come on Over*—each sell in excess of 11 million units.

The Velvet Fog, jazz singer Mel Torme (b. 1925), dies.

Gene Simmons of Kiss turns 50.

Backstreet Boys set first-week sales record with *Millenium*. It sells 1.25 million copies its first week.

Wayne Gretzky hangs up his skates and (once again) Michael Jordan hangs up his Air Jordans.

Quarterback John Elway leads his Denver Broncos to a second consecutive Super Bowl victory.

Bill Clinton is the first U.S. president to be impeached since Andrew Johnson in 1868.

Two students open fire on classmates at Columbine High School in Littleton, Colorado, leaving 15 dead including the gunmen.

Baseball legend Joe DiMaggio (b. 1914) dies.

John F. Kennedy Jr., his wife Carolyn Besette Kennedy, and sister-in-law Lauren Besette die in plane crash off Martha's Vineyard.

THE STARS

LEGENDS

IT ALMOST MAKES YOUR TEETH HURT. Imagine, had the technology existed to make it possible, if *Austin City Limits* were celebrating its seventy-fifth anniversary instead of its twenty-fifth. Think of all the masters of American music who might have plied their trade on the stage in Studio 6-A: Hank Williams . . . mysterious blues genius Robert Johnson . . . Billie Holiday . . . Maybelle, Sara, and A. P. Carter . . . Charlie Parker . . . Ella Fitzgerald scatting Gershwin lyrics . . . the Gershwins themselves, for that matter . . . Frank Sinatra in his saloon-singing prime . . . Duke Ellington . . . Muddy Waters . . . not only Bob Wills, but his fellow western swing pioneer, Milton Brown, with his Musical Brownies . . . Miles Davis . . . Patsy Cline . . . Count Basie . . . Elvis, by God, Presley.

PANCHO WAS A BANDIT, BOYS . . .

Dammit, it *does* make your teeth hurt.

Still, in its quarter-century tenure, *ACL* has done a laudable job of chronicling some of the cream of this country's musical innovators and stylists in an array of disciplines. Some have been founding fathers, some have put a fresh spin on a familiar form, some have been native geniuses unfettered by formal training, and some, in Mark Twain's wonderful phrase, just lit out for the territory.

There is a category of musician that aptly merits the honorific title of "legend." Other superlatives have become debased in our media-saturated age. Someone is "nearly unique" because he or she possesses something "almost priceless." The glittering adjective "superstar" has become so devalued that superstar winos and superstar meter maids are vying for attention on the next *Entertainment Tonight.* But "legend" still connotes something a little different, a trifle more stratospheric.

ROY ORBISON (1982)

Combining magic and mystique and an angelic voice straight from heaven, Roy Orbison received more standing ovations than any other performer on any other show. Producer Terry Lickona remembered it as "one of the few times I can honestly say I had chills running up and down my spine from watching a performer on our own stage."

CARL PERKINS (1980)

Carl Perkins ranks up there with Elvis, Jerry Lee, Little Richard, Buddy Holly, and Chuck Berry as the founding fathers of roots rock and roll. A gentle spirit offstage, he brought his blue suede shoes twice to Austin City Limits.

JOHN DENVER (1989)

"Fort Worth native John Denver appeared on the show only once, as part of a show with many other musicians. He sang only a few songs, but he made a big impression on me," recalls Scott Newton. "I'd always heard him referred to disparagingly, kind of like a folk-country Barry Manilow, popular but holding no substance. Nothing could be more wrong. John Denver had huge personal charisma. If he was in the room, your attention would be on him. If you never saw him perform, let me tell you that there was more than a touch of what I call 'Elvis power' in him."

DANNY GATTON (1991)

The late Danny Gatton had a way of using a beer bottle as a slide when he played his blazing riffs.

JOHNNY CASH (1987)
Pride. Experience. Dignity. Class. Street smarts. Been there, done that. Johnny Cash still has a lot to say. The Man in Black may not be in a class by himself, but it doesn't take long to call the roll.

STEVIE RAY VAUGHAN (1989)
"I remember being fascinated by the fact that he never, ever seemed to be lost in any way," Eric Clapton recalls of Stevie Ray Vaughan. "I mean it wasn't ever that he took a breather, or paused to think where he was gonna go next. It just flowed out of him. And actually even that doesn't come just with virtuosity or practice. It's not a question of doing it over and over again or anything like that. It's just that he seemed to be an open channel. And it just flowed through him."

LEON RUSSELL (1986)
The mystery man of '60s rock hasn't stopped rockin' yet. Still walking that "Tightrope."

JERRY LEE LEWIS (1983)
According to Scott Newton, "The Killer" delivered one of his trademark performances in 1983. Powerful, raucous, and riotous, Jerry Lee Lewis knows how to entertain. He's one of the founding fathers of rock and roll. Enough said.

ALLMAN BROTHERS BAND (1995)
Deservedly legendary, the Allman Brothers Band set the standard for southern rock. They are the best of their genre and Greg Allman's voice is among the best in the rock world. Dicky Betts's guitar work is unparalleled for its soaring heights and emotional intensity.

Bob Wills and Bob Marley both merit that appellation, since both were the prime exponents for ground-breaking new kinds of music. Ditto Bill Monroe and Louis Armstrong, who seem in retrospect to have invented their respective genres of bluegrass and jazz, so large are the shadows they cast. The same might be said of the king of zydeco, Clifton Chenier, and the queens of country, Loretta Lynn and the late Tammy Wynette.

Elvis Presley took bits and pieces from sources as disparate as Big Mama Thornton and Dean Martin and (with producer Sam Phillips's help) created something so much bigger than the sum of its parts that the reverberations are still echoing today.

Like many another legend, Elvis didn't create art out of thin air, but he combined familiar sounds in new and unforgettable ways. The same thing goes for Ray Charles, who did something in the early sixties even better than crossing the line between blues and country and western: He made the line irrelevant.

JOAN BAEZ (1993)

Immaculate delivery with a voice as clear as a mountain stream, Joan Baez is a bona fide legend. She has set the standard for all folk singers for time immemorial.

STANLEY JORDAN (1988)

An impeccable jazz guitarist with impeccable style and taste, Stanley Jordan has the uncanny ability to play two guitars at once.

DWIGHT YOAKAM (1985)
This in-between, off-beat shot by Scott Newton captures some of the frenetic fun of a Dwight Yoakam performance.

GLEN CAMPBELL (1984)
One of the first country "crossover" artists, Glen Campbell is a true guitar virtuoso with real class.

KRIS KRISTOFFERSON (1981)
Air Force brat from Brownsville, Texas, Rhodes scholar, and ex-Nashville janitor, he's written some of pop and country's most compelling songs, not to mention his many motion picture and television acting credits.

NEIL YOUNG (1985)
American music's Proteus was in a country-folk phase. Neil's music and imagery represent the best of a generation's lyrical tradition, as Scott Newton points out. His biting guitar and distinctive singing voice are totally original and unique.

BUDDY GUY (1990)
One of the most passionate performers in any style, Buddy Guy was a major influence on Stevie Ray and Jimmie Vaughan, and was Eric Clapton's favorite guitar player.

RAY CHARLES AND THE BAT

Getting Ray Charles to do *Austin City Limits* wasn't easy. He wasn't used to doing television for union scale plus expenses. Although the program had growing legions of fans, it was still a well-kept secret to some honchos in the music industry. I talked my way backstage after a Ray Charles concert in Austin in 1979, to try the direct approach. I walked into Ray's dressing room to find him standing in his red underwear groping for his pants. Ray was a congenial host—oblivious to any hint of embarrassment—and it turned out he was familiar with the show, and within a few months he was booked to play it.

The taping day was tough; Ray wasn't happy with rehearsal and the band didn't seem especially happy to be there either. But minutes before show time, everything seemed under control. Ray was chilling out in his dressing room and the crowd was buzzing upstairs in the studio.

One of Austin's most famous tourist attractions is the migratory colony of Mexican free-tail bats, and although the critters are harmless, they do occasionally find their way into big buildings; the cavernous studios of KLRU must have seemed like home away from home. It wasn't unusual for two or three to find their way through the air-conditioning ducts to buzz the audience (and stage) during a show. On this particular night, one of them decided to target Ray Charles's dressing room.

Suddenly his door burst open and his road manager sprang out, looking like he'd just met Dracula himself. "There is a *bat* in Mr. Charles's dressing room! Mr. Charles will *not* go on until somebody removes that bat!"

Security chief Joe Cook peeked inside, where Ray seemed to be sitting contentedly, humming some song he would no doubt be singing for a national TV audience in a matter of minutes. Neither he nor the bat seemed to care about each other in the least. Joe dispatched a crew person to fetch the official *Austin City Limits* bat net, and within a very short time the bat was history. And Ray's show still ranks as one of the best episodes in the twenty-five years of *Austin City Limits*.

TERRY LICKONA, Producer

RAY CHARLES (1984)
Ray Charles can rock out as well as anyone. He's a giant of American music—a true musical and creative force. He may be blind, but his vision is crystal clear when it comes to emotional states and the human condition.

A cynic might say that the prime—but by no means essential—attribute of a legend is that he or she be, well, dead. That's an observation with a lot of hard bark on it. But it is true that their untimely passing has lent a certain resonance to, and deferred appreciation of, *Austin City Limits* guests such as gentle songwriters Keith Whitley, Kate Wolf, and Steve Goodman, as well as cowboy/pop balladeer Marty Robbins, and Roy Orbison, whose prodigious talent was balanced by a rare sweetness of spirit, as well as the guitar-slinging quartet of Danny Gatton, Albert Collins, Roy Buchanan, and Stevie Ray Vaughan.

Happily still among the living are artists whose *Austin City Limits* appearances have chronicled their mastery of their chosen forms: country stars George Jones, Buck Owens, and Johnny Cash; blues stars Ruth Brown, Buddy Guy, B.B. King, and Ray Charles; rock stars Jerry Lee Lewis, Neil Young, and the Allman Bros. Band; folk stars Billy Bragg and Joan Baez; and contemporary hitmakers from Reba McEntire to Stanley Jordan to the Neville Brothers. Though they share little in common musically, all tower over the musical landscape with a larger-than-life presence.

In the end, the difference between a mere star and a legend is, as Mark Twain put it, the difference between the lightning bug and the lightning.

THE NEVILLE BROTHERS (1994)
The Neville Brothers possess incredible power. Their concerts are, in the words of Scott Newton, "orgiastic religious experiences." Austin likes to tout itself as the Live Music Capital of the World, but as long as the Nevilles live in New Orleans, the issue is in doubt. Here they rocked the house in 1994.

WILLIE NELSON

Without Willie Nelson there would be no *Austin City Limits*. He did the original pilot in 1974 that launched the series on PBS, he helped sustain the show's popularity through the early years, and he's been associated with the series in real and symbolic ways ever since. He's the living essence of *Austin City Limits*, right down to his Texas roots, and the show has grown, evolved, and reached new audiences just as Willie's own music has.

In 1977 he used the program to showcase his ground-breaking *Red-Headed Stranger* album—the record that catapulted his career to platinum status and put him on the covers of *Time* and *Newsweek* in the same year. He was the centerpiece for the songwriters-in-the-round prototype, and he has appeared in more Songwriters' Specials than any other single artist. He's appeared with and without his Family Band, and he even did a show (once) without his trademark guitar. (That battered icon, "Trigger," was the only thing Willie took pains to hide from the I.R.S. during his tax travails.) He would show up unannounced to sit in with pals like Roger Miller and Merle Haggard, or to guest with Bob Wills' Original Texas Playboys.

SMILING WILLIE (1980)

"Perhaps no one connects as directly with an audience as Willie Nelson," says Scott Newton. "He has a way of looking directly into every audience member's eyes while he's performing, establishing instant and permanent rapport. He personifies positive, integrating energy, dissolving the audience-performer separation." Newton captured "Smiling Willie" during the first Songwriters' Special, which set the template for many more to follow.

Over the years, Willie's "family" has consisted of a cast of characters that deserves its own TV sitcom (or at least a Kinky Friedman novel . . . oops, that's been done).

Whenever Willie's bus is parked down in the service driveway outside the studio, it always has a unique aura about it. Once, during a taping of a non-*ACL* show featuring Willie and Ray Charles, I went down to the bus to find the two of them engrossed in a game of chess. Willie said that the night before, playing in a hotel room, Ray had beaten him at the game. "The next time," he added, "I'm gonna make him leave the lights on."

In many ways, Willie seems ageless. At other times he seems as old as Methuselah. He was forty-one when he taped that original *ACL* pilot, and at the time some people joked that he looked sixty-five. As the twenty-fifth anniversary draws near, he'll be approaching sixty-seven (Willie is collecting Social Security!), but now he looks ten years younger, with his long, braided hair still red, and those piercing, dark eyes that are laughing, not crying, in the rain.

TERRY LICKONA, Producer

THE RED-HEADED STRANGER (1990)

This face should be chiseled into a musical Mount Rushmore some day.

COUNTRY

If You Don't Think I Love You, Ask My Wife

COUNTRY MUSIC CAME TO TEXAS by way of England, Scotland, and Ireland, not to mention Mexico and the Deep South. Country music and the blues are, after all, first cousins—just ask Jimmie Rodgers or Ray Charles. Since it took up tenure on these shores, country has absorbed elements of jazz, Tin Pan Alley pop, rock and roll, Hollywood singing-cowboy soundtracks, rhythm and blues, and cynical crossover calculation.

Country music is both a sponge and a mirror. It absorbs the musical fillips of each era, and reflects its audience in a funhouse mirror of idealized hopes and dreams. Who *doesn't* at some point want to grow up to be a singing cowboy, a stoic, lonesome figure heading for the horizon, or a badass gunslinger in a smoky saloon?

Country's Texas-based practitioners have ranged from Jimmie Rodgers (whose blue yodels imitated the trains he rode, and who bragged, "I got my name painted on my shirt/I ain't no ordinary dude/I don't have to work") to Willie Nelson, who combines the gypsy jazz guitar of Django Reinhardt, an unflinching eye for the foibles of the human heart, and a Zen-like faith in the circularity of fate.

George Strait, a real working cowboy from Pearsall, Texas, became the white-hatted heir to Hoppy, Gene, and Roy, and he performed the singularly heroic feat of making the airwaves safe once more for western swing. On the flip side, San Antonio-bred Steve Earle sings of Death Row and dead ends with a gritty, hardscrabble fatalism. "I wanna know what's over that rainbow," sings one of his hapless small-town protagonists; "I'm gonna get outta here someday," he vows, not believing it for a minute. And way on out past the far end of that rainbow is

MICKEY GILLEY (1982)
Best known for his legendary Gilley's Club in Texas that spawned the "Urban Cowboy" craze (for better or worse), Mickey could pound the piano as well as cousin Jerry Lee Lewis any day.

the late, great Townes Van Zandt, whose darkest musings such as "Waiting Around to Die" and "Tecumseh Valley" make Earle sound like Mister Rogers.

Houston native Rodney Crowell's best songs are luminous with humanity, as resonant as a Raymond Carver short story. Joe Ely, from the opposite end of the state, in Lubbock, blazes through some of the same emotional landscape as Crowell with the heedless rush and bustling energy of a West Texas cyclone.

And then there is Asleep at the Wheel, whose scattershot big-band eclecticism yields a show that does a joyous bump-bounce-boogie from cowboy ballads and two-steps to Kansas City jump blues and postwar Bob Wills twin-fiddle western swing classics. At the other end of the emotional spectrum lies George Jones, seemingly impervious to the malleable styles of the passing decades, his music a timeless teardrop wrapped in a heartache. Jones hails from Beaumont, which in recent years has yielded new young country stars Mark Chesnutt, Tracy Byrd, and Clay Walker.

STEVE EARLE (1986)
When you listen to a Steve Earle song, you know he's been there. He learned at the knee of the master, Townes Van Zandt, but he's a survivor.

GEORGE STRAIT (1988)
George Strait has come a long ways from his cattle-ranching days to the pinnacle of country music. Through sheer talent and unwillingness to compromise, he has hewed to Texas tradition and yet become a modern country superstar. He came from playing the fraternity party circuit to his first Austin City Limits in 1981 (sporting longer locks), and returned three more times (last appearance 1988).

REBA McENTIRE (1987)
Reba McEntire sings from the heart—down-home and loveable.

RODNEY CROWELL (1981)
Born and bred in Houston, Crowell brought an edge to country music in the '80s—when the powers that be let him.

THE GEEZINSLAWS (1985)
Sammy and Son—country music and schtick with an Austin edge. From Arthur Godfrey through Johnny Carson and Ralph Emery, perennial favorites continue to pack 'em in at Austin's legendary Broken Spoke.

JOE ELY (1985)
Joe Ely is a dynamic, powerful performer. He has been called "the Texas Springsteen," and the description is apt. What is it about West Texas that generates such powerful performers? Maybe it's in the water; maybe it's in the wind; maybe it's in the huge sky with the correspondingly low, flat horizons. Whatever it is, Joe has it.

No-Show Jones

George Jones, country music's golden voice, is equally famous for his bouts with the bottle as he is for his missed show dates, both of which seem to be, thankfully, in the past. George pulled his own "no-show" at *Austin City Limits* in January of 1985.

Ironically, it wasn't Jones's fault, contrary to his reputation. But there were more than a few skeptics at the time. Actually, George had been on the wagon for at least two solid years at that point; he was under new management and under the watchful eye of his new wife, Nancy. But from the minute I booked the show, I was grilled daily by other people: "But is he going to show up?"

On taping day the band came in for the afternoon rehearsal, but George and Nancy were due to fly in on a private plane from their East Texas home just before show time. By 7 P.M., an hour before curtain, there was still no George, and I was very nervous.

A few minutes later the phone rang and it was George, stranded in some private airport because his pilot, not he, had pulled a no-show. He apologized profusely, but said there was no way he could make it in time for the show that night.

Meanwhile, 450 diehard fans were waiting upstairs to see their hero, and I knew they weren't going to believe *me.* So I talked George into recording a personal apology over the phone, explaining his predicament; then I went onstage and played the tape. It sure sounded like ole Possum, and thank God George's fans are the most forgiving in country music.

Not so the press. The national media picked up the story ("No-Show Jones Strikes Again!") and it took another year to convince George that the *ACL* staff weren't the ones trying to make him look bad and lure him back to the show.

TERRY LICKONA, Producer

GEORGE JONES (1985)
If Scott Newton had to pick just one voice to represent country music, it would be that of George Jones, the perfect distillation of the form.

And there is, of course, Ernest Tubb. He helped popularize the use of electric instruments in country bands during the postwar transition to the harder-edged "honky-tonk" sound, with hits like "Walking the Floor Over You" and "Thanks a Lot." He was also one of the kindest and most generous men in any genre of music. Decades after E.T. came on the scene, his stylistic heir, the guit-steel-slinging Junior Brown mournfully intones, "My Baby Won't Dance To Nothin' But Ernest Tubb." Waltz across Texas, indeed.

Brown's music is informed by the Texas honky-tonk tradition that gave rise to Tubb, Johnny Horton, Lefty Frizzell, Ray Price, and Hank Thompson, but the kids listening to Junior don't have to know all that before packing a dance floor. If they pause to reflect, however, they might be surprised how deep country music's Texas roots run.

Indeed, the first million-selling country music record, 1924's "The Prisoner's Song," was the product of a Texas-born, New York-based vaudeville and light opera singer named Vernon Dalhart (a moniker that strung together two West Texas towns to replace his own name, the less-than-melodious Marion Try Slaughter). Country music and Texas go together like chicken-fried steak and cream gravy.

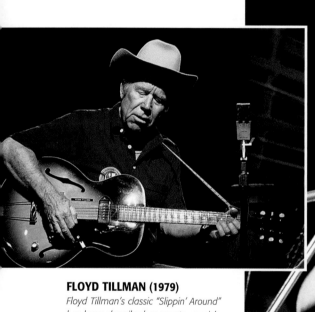

FLOYD TILLMAN (1979)
Floyd Tillman's classic "Slippin' Around" has been described as country music's first cheatin' song. But Floyd is also a legendary singer and writer whose hits have been covered by everybody from Willie Nelson to Ray Charles to Ella Fitzgerald.

ERNEST TUBB (1977)
A ground-breaking Texas artist, Ernest Tubb dominated country music—and Nashville—in the '40s and '50s. He took the raw honky-tonk sound to a national audience, and was the first artist to perform with amplified instruments at the Grand Ole Opry. He popularized and revolutionized country music for his times.

CHET ATKINS (1990)
The world's most famous guitar player and the first major country artist to appear on the show, Chet Atkins came back many more times, including this appearance in 1990.

JUNIOR BROWN (1994)
Junior is an amalgam of seemingly conflicting styles—Ernest Tubb meets Jimi Hendrix—the '50s meet the '90s. Oklahoma meets Texas, AM meets FM. Then there's that instrument—the guit-steel, fashioned specifically for him, which marries a guitar and a pedal steel into one. He's one of the hottest pickers around. Much of country music has gone formula, but Junior's bass voice booms out that it just ain't necessarily so.

RAY PRICE (1998)
Some call Ray Price the Frank Sinatra of country music, but maybe Frank was the Ray Price of pop. Pure class; still goin' strong.

HANK THOMPSON (1998)

Hank Thompson is another native Texan who still carries on the western swing tradition for a new generation of '90s honky-tonkers.

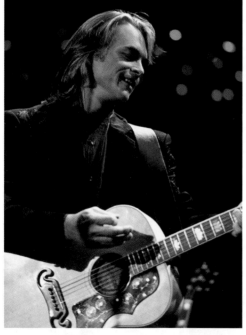

MARTINA MCBRIDE (1998)

Reba McEntire says that Martina McBride has "one of the purest and most powerful and soulful voices in the business," and you know what? She's right.

HAL KETCHUM (1993)

"I used to come up and watch all these remarkable artists and think to myself, 'I would like to be that guy someday. I'd like to be on that stage,'" Ketchum remembers. "We approached it like a live show, warts and all. . . . I think the energy of the whole show is better conveyed just start to finish."

KEITH WHITLEY (1988)

Keith Whitley was just hitting his stride as one of country's brightest young singers when he died tragically from alcohol poisoning only a year after his 1988 appearance.

KATHY MATTEA (1989)
Possessed with one of country music's most powerful yet poignant singing styles, Kathy Mattea never sold out to slick commercialism or country-pop.

DON WILLIAMS (1979)
Texas-born Don Williams was dubbed country's "Gentle Giant"— a testament to his easy-going style and string of hits in the '70s and '80s.

MEL TILLIS (1979)
Mel Tillis recorded a string of honky-tonk hits and country weepers for two decades, and is still a popular fixture on the Branson, Missouri, circuit.

HANK WILLIAMS JR. (1980)
The son of a legend, Hank Jr. was thrust into his own career by his mother at the age of eight and became a country superstar in his own right.

VINCE GILL (1998)

A giant talent with a gentle spirit who can sing like a bird and tear it up on guitar, Vince is a big fan and perennial favorite. From his first long-locks appearance with Pure Prairie League in 1979 to his recent shows in the '90s, Vince loves to do Austin City Limits *because it "makes him feel like a musician again."*

Of course, country music has always eclipsed Texas, though it pains natives to admit it. A little burg called Nashville had some passing influence on the genre, it's rumored, as did locales from California to Kentucky. Hollywood and Tin Pan Alley have also laid a historical claim to a big chunk of country music's classic repertoire. "There were always times throughout country music's entire history when it fragmented off into different things," said Vince Gill, who returned to his own country roots with the album *The Key.* "In the fifties, they started to put that cosmopolitan sound to it. They put strings on a Ray Price record, and people were going, 'What is the deal?! Is this the end of the world?' Buck Owens came along and he is now really considered hard-core country. But in the sixties he was really kind of a rebel, and it was rockin' a little bit because it had such a neat groove to it."

Many, if not most, of the stylistic and geographic permutations of country music have been represented on the *Austin City Limits* stage over the years. Texas artists have been abundantly represented, but so have Nashville's biggest hitmakers, from the late Tammy Wynette to Garth Brooks, Vince Gill, Reba McEntire, Alabama, Emmylou Harris, and Alan Jackson.

BUCK OWENS (1988)

Born in Texas, Buck Owens became associated with the burgeoning "Bakersfield sound" in the '50s and '60s. Hee-Haw made him one of country's most identifiable stars, but as far as producer Terry Lickona is concerned, Buck and the Buckaroos helped define the modern country band sound.

DOTTIE WEST (1983)

With Patsy Cline as her mentor, Dottie West became one of country music's most popular song stylists of the '60s and '70s.

MERLE TRAVIS (1977)

Legendary guitarist Merle Travis inspired Chet Atkins to learn how to pick; he was also the first to experiment with a solid-body electric guitar. As if that weren't enough, he wrote country classics like "Sixteen Tons" and "Smoke, Smoke, Smoke that Cigarette."

RANDY TRAVIS (1986)

Now they call him "the grandfather of the new country traditionalists," whatever that means. He was one of the first in the '80s to lead the movement "back to the future"—back to the roots country sound that gave country music its distinct quality.

TRAVIS TRITT (1996)

Maybe a country outlaw for the '90s, Travis Tritt borrows from both country traditions and southern rock.

MARTY ROBBINS (1979)
A singer-songwriter best remembered for the immortal classic cowboy ballad "El Paso," Marty Robbins was a genuine country-pop star with legions of rabid fans. He also had a love affair with the television camera.

JERRY REED (1981)
Despite his "Smokey and the Bandit" movie fame, Jerry Reed is a certified, country-fried guitar whiz—signed by Chet Atkins, no less.

JOHNNY PAYCHECK (1979)
They might've called Willie, Waylon, and the boys "outlaws," but Johnny Paycheck was the real deal. "Take This Job and Shove It" is about as subtle as he gets.

K.T. OSLIN (1988)
K.T. Oslin's hit song "80's Ladies" set a new standard for country song stylists and helped female country artists find a new voice.

Country music has always been regarded as *ACL*'s special forte, and the depth of its coverage over the years has been lavish. Genuine pioneers such as Bob Wills' Original Texas Playboys, Loretta Lynn, Merle Haggard, Ray Price, George Jones, Chet Atkins, Merle Travis, Floyd Tillman, and Johnny Cash have taped episodes of the show. But so have the cream of a new generation of stars—Faith Hill, Dixie Chicks, Deana Carter, Trisha Yearwood, Patty Loveless —and many of the standard-bearers of the Americana-style country youngbloods such as the Old 97's, Whiskeytown, Robbie Fulks, Junior Brown, Son Volt, and Robert Earl Keen.

THE LEARNING CURVE ON WESTERN SWING

Willie did the *Austin City Limits* pilot and they bought it, so (talent booker) Joe Gracey sold them on the idea of doing a Texas Playboys/Asleep at the Wheel show, because we were the young western swing band, and we were having a top ten album and had a big hit at the moment with "The Letter That Johnny Walker Read," so they were all excited about having us.

Well, all anyone at the station knew was that we were a hot country western act, and we were going to have these old guys. Paul Bosner, the producer of the show at the time, was saying, "Well, you'll do forty-five minutes and we'll let the old guys do fifteen minutes." He didn't know the history of the band, and the Playboys had not been together for years. And we were, like—Whoa! Wait a minute!

So me and Gracey sat down and explained it to them, and they went, "Oh . . . okay." The people at the station were wonderful, they just didn't know. And that show wound up going into the Smithsonian.

RAY BENSON, Asleep at the Wheel

ASLEEP AT THE WHEEL (1995)
Ray Benson, leader and founder of Asleep at the Wheel, has carried the flame of western swing from the days of post Bob Wills' Texas Playboys into the present. Ray's rich baritone and highly entertaining performances have enlivened Austin, and the entire country, for more than twenty-five years. Ray also sits on the board that directs KLRU, ACL's home station, and he was instrumental in getting the idea for this book off the ground.

BOB WILLS' ORIGINAL TEXAS PLAYBOYS (1977)
The Playboys' second appearance included bandleader "Take It Away" Leon McAuliffe, one of the pioneers of the steel guitar.

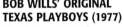

ROGER MILLER (1983)

Roger Miller won more Grammys in one year than any other artist (with songs like "King of the Road" and "Dang Me"). He was a prolific songwriter, comic genius, and everybody's friend.

OAK RIDGE BOYS (1984)

The Oak Ridge Boys were huge when they came to do the show in 1984. They brought their high-tech lights, fog machine, and a touch of Las Vegas, and their fans loved it all.

ALABAMA (1980)

One of the most successful bands of all time in country music, Alabama only did ACL once. They wouldn't be caught dead in those jump suits today, and they've long since outgrown the road-weary RV they drove up in when they did the show.

LORRIE MORGAN (1990)

With country music in her blood (her father was country crooner George Morgan), Lorrie Morgan can belt out ballads or songs about hard livin'.

LORETTA LYNN (1983)

A large part of Loretta Lynn's appeal is her apparent vulnerability. She withholds nothing, giving it everything she has, with no sense of guile or reserve. This shot was taken at the end of her first show, and her glee at exposing her emotions and having the audience respond with obvious appreciation is easily seen.

CHARLEY PRIDE (1981)
Charley Pride was one of the few black artists to break through to true country stardom. Truth is, country music always crossed racial lines in the rural South, but the black voice was seldom heard.

FAITH HILL (1996)
Faith Hill is one of the '90s purest country vocalists. Her soul-mate Tim McGraw has yet to do the show, but it sounds like a great idea for the future, doesn't it?

THE JUDDS (1984)
This classic photo of the Judds has almost a fairy-tale quality about it—both mother and daughter radiate beauty and innocence, not to mention two of the best voices country music has ever heard.

SON VOLT (1996)
They may dub it "alternative country," "alt.country," or "no depression," but whatever it's called it's just good original music that doesn't fit any commercial labels. Derived from the near-legendary Midwest band Uncle Tupelo, Son Volt is led by songwriter-guitarist Jay Farrar.

RONNIE MILSAP (1986)
Ronnie Milsap never let his handicap get in the way of his music. A child prodigy, he rose to become a country pop superstar in the '80s, and rocked the Austin City Limits *stage in 1986.*

PATTY LOVELESS (1993)
Country to the core, Patty Loveless would rather spend an hour in the studio with George Jones than fret about a "crossover" hit. Her live shows mix energy with country soul.

RIDERS IN THE SKY (1986)
You might think it's hard to take these guys seriously (left to right: Woody Paul, Ranger Doug, Too Slim; Two Jaws onstage), but looks aren't everything. Not only do they promote and preserve traditional western heritage music, they are three of the best performers of the genre, bar none.

Perhaps the country subgenre to receive the most attention on *ACL* has been bluegrass. Bluegrass is not native to Texas—its origins lie in the back-country hollows and misty ridges of Appalachia—but its essential elements of instrumental virtuosity and narrative tradition fit in well in the local musical mosaic.

Over time the show has presented many permutations of the music, from the old-rock founders (including patriarch Bill Monroe, who practically invented the genre, and Earl Scruggs, Doc Watson, Ralph Stanley, and Jethro Burns) to the "newgrass" inheritors whose ranks include Bela Fleck, Alison Krauss, Ricky Skaggs, and Austin's inimitable Bad Livers.

DOC WATSON (1977)
Nobody can flat-pick a guitar like Doc Watson.

WHISKEYTOWN (1998)
Whiskeytown brings a dose of rock and roll attitude to country music. With influences ranging from Merle Haggard to punk rock, they're blazing new trails in the "alternative country" movement.

RALPH STANLEY (1979)
Bluegrass pioneer Ralph Stanley and the Clinch Mountain Boys remain one of the constants of bluegrass music, with a traditional sound reminiscent of the hills and valleys of rural western Virginia. Ralph's unique clawhammer banjo style and high mountain tenor rank with Bill Monroe in the bluegrass hierarchy.

RICKY SKAGGS (1987)
Ricky Skaggs is one of the few bluegrass artists to cross over successfully to mainstream country—and without compromising his basic style. He apprenticed with Ralph Stanley while he was still in high school, and today seems the heir apparent to the late Father of Bluegrass, Bill Monroe.

EARL SCRUGGS (1976)

Few musicians are associated with a single instrument as Earl Scruggs is with the banjo, but then few musicians have written classics like "Foggy Mountain Breakdown." Earl ventured to Texas for an early show with his sons as part of the Earl Scruggs Revue.

ALISON KRAUSS (1995)

In a bluegrass world dominated by men, Alison Krauss and her band Union Station brought a breath of fresh air to the genre. She also rocked the country music world when she won the prestigious Female Vocalist of the Year Award.

JOHN MCEUEN AND FRIENDS (1978)

A founding member of the Nitty Gritty Dirt Band, John McEuen (on banjo) staged one of the first "concept" shows on Austin City Limits, including then-twenty-year-old Marty Stuart (on mandolin).

BILL MONROE AND RALPH STANLEY (1986)

Bluegrass summit—a rare stage appearance by Bill Monroe (left) and Ralph Stanley.

SAN ANTONIO ROSE

Willie Nelson's hit pilot show launched *Austin City Limits* on PBS. But for me, what *ACL* was really all about was having Bob Wills' Original Texas Playboys perform on the very first program of Season 1, bringing together on national television all the history, the music, the original musicians, a new generation of fans, and a new music showcase. Bob had just died a few months before the show was taped in September 1975, and it was the first time in more than thirty years that the original members of his Playboys had performed together in public, let alone on TV, though Wills and later configurations of Playboys had toured until 1969.

Three generations of fans comprised the studio audience that night, all groovin' to the same beat. The atmosphere was charged like a tent revival, a revival of music that had been nearly gone but not nearly forgotten, with the Texas Playboys leading the charge of "Bob Wills Is Still the King!" Western swing was alive again.

The old pros picked up where they left off without missing a beat, under the leadership of "Take It Away" Leon McAuliffe, one of the pioneers of the steel guitar. It was a reunion that would last over a decade as various members of the original Playboys toured and recorded together, and they returned to *Austin City Limits* as well.

It was only fitting that when the show celebrated its tenth anniversary, it would mark the occasion by blocking off Congress Avenue in downtown Austin and setting up a stage for the Texas Playboys to play a street dance for five thousand fans—much as they played many times from a flat-bed truck in some dusty burg in West Texas in the thirties. The plaque at Bob Wills' grave reads, "Deep within My Heart Lies a Melody," and that melody will forever flow through *Austin City Limits.*"

TERRY LICKONA, Producer

BOB WILLS' ORIGINAL TEXAS PLAYBOYS (JUNE 16, 1984)
For the Austin City Limits *tenth anniversary celebration, early on a Saturday evening five thousand people filled the streets in the middle of downtown, with the real Texas state capitol as backdrop. It was the Playboys' final regular appearance on the show.*

NEW GRASS REVIVAL (1983)
They tried to revolutionize bluegrass with their mix of traditional and modern sounds, but bluegrass wasn't ready.

BELA FLECK (1991)
Nobody makes banjo jokes when Bela Fleck picks up the instrument. You've got to hear this one-man banjo crusader to believe it (ever heard jazz or funk on a five-string banjo?).

WILL THE CIRCLE BE UNBROKEN (1989)
Jimmy Martin (far right) is without question one of the most colorful characters in all of bluegrass, joined here by (left to right) Jeff Hanna (Nitty Gritty Dirt Band), son Ray Martin, and mandolin-man Sam Bush.

CHARLIE DANIELS (1988)
Charlie Daniels in a moment of rare exuberance—hats off!

THE ONE AND ONLY JOHNNY GIMBLE

JOHNNY GIMBLE (1981)
Country's premier fiddler, he holds the record for most appearances on Austin City Limits *by a single performer.*

He's from Texas, he was one of Bob Wills's favorites, he tells the best stories, he has the brightest smile, he loves what he does—and what he does is play the hell out of the fiddle (oh yeah, and the mandolin, too). He's Johnny Gimble, an *Austin City Limits* mainstay who came as close to being a member of the house band as any musician in the history of the series. He gave up cutting hair in Waco to cut a niche for himself as country music's finest fiddler over the past four decades. He's got a shelf full of CMA Instrumentalist of the Year awards, but more important, he's always been the artists' favorite.

It was not uncommon throughout the eighties for visiting country stars to call Johnny to sit in for their *Austin City Limits* performances (he lives conveniently close to the city, which helps). Over the years Willie, Merle Haggard, Roger Miller, Chet Atkins, Garrison Keillor, George Jones, Floyd Tillman, Asleep at the Wheel, and more all made the call. He played with Bob Wills' Original Texas Playboys, organized a "Texas Swing Pioneers' Tribute," starred in a "Mandolin Special" with Tiny Moore, David Grisman, and Jethro Burns, and did a show with his own band. He and the fiddle are one entity, and country, swing, jazz, and blues flow from that persona with joyous abandon.

My favorite memory of Johnny Gimble? Well, he was on the road with Willie for several tours with the Family Band. I remember one night after a show, the band was winding down on the bus, looking like they had literally been rode hard and put up wet—not a J. Crew model in the bunch. Suddenly, out of the back comes Johnny, ready to bed down in his bunk, wearing crisply pressed flannel jammies and a cherubic grin. He looked like the Easter Bunny in a pen full of timber wolves. You gotta love it.

JOHN T. DAVIS

THE NIGHT THE LIGHTS WENT OUT IN AUSTIN

On September 13, 1981, *Austin City Limits* went into the black—literally. Everybody has a blackout story, and so do we. Ours begins when Kris Kristofferson and his band were onstage and about to be introduced when without warning, Kris, the band, the crew, and nine hundred people in the audience were plunged into a darkness as total as the depths of Carlsbad Caverns with the lights out. That's when we realized there was no emergency lighting in the studio.

Minutes later there were still no lights. Out came the cigarette lighters. Somehow somebody found a flashlight. Outside a thunderstorm raged and sheets of rain pounded the pavement. The lights never did come back on that night.

As it turned out, a third of the enormous University of Texas campus had been blacked out by an unexpected intersection of technology and rodent. An errant rat had gotten himself between two power lines and was promptly fricasseed. But in the process he shorted out the entire system. (The campus utility department saved the evidence, which may still occupy freezer space in the basement of the University of Texas Zoology Department.)

Meanwhile, the audience was led safely down dark stairwells and out into the pouring rain while someone instigated a singalong of the *ACL* theme song, "London Homesick Blues." No one was hurt. Kris himself headed to the building rooftop to watch the storm, and came back the next night to do the show for real.

After that, the crew installed emergency lights and drew up an evacuation plan. The fire marshal also restricted attendance in Studio 6-A from the previous 800 or 900 audience members to about 450 people, where it remains today.

TERRY LICKONA, Producer

That passage of styles and generations is part of the program. Young musicians who have seen their idols perform on the show may one day fairly dream of standing on the same stage. Even veteran performers can sense the turning of the wheel.

"*Austin City Limits* is a way of timing my life," said Merle Haggard, who has made multiple appearances on the *ACL* stage. "As I look back on the different appearances I've done, it's probably the most truthful [representation] about that particular period in my life. It's like a photo album, I guess."

MERLE HAGGARD
(1978, 1981, 1983, 1985, 1995)
Merle Haggard sings directly to and for the everyday working man, accomplishing this easily, with the working man's innate pride and dignity pervading his work. As this scrapbook montage makes clear, Austin City Limits *serves as a sort of photo album, "a way of timing my life," says Haggard.*

1985

1981

1995

1978

1983

BLUES

There's The Blues and There's Zip-A-Dee-Do-Dah

THE BLUES IS THE TRUE SOUNDTRACK OF AMERICA, embodying all the dichotomies of this troubled republic, the hopes and joys, the secret shames, the skull behind the smile. The blues is as pervasive as sex and as inescapable as death. It is, finally, our shared American heritage, and a measure of the distance between Puritan leader John Winthrop's vision of "the shining city on the hill" and the raw reality of our common history.

Derived from Africa and the Caribbean but born in the American South, the blues is our native offspring. It has informed practically every note of music played on the continent. The direct precursor of jazz, it has also left an indelible indigo tint on rock, pop, country, the Broadway musical, and even opera (*Porgy and Bess,* anyone?). Townes Van Zandt summed it up best. "There's only two kinds of music," Townes used to say. "There's the blues, and there's zip-a-dee-do-dah."

The Rolling Stone Encyclopedia of Rock & Roll accurately but dryly categorized the blues as "a 12-bar song form . . . in which one line of lyrics was repeated, then answered—AAB—over a chord progression of four bars of tonic, two of subdominant, two of tonic, one of dominant, one of subdominant, and two of tonic." Fine as far as it goes, but that's like trying to describe *Mona Lisa* by listing paints, gesso, and the number of hairs in the artist's brush. Technique is useless unless combined with spirit and passion. And that passion can lead the blues singer—and the audience—either to despair or to ecstasy.

B.B. King, who ought to know, said, "When I think in terms of the blues, I don't think of it like some other people do. The blues started, of course, from pain and sorrow. But then, there were happy blues back then. A lot of slaves would be singing, 'Hey, the boss is coming.' But the blues in my opinion have always been on two sides of the coin. If I sing, 'Nobody loves me but my mother,' that's the pits, that's down. But if I sing, 'I got a sweet little angel,' I'm not blue at all."

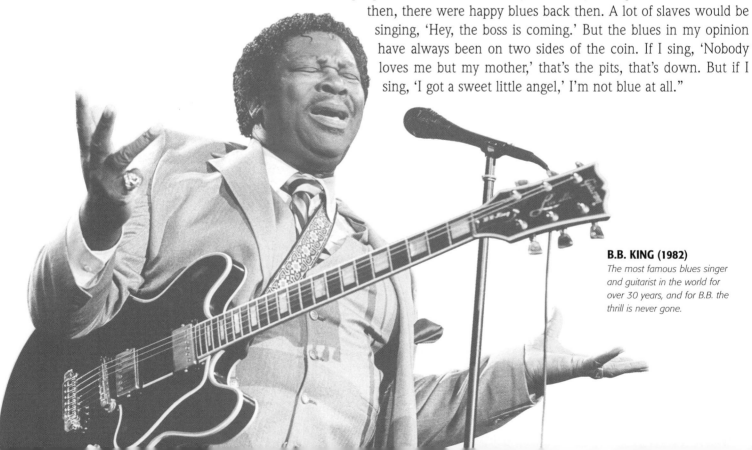

B.B. KING (1982)
The most famous blues singer and guitarist in the world for over 30 years, and for B.B. the thrill is never gone.

ELIZABETH COTTEN (1978)
The composer of the folk-blues classic "Freight Train," Elizabeth Cotten worked as a maid well into her sixties until she was "discovered," and she delighted audiences well into her eighties.

Or, as the ageless Gatemouth Brown put it, "I don't just get up there and play hard-core blues, feeling sorry for myself, and how my woman left me—who cares? All that old downer stuff makes people think about the bad days. I try to make people think of their good days."

Joy as a poultice to salve pain is the essence of the blues, laughing to keep from crying. The Devil at the crossroads, the unfaithful woman, the white man with ice in his veins and a whip in his hand, the hovering specter of bad luck and troubles—the bluesman knew them all.

CLARENCE "GATEMOUTH" BROWN (1996)
"I don't just get up there and play hard-core blues, feeling sorry for myself and how my woman left me— who cares?" says Brown. "All that old downer stuff makes people think about the bad days. I try to make people think of their good days."

"The Iceman" cometh. Texan Albert Collins had a raw edge, and his death left a void that no one can fill.

THE BLUES 'N' THE GREEN

LIGHTNIN' HOPKINS

The late Lightnin' Hopkins was the real deal: a first-generation bluesman who inspired all the big rock bands of the sixties, from the Rolling Stones and Cream to the Grateful Dead. A product of Houston's Fifth Ward, he lived and personified the blues. He had no idea what *Austin City Limits* was, but his ambitious young bass player, Ron Wilson (now a veteran Texas state legislator), somehow talked him into taping the show in 1979.

But there was a hitch. Nobody told us that Lightnin' liked to get paid before the show—cash in hand, please. Public television policy—paying by check within fifteen business days—just wouldn't cut it. The amount in question was only about $400, but Lightnin' had been burned enough times that he wasn't in a mood to compromise. To begin with, it was Sunday, so the banks were closed, and this was long before the days of handy ATMs in every convenience store. What to do?

I took up a collection from the crew—try coming up with $400 from a public television production crew!—but we did it. Lightnin' got his green, and that plus a little Jack Black made him a happy camper. It was the most singular classic performance ever captured on videotape of one of the latest and the greatest blues legends. He died three years later.

TERRY LICKONA, Producer

BOBBY BLUE BLAND (1999)
Bobby Blue Bland: Grammy Lifetime Achievement Award winner, R&B pioneer. No imitators.

GATEMOUTH BROWN WITH ROY CLARK (1979)
Gatemouth Brown and Roy Clark may be one of the strangest pairings in all of country music, but together they mean two strokes of genius on the same stage.

Greil Marcus, in his wonderful book *Mystery Train,* summed it up when writing about the protean blues singer Robert Johnson: "He sang about the price he had to pay for promises he tried, and failed, to keep; I think the power of his music comes in part from Johnson's ability to shape the loneliness and chaos of his betrayal, or ours. Listening to Johnson's songs, one almost feels at home in that desolate America; one feels able to take some strength from it, right along with the promises we could not give up if we wanted to."

Johnson left a tiny recorded legacy—only some thirty-odd songs—but his influence is profound, stretching from his contemporaries like Johnny Shines and Son House to rock and roll giants such as the Rolling Stones and Eric Clapton and youngbloods like Jonny Lang and Robert Cray. As it happened, Johnson recorded all of his immortal music in Texas, in San Antonio and Dallas. And that's only one instance of a long association between Texas and the blues.

RUTH BROWN (1998)
As she says, R + B = Ruth Brown, and this Rock and Roll Hall of Famer is still the queen of rhythm and blues.

BOZ SCAGGS (1997)
Over all the years of witnessing all the great shows, photographer Scott Newton's favorite song was Boz Scaggs's rendition of "Brother Can You Loan Me a Dime."

FATS DOMINO

I've always believed that persistence and perseverance pay off when it comes to getting legendary artists to do the show. Antoine "Fats" Domino was the ultimate challenge; I worked over ten years and every angle I could think of before it finally paid off in 1986. The "Man Who Put the Roll in Rock 'n' Roll" was just too important a figure in American music—and too elusive at that—to make only a token effort.

I was determined to hear "Blueberry Hill" performed on our stage, in front of our cameras, so I sent *Austin City Limits* tapes of contemporaries Jerry Lee Lewis, Roy Orbison, and Carl Perkins to Fats's home address in New Orleans to tweak his interest. He talked to his son, Antoine Jr.; his long-time road manager, Ike; his record distributor, Rita; bandleader Herbert Hardesty; John Foose, a mutual friend and music writer; and booking agent Al Embry. The director of the New Orleans Jazz and Heritage Festival, Quint Davis, was extremely helpful and went to Fats's house to talk to him about it. We came close many times, but no cigar.

Money had a lot to do with it, plus Fats made it a point not to travel outside New Orleans much (something about paternity suits). I went to see him at a show in San Antonio and actually met him backstage, but came away with nothing more than an autograph. To this day I'm still not sure why, but what finally clinched it was when I got to sit down with Fats face to face in his suite at the Las Vegas Hilton (the "Elvis suite") one Sunday morning after a weekend gig there. I was ushered into the lavish digs, where I found Antoine sitting in his bathrobe, wearing a hairnet and peeling shrimp that had been specially flown in from New Orleans.

We talked for about fifteen minutes and I sincerely doubt if either one of us had the slightest idea what the other was saying. Between Fats's New Orleans jive and my Yankee-by-way-of-Texas blather, somehow there emerged a deal for him to do the show. There were a few more bumps along the road before he finally hit the stage, but I do believe we captured the best Fats Domino performance on film or video ever.

By the way, there's a clause in Fats's contract that all house air conditioning must be turned off when he's on stage—no exceptions! With a ton of TV lights blazing away and 450 fans going nuts, it was literally one of the hottest nights on the *Austin City Limits* stage.

TERRY LICKONA, Producer

FATS DOMINO (1986)

Fats Domino brought his brand of New Orleans blues to the show in 1986. Living legend and master showman, he does unique things with the piano, like bumping it across the stage while he's playing.

B.B. KING

A few artists truly personify an entire genre of music, like Johnny Cash for country, or Bill Monroe for bluegrass. Or B.B. King, the king of the blues. Meeting B.B. King for the first time in 1982 really was like meeting royalty.

B.B. hadn't done a lot of national TV back then, but he was given the full hour of the show. Within minutes, he had the audience totally mesmerized. His face showed either pain or ecstasy for every note he squeezed out of his trademark Gibson guitar, Lucille. A lot of artists are fickle about eating before they go on, but not B.B. He and the band scarfed at least thirty pounds of barbecue ribs about an hour before they hit the stage.

When he returned thirteen years later in 1996, he was pushing seventy, a bit grayer and thinner, but still touring practically nonstop around the world, even playing for the Pope. But there has never been any pretense about B.B. After the afternoon rehearsal I discovered him sitting alone behind a curtain, catching a quick nap with his head nodding. I couldn't help but stare, thinking, "There sits one of the most celebrated artists of the twentieth century enjoying a rare moment of peace amidst all the commotion and swirl of activity in a television studio."

TERRY LICKONA, Producer

B.B. KING (1996)
"King of the Blues" doesn't begin to describe B.B.'s position in the blues world. He's much more than that. Not only does he continue to create living, vital, significant music into his seventies, his exuberant attitude permeates everything he does. He is, according to Scott Newton, a prototypical American, in the best sense, our Blues Ambassador to the world.

JOHN HAMMOND (1990)

Hammond carries on a family tradition of preserving American blues by being one of its best contemporary practitioners.

OMAR AND THE HOWLERS (1986)

Omar and the original Howlers came to Austin from their native Mississippi in the late '70s. Omar stayed and still growls his distinctive blues. He adds southern spice to the musical melting pot that Austin has become.

A great disc jockey named Jim Lowe, on Dallas's WRR, used to ask a signature question: "How blue can you get?" The answer in Texas, historically, was "pretty damn blue indeed." The blues didn't originate in Texas, but it got there as quick as it could. Slaves brought their music with them through the port of Galveston. Workers in the East Texas pine tar camps, sharecroppers chopping cotton, and convicts cutting cane on the Brazos River for The Man up in Huntsville all refined the form through a brutal distillation process composed in equal parts of numbing labor, hard times, and cultural and economic disenfranchisement.

As the decades passed, country bluesmen in the Lone Star State like Blind Lemon Jefferson, Leadbelly, and Mance Lipscomb saw their acoustic art transformed by urban blues players who plugged in, turned up, and made magic in the Third, Fourth, and Fifth Wards of inner-city Houston, the Stop Six precinct in Fort Worth, East Austin, and the Deep Ellum district in Dallas.

JIMMIE VAUGHAN (1998)

"That's what it's all about, is just coming out and letting it out," declares Jimmie Vaughan. "If you're gonna bare your soul for everyone, it might as well be at home."

STEVIE RAY VAUGHAN (1989)

Joy is written all over this shot. Photographer Scott Newton explains, "When a musician expresses and mirrors with his body language and facial expression exactly what he's playing, and when what he's playing is great, and you push the shutter button, and you know you've got it on film, there's a big rush and the hair on the back of your neck stands up. It doesn't happen all of the time, but it happened to me when I took this shot."

RORY BLOCK (1993)

For whatever reasons, Rory Block is in rarified company when it comes to women playing the blues. She bridges the cultural divide with her own deeply personal style.

JONNY LANG (1998)

Only seventeen years old when he appeared in 1998, Lang told the audience he had already been dreaming of doing Austin City Limits "for years." His sizzling guitar shows he learns well and fast.

SUSAN TEDESCHI (1999)

As Scott Newton says, "If you saw Susan Tedeschi walking down the street, you'd think she was an accountant; you'd never guess what power lies beneath the surface. As soon as she opens her mouth to sing, all doubt is dispelled about who the best female contemporary blues vocalist is. If she comes to your town, drop everything and go bear witness."

JOHN MAYALL (1993)

"The Patriarch of English Blues," according to Scott Newton. "You'd think that a patriarch would be over the hill, but I can assure you that it ain't so. John Mayall is the King. There's a reason all those wunderkind have apprenticed to him over the years; he has the Holy Grail."

In the thirties and forties, Teddy Wilson, one of the great piano players of any genre, put smoke and soul behind the timeless voices of Ella Fitzgerald, Sarah Vaughan, and Billie Holiday. In the same era big band leader Benny Goodman introduced a Texas jazz guitar prodigy, Charlie Christian, to a national audience. Together with his protégé and successor, T-Bone Walker, Christian popularized a stinging, single-string electric guitar style that would go on to influence the playing of everyone from B.B. King and Albert King to fellow Texans Albert Collins, Freddie King, and the young Vaughan brothers, Jimmie and Stevie.

In the fifties, Bobby "Blue" Bland, along with Junior Parker, Big Mama Thornton, Gatemouth Brown (who could play western swing, big band jazz, or Cajun music with the same virtuosity he applied to the blues), Memphis Slim, and others cut some of their greatest sides for Don Robey's Houston-based Duke and Peacock labels.

In the sixties, Texans Janis Joplin, Boz Scaggs, Sly Stone, Steve Miller, and Johnny Winter put a psychedelic spin on the blues.

From the seventies through the present, older, more traditional blues musicians began to receive their long-deferred due. Austin's famous Armadillo World Headquarters became known as "the house that Freddie built," thanks to Freddie King's memorable performances. Antone's blues club, for a long time located just down the street from the *ACL* studios, became a literal shrine to veteran Chicago and Texas bluesmen.

Younger white musicians in Austin, like the Vaughan brothers, Angela Strehli, Paul Ray, Lou Ann Barton, and the Fabulous Thunderbirds learned from, and worked alongside, their black mentors. Up-and-coming musicians in other Texas cities did the same thing.

Since its inception, *Austin City Limits* has showcased an enviable array of blues stylists and innovators from Austin, from Texas, and from all the points on the map where the blues flame still burns hot. In so doing, the show has helped preserve the form in an era in which radio has turned its back on the genre.

With its cold beer, warm audience, and nightclub-like ambiance, the *ACL* set seems particularly receptive to a blues-R&B groove. As B.B. King said following his performance, "This is one of the few times in my whole career that I felt very comfortable doing a television show and not paying any attention to it. Tonight it was like I was on stage, just playing. It was hot to us [and] if the cameras saw it that way, then that's okay."

ROBERT CRAY (1990)

One of the few of his generation not to ignore his musical heritage, Robert Cray brought passion and flair to modern blues that had been missing for years.

DELBERT McCLINTON (1992)

McClinton, a Fort Worth native, is the archetypal blue-eyed blues vocalist. They broke the mold after he was made—his voice and performances are world-class. He's been performing so long that he literally taught John Lennon how to play harmonica. And like a fine wine, he's gotten better with age.

DELBERT McCLINTON (1997)

Delbert McClinton loves to make music with his friends, like Texas buddies Lee Roy Parnell (far right) and Lyle Lovett (second from right).

TEJANO AND CONJUNTO

"CHULAS FRONTERAS"

I T TOOK THE VIOLENT DEATH of twenty-three-year-old Tejano music queen Selena Quintanilla Perez in March of 1995, and a subsequent movie based on her life, to catapult "la onda Tejano" ("the Tejano wave") onto the international cultural radar.

Tejano and its acoustic predecessor and complement, conjunto, have been popular for decades in South Texas, northern Mexico, and wherever migrant Mexican farmworkers followed the harvests, from California up to Washington, the upper Midwest, and east as far as Florida. But although both styles are ubiquitous soundtracks along the Rio Grande Valley, in South and West Texas, and in the music's mecca, San Antonio, neither conjunto nor Tejano have been accorded the trendy status or commercial acceptance of other Latino pop music styles such as salsa, tropical, merengue, or banda, nor have they been embraced by other Latino cultures.

With her fresh, smoldering good looks, unfettered Tejano brio, and limitless crossover potential, Selena was the best bet to change all that. With the right career moves she could have become for South Texas what Gloria Estefan was for Miami's Latino population—an ambassador to the Anglo mainstream, and a groundbreaker for her peers. But if a gunshot in a Corpus Christi hotel room ended those dreams, her short life and ascendant career at least served notice to the rest of the world that here was a vibrant, indigenous musical form worth cultivating.

Down in the Valley, and over in San Antonio's El West Side barrio—and even through the United States and Latin America at large—candles were lit and murals were painted in Selena's memory, and the first corridos—the story-songs that were the norteño precursor to CNN—began to chronicle the life and death of the young Tejano queen. The following November, on the Day of the Dead, Selena's photo and album covers found their way onto many an *ofrenda,* the small family altars in many Mexican and Texas homes. "So young," everyone said. "Que lastima." An entire hemisphere mourned her.

But music has always served to bridge the border between Texas and Mexico. The Rio Grande has been an arbitrary boundary since 1848, a demarcation that the people on both sides of the border regard as a tangible political reality only in moments of personal convenience or unavoidable necessity. Otherwise the border is a porous and permeable thing. The land, the people, and the culture that exist between San Antonio and Monterrey form, in reality, a third country, La Nacíon del Rio.

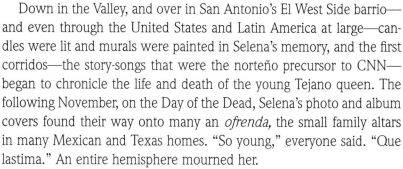

FLACO JIMENEZ (1990)
Flaco is a charismatic performer who's king of the accordion. In the Tex-Mex universe, he's definitely considered royalty. For the last decade he's also been one of the four principals who make up the Texas Tornados.

FREDDY FENDER (1994)
A pop star in the '70s ("Until the Last Teardrop Falls," "Wasted Days and Wasted Nights"), Freddy Fender returned to his Tex-Mex roots on a Tejano special in 1994.

LITTLE JOE Y LA FAMILIA (1978)
One of the pioneers of Mexican-American music, Little Joe y la Familia has always stayed one step ahead of everybody else, blending pop, Tejano, and conjunto, with a brassy punch.

TISH HINOJOSA (1993)
*"It's amazing the audiences that watch
this show, and it's not just the intellectual
PBS watchers," declares Tish Hinojosa.
"I felt like I was in my living room, which
was really wonderful."*

LOS LOBOS (1991)
*Cesar Rosas (left) and bandmate
David Hidalgo are the yin and yang
that make Los Lobos so unique.*

LOS LOBOS (1988)
*The members of Los Lobos transcend
their cultural heritage, even when
singing in Spanish, and speak eloquently
to human beings of all extractions in the
universal language of music.*

The music of that region—modern Tejano music, along with its elder antecedents and cousins such as conjunto, norteño, and corridos—has demonstrated an elastic ability to absorb influences from European polkas to South American cumbias to mainstream American pop, disco, rhythm and blues, and country.

"When you hear Tejano, know that we are sharing each other's culture," says Flaco Jimenez, scion of Texas's first family of conjunto accordion. "We are sharing our music, our language—Tejano-country, Spanish-English. That's what I like about performing this music, there's a sense of brotherhood, and that keeps us together. It shows that we can all get along."

Chris Strachwitz conceived, produced, and recorded the audio tracks for Les Blank's wonderful 1976 documentary film, *Chulas Fronteras* (Beautiful Borders). In the liner notes to the film's soundtrack, Strachwitz described the rise and evolution of Música Norteña: "The diatonic, button accordion, first developed and mass-produced in Germany in the middle of the 19th century, made its appearance in the Texas-Mexican border region before the turn of the century. The instrument was well distributed in the northeast of Mexico and in South Texas, due to the large influx of Central Europeans in that region. The rugged little black box quickly became popular, especially with rural musicians and dancers, because of its volume, low price, portability, sturdiness, light weight, and ability to play both melody and bass." Strachwitz also noted, "Norteño/conjunto is immediately recognizable by the accordion as the lead instrument." In addition the usual conjunto norteño includes a *bajo sexto* (a solidly built twelve-string guitar), a string bass (today usually an electric one), drums, and sometimes an alto saxophone.

Freddy Fender (born Baldemar Huerta), in the liner notes to the *Los Super Seven* album, recalls the *acordeonistas* of his youth in the Rio Grande Valley town of San Benito: "We didn't have streetlights in San Benito then," Fender said. "I would hear the music and sneak out onto the street and see these little fireflies of light, which were the cigarettes in the hands of the players, and that was where it was happening. I learned the chords watching guys' fingers."

Strachwitz continued, "The music represents a cultural treasure trove with its great variety of rural dances, such as the polka, waltz, redova, mazurka, huapango, schottische, cumbia, danzón, etc. It also offers a huge repertoire of songs and types, ranging from rancheras to boleros."

ESTEBAN JORDAN (1978)
From the streets of Corpus Christi, Texas, to the Austin City Limits *stage, accordion in tow: twenty years later, Esteban Jordan is still playing conjunto his way.*

Inevitably, conjunto migrated to the cities and became modernized. In the thirties and forties, San Antonio became the hub of Latin music in Texas, with spokes that led out to Alice, Corpus Christi, and the Valley. With the advent of electronic recording technology, small labels like Ideal and Falcon sprang up (similar indies, such as Chief, Freddie, and Barb Wire, still survive today). During and after World War II, the enormous military bases encircling the city attracted an equally massive influx of Chicano servicemen and their families, and the music itself became more urbanized with big band orchestra elements injected into the music.

Meanwhile, San Antonio-based musicians Valerio Longoria and Don Santiago Jimenez and the Rio Grande Valley's Narciso ("El Huracan del Valle") Martinez largely codified and popularized the conjunto form through their early records and performances. Both of Don Santiago's sons have kept the tradition alive: Santiago Jr. has hewed closer to a traditional, regional style, while Flaco has gone on to record with the Rolling Stones, Dwight Yoakam, Ry Cooder, the Texas Tornados, the Mavericks, and many others, though he can still throw down in a *baile grande* (a big dance) in a South Texas dancehall as well as anyone. At the same time, balladeer Lydia Mendoza arose to become the region's first great norteña chanteuse.

In much the same fashion as the blues and country combined to form, and were transcended by, rock and roll, so too conjunto and other Música Norteña styles evolved into modern Tejano. Elements of classic big band music, rock, seventies-era disco, and, recently, hip-hop also figure into the mix.

FLACO JIMENEZ (1994)

"When you hear Tejano," says Flaco Jimenez, "know that we are sharing each other's culture—our music, our language, Tejano-country, Spanish-English. That's what I like about performing this music, there's a sense of brotherhood and what keeps us together."

THE SQUEEZEBOX KING

Leonardo "Flaco" Jimenez came from squeezebox royalty. His father, Don Santiago Jimenez, practically invented the genre of accordion-accented conjunto music, and his brother, Santiago Jr., followed in the same footsteps. But Flaco (a nickname that means "skinny") had the joy, the infectious spirit, the funk, and the charisma that overflowed onstage. He was already an institution in San Antonio, and word was quickly spreading. He had appeared on *Austin City Limits'* first season with Ry Cooder, but as a new producer, I was anxious to get him back for an encore performance.

But I couldn't find Flaco, who didn't exactly have a manager at the time, and didn't really have a telephone either. I finally tracked him down at an accordion repair shop, and then found out he was playing a couple of gigs that weekend. So I figured he'd just drive down from Austin and work out all the details.

It turned out to be an exciting adventure on San Antonio's Lockhart Highway, where I found Flaco at the Rockin' M Club. After a weapons search at the door (I was clean), I settled in for a new cultural experience. He was excited that I was there, and he introduced me and then went on and on (en Español, of course) about *Austin City Limits.* There were probably more eyes on me than on Flaco that night, but after a few cervezas, I felt right at home.

TERRY LICKONA, Producer

TEXAS TORNADOS (1990)
Hotter than any salsa or chile pepper known to man, the Texas Tornados lived up to their name. They are (left to right) Augie Meyers, Doug Sahm, Freddy Fender, and Flaco Jimenez.

"Tejano music developed from traditional accordion music, orquestas and conjuntos," Freddy Fender explained. "It's combining arrangements and intonations, and blending with Anglo musical traditions. The arrangements are almost rock and roll. Creatively, it's an art that belongs solely to South Texas. Because of the blending of our cultures down there, we have this. It's an evolution of what was and has been our music. We're feeding each other's music."

In the wake of the political awakening embodied by the Chicano Movement and La Raza Unida in the sixties and seventies, Tejano music became the anthem for an explosion of cultural pride. Rick Treviño, who grew up in a white-bread suburb of Austin and in whose house Spanish was not spoken, recalled being profoundly moved as he began to delve into his musical heritage, via his own bilingual recordings (for which he had to study Spanish in Mexico) and the Los Super Seven project. "That's my culture, but it's something I didn't do growing up," Treviño said. "This is giving me a good chance to grow into my own culture."

"Tejano means Texan," said Tejano-country crossover performer Rick Orozco, who recalled seeing George Strait and Garth Brooks on *Austin City Limits.* "It brings together many varieties of music—pop, Latin, country. . . . It's energetic and it transcends a lot of boundaries. Mexicans consider this American music." Orozco appeared on *ACL* in 1995, along with Jimenez, Fender, Joel Nava, and the band La Diferenzia. All represented, to varying and lesser degrees, the cross-cultural, crossover potential of Tejano.

In 1998 a project of border music enthusiasts dubbed Los Super Seven released an all-star album of largely traditional material. From that recording project arose another *Austin*

City Limits summit meeting, dubbed the "Mexican Roots Music Celebration," which included members of Los Lobos, Flaco Jimenez, Joe Ely, Tish Hinojosa, Ruben Ramos, Freddy Fender, and the mariachi group Las Campanas de America.

In 1999, for the first time, Tejano music received its own category in the Grammy awards; nominated were Flaco Jimenez, Corpus Christi's Leyendas y Raices (which includes Chicano legends Sunny Ozuna, Agustin Ramirez, and Freddie Gonzalez), Fiebre, and the Tejano standard-bearers for thirty years, Little Joe y La Familia. Conjunto was also represented at the Grammys, as Texans Los Terribles del Norte, Jaime y los Chamacos, Vicente Fernandez, Introcable, and Ramon Ayala were all nominated in the Mexican-American category.

MEXICAN ROOTS MUSIC CELEBRATION (1998)
A cross-cultural celebration of traditional Mexican music brought together (front, left to right) Tish Hinojosa, Joe Ely, Cesar Rosas from Los Lobos, and Ruben Ramos, as well as (background) San Antonio mariachi band Campanas de America and Rick Treviño (far right), as well as Freddy Fender and David Hidalgo (not seen here).

Today, stars such as Emilio Navaira (or simply Emilio, as he prefers to be known) and Rick Treviño are making inroads in the country market; Emilio even has his own beer sponsorship, a sure sign of mainstream acceptance ("Esta Miller Time!").

Emilio has not appeared on *Austin City Limits*—at least not yet—but many of the traditional and modern exponents of this Texas-Mexico fusion have done so, including both Flaco and Santiago Jimenez Jr., Little Joe y La Familia, Los Lobos, Johnny Rodriguez, Las Campanas de America, the Texas Tornados, Tish Hinojosa, Rosie Flores, Esteban Jordan, and others. "La onda Tejano" is still rolling, and anyone with an appreciation for the way cultures can combine, evolve, and emerge as something wholly new and delightful is free to ride the wave.

Los Siete Magnifico

The "Mexican Roots Music Celebration" in Season 24 had its origins in a pair of private showcases held at Austin's annual South by Southwest Music and Media Conference each March. Dan Goodman, who runs a management company in Nashville that handles Austin country star Rick Treviño, noticed the paucity of attention paid to conjunto and Tejano at SXSW, despite its Texas locale.

"A lot of shows at SXSW were just mob scenes and nobody was covering border music," Goodman said. "I thought it might be nice to do something in a real small setting and invite the press to see music that otherwise wasn't being presented." To that end he and co-producer Paula Batson took over the back patio of Las Manitas, a beloved downtown Mexican café, and in 1997 and '98, on the patio's tiny stage, assembled a remarkable acoustic crew: Doug Sahm and Augie Meyers of the Texas Tornados, Joe Ely, San Antonio country roots rocker Rosie Flores, Treviño, and the mariachi band Las Campanas de America.

The shows were rocking, joyous affairs that were quickly elevated into legend. Treviño, who grew up in a suburban, mainstream environment, was visibly moved as he delved into the traditional repertoire. Actress Sandra Bullock, newly moved to Austin, was among those sitting in the back of the tiny patio, sipping a beer and "ay-yi-yi-ing" with the best of them.

Out of those shows grew the Grammy-winning Los Super Seven recording project, which combined the talents of David Hidalgo and Cesar Rosas of Los Lobos, Treviño once more, Freddy Fender, Joe Ely, conjunto accordion master Flaco Jimenez, and one of Austin's musical giants, bandleader and singer Ruben "El Gato Negro" Ramos.

The album project, with its emphasis on traditional material, gave rise to *ACL*'s celebration of Mexican roots music, which featured Hidalgo and Rosas, Jimenez, Ely, Ramos, and Fender, along with Las Campanas de America (who even went outdoors and serenaded the ticketholders as they waited outside the studio doors), and Austin songstress and activist Tish Hinojosa.

To regional roots music fans of all complexions, the sounds that night were like visits from old friends. *Austin City Limits* fans across the country had the opportunity to sample, perhaps for the first time, the rich Tex-Mex musical heritage of the border country.

JOHN T. DAVIS

SINGER-SONGWRITERS

AS THE STORY GOES, a young apprentice approached Michelangelo one day and asked him how to become a great sculptor. Piece of cake, the master replied. You just get a big block of marble and chip away everything that doesn't look like David.

Any songwriter who has gone to the mat with the muse can appreciate the hard-won wisdom of that story. Historically there have been people in Broadway's Brill Building or on Nashville's Music Row who approach songwriting as a nine-to-five day job, cranking out songs with assembly-line regularity. But for the most part those tunesmiths were crafting their ditties for others to sing. Songwriters who stare at a blank sheet of paper until small drops of blood form on their forehead and then stand impaled by the spotlight while pouring their hearts out to people in the dark are a special breed unto themselves.

"Hank Williams wrote [songs] in twenty minutes," Leonard Cohen once marveled. "There's two tribes. There's those guys, and then there's us who have to sweat over every word. It just is the way it is."

"What I set out for is, first of all, to feel like it's my true voice that's coming through," says Mary Chapin Carpenter, an adept songwriter with the hit albums and big shiny awards to prove it. "When singer-songwriters write personal music, people say, 'Doesn't that make you uncomfortable?' To me, no, that's just our voice expressing itself. There's a difference between expressing yourself and exposing yourself."

For piano player and songwriter Bruce Hornsby, writing songs was never an end unto itself; it was only a beginning. "I was a jazz major in college," Hornsby said, "I got my degree in jazz music and improvisation, and that's what I've always been about. It sort of opened me up [as a pop songwriter], much to the record company's chagrin. It was a wonderful accident that I had three hit singles on my first record, but that's not where I was headed. I'd be stretching and blowing and playing ten-minute songs and sort of deconstructing the songs, playing them in different ways. And I'm sure a lot of those people who were there to hear the song just like they know it on the radio were disappointed. *Austin City Limits* is an important show, because it's one of the few areas where the mass populace can see someone do more than just their hit single, like you do on Letterman and Leno."

You Got to Sing Like You Don't Need the Money

BRUCE HORNSBY (1998)

"Austin City Limits is an important show for me because it endures. . . . It's also one of the few places where the mass populace can see someone do more than just their single like on Letterman and Leno. It's great, I'm a huge fan."

MARY CHAPIN CARPENTER (1989)
Singer-songwriter from the Washington, D.C., area, Mary Chapin Carpenter rewrote the Nashville songbook when she won the coveted Country Female Artist of the Year award. She first appeared in 1989.

JOHN PRINE (1991)
Who has a better way with words? John Prine is the premier lyricist of our generation, barring Bob Dylan or maybe Neil Young. "Sam Stone is the saddest song I've ever heard," says Scott Newton. "The guru will tell you that the greatest task you can take on in this life is to learn to 'walk with joy in this vale of sorrows.' With his mischievous grin, John Prine shows us that this can be done."

LOUDON WAINWRIGHT III (1987)
Witty and winsome, Loudon Wainwright combines razor-sharp humor with wry introspection.

JOHN HIATT (1993)
An energetic and forceful entertainer, John Hiatt is also a perceptive songwriter. Scott Newton believes that watching Hiatt perform is akin to having a ringside seat at a tornado.

ROGER MCGUINN (1985)

With songs like "Eight Miles High" and "Turn, Turn, Turn" to his credit when he was a founding member of the Byrds, Roger McGuinn brought his '60s songbook to the stage for a solo performance.

DON MCLEAN (1981)

He broke a string in the middle of "American Pie," but there was no way he was going to repeat his seven-minute classic from the top, so he kept right on singing and changed strings without missing a beat—a feat of magic mixed with music.

The triptych of singer, instrument, and song are perhaps the classic combination in American music. Whether it's the cowboy and his guitar on the range, the bluesman on the back porch, the torch singer at the piano signaling for one more for her baby and one more for the road, or the lonesome hobo troubadour hopping a westbound freight, the self-contained singer-songwriter seems to embody the gritty essence of the musical creative process.

Sheryl Crow, whose growth and insight over the course of three albums reveals a rapidly maturing talent, nevertheless confessed that the alchemy of songwriting was something of a mystery. "I think a lot of the time you write songs and you think nobody's ever going to hear them. When you're writing a song that's coming from sort of a gut feeling, a broken heart or from your own experiences, your own insights, your own perspective, or whatever, it never occurs to you that somebody else is going to relate to it. But you know as early as sixteen or seventeen, when I was writing my own songs, there were always people around saying, 'Wow, I can relate to that.' But as a kid, you don't really believe anybody can understand you. Songwriting's funny, because it's like keeping a diary. You can go back and see where you've grown, what you've been through. And there are things that are hard for me to listen to now, and things that I still think really apply."

SHERYL CROW (1997)
Everything a modern rocker (male or female) ought to be, Sheryl Crow wowed the crowd.

Singer-songwriters have always been central in Texas music precisely because they come in so many guises: the storytelling corridas of South Texas; the country blues of the Piney Woods; the cowboy balladry of the Panhandle; the psychic self-dissection of the angst-ridden urban introvert in the backstreets of Houston or Dallas, all spring from the songwriter's pen.

Jerry Jeff Walker, one of a long line of musical immigrants to the Lone Star State, figured out early in his creative life that if you lived your own adventures, you could sing about them instead of about somebody else's. After years of rambling from his home in upstate New York to Key West to New Orleans, Walker finally put down roots in Austin in 1971. He was drawn to Texas in part, he said, because music was central in people's lives there, and people thought the things they did and the place they lived were important and worthy of singing about. That natural connection between people, places, and songs is central to Walker's own artistic personality, and he began a long and fruitful association with Texas and things Texan.

It's funny how destinations can shape destinies. As songwriter Jimmy LaFave recounted, "The other musician to come out of my hometown of Stillwater, Oklahoma, is Garth Brooks. I was playing music there before he was, and . . . my friends always said, 'Jimmy, we always thought you'd be the first person out of Stillwater to be on *Austin City Limits.*' But Garth went to Nashville, and I went to Austin."

Other songwriters have also migrated to Texas, from the father of country music, Jimmie Rodgers (who lived his last years in the Hill Country town of Kerrville), to recent immigrants such as Shawn Colvin, the Grammy-winning songwriter who drifted through Austin in the 1970s with a country-rock band called the Dixie Diesels and returned two decades later to put down roots and start a family.

"It's for reasons like a show called *Austin City Limits* that I moved here," Colvin explained. "It was huge! For me it was like being asked to do *The Tonight Show.* To have enough notoriety to be asked to be on *Austin City Limits* was a major validation. I remember the whole day—I remember the rehearsal, I remember going to dinner with my sister, I remember the taping. . . . It was a really, really big deal."

Texas has also given rise to native generations of songwriters. The breed seems to have a particular avidity for West Texas, to the eternal mystification of much of the rest of the populace, who look at the region's endless, flat vistas, the overpowering sky, the relative lack of any sort of intellectual tradition, and wonder just precisely where in the hell all that music is coming from.

Some folks say it's the wind. According to Butch Hancock, it comes sweeping down from Canada. Hancock, one of the heirs to the West Texas songwriting tradition of Buddy Holly and Roy Orbison, insists, "All the way down it keeps picking up dreams and images, and when it hits Yellow House Canyon, outside of Lubbock, all that stuff sorta spills outta there."

DAVE ALVIN (1999)
A unique voice from L.A. that resonates with music fans everywhere, Alvin appeared for the first time in 1999. He writes about real people and places that play with the imagination.

JERRY JEFF WALKER (1979)
In his hell-raisin' days of the '70s, Jerry Jeff Walker had no match. Everybody's got a favorite Jerry Jeff story.

HARLAN HOWARD (1988)
The dean of country music songwriters, Harlan Howard boasts more than four hundred songs, including "I Fall to Pieces" and "Busted." In 1988 he did something he almost never does—he went on stage—on national TV, no less!—and joined a group of Nashville cohorts for another Songwriters' Special.

SHAWN COLVIN (1994)
Multi-Grammy Award winner (best song, best record, 1998), Shawn Colvin's songs are direct, passionate, and pure. Austin is proud to claim her as one of its own.

Lubbock-raised Terry Allen, a songwriter and visual artist who is one of Hancock's contemporaries, thinks the region breeds a naturally restless curiosity: "Lubbock is so flat in every direction, that if you grow up in it (and are blessed with any curiosity at all), your attention just naturally runs to the horizon, the edge. . . ."

Beyond that horizon is another native tradition of urban songwriting, with Houston as one of its hotbeds. Houston folk clubs such as the Old Quarter, Anderson Fair, and the Mucky Duck proved valuable training grounds for Lyle Lovett, Robert Earl Keen, Nanci Griffith, Townes Van Zandt, Guy Clark, Jerry Jeff Walker, and others. A similar scene in Dallas helped nurture Michael Martin Murphey, the late B. W. Stevenson, and Steven Fromholz.

And, of course, there was Austin. "If you were trying to describe it to someone who's never been here," mused Willie Nelson, who has been known to pen a hummable tune or two himself, "I dunno. It's indescribable. It's everything imaginable, the people, the weather, the freedom. Those of us who are really touched by it, we don't find it anywhere else. Plus, the sunsets are the best in the world."

LYLE LOVETT WITH WILLIE NELSON AND RODNEY CROWELL (1993)
Three Texas songwriters in the round (left to right): Lyle Lovett, Willie Nelson, and Rodney Crowell.

OUTLAW SUMMIT (1996)
From left to right, Waylon Jennings, Kris Kristofferson, and Willie Nelson.

SONGWRITERS' SPECIALS

The inspiration for the Songwriters' Specials came from University of Texas football legend Coach Darrell K. Royal, who's also a legendary music fan. Coach values songwriters more highly than quarterbacks. Back in the late 1970s and early 1980s, he used to have regular "guitar pulls" at his house in West Austin. Willie was part of the original crowd, and Darrell would have obscure scribes and million-seller writers come and hang out at his house every now and then. Everybody would stay up all night singing and picking, with "The Coach" in command. But when folks got to talking too much or too loud, Coach would shout "Red Light!" and instantly you could hear a pin drop in the room.

Coach knew all the great writers in Nashville, and they loved to escape to Austin to play golf, hang out with Willie (that's redundant), and end the day at Darrell and Edith's house.

In 1980, we decided to re-create the scene for *Austin City Limits.* Willie had to be the centerpiece, of course, but we also invited Floyd Tillman, who practically invented the country "cheatin' song" (with "Slippin' Around"), Hank Cochran (who gave Patsy Cline "I Fall To Pieces"), Whitey Shafer (Lefty Frizzell's and Merle Haggard's favorite writer), and contemporary hit-makers Sonny Throckmorton and Red Lane.

It was utterly unlike anything else we had ever done on that stage—pure magic. It really was like the cameras were invisible and the audience was privileged to sit in on a pickin' party at Coach's. It was so good, in fact, that we had to make two episodes out of it instead of one.

TERRY LICKONA, Producer

PURE MAGIC (1979)
The first Songwriters' Special featured (left to right) Floyd Tillman, Sonny Throckmorton, Rock Killough (background), Hank Cochran, Willie Nelson, Whitey Shafer, and Red Lane.

A SIT-DOWN SONG SWAP (1983)
Freddie Powers (center) was the man who brought together Willie Nelson and Merle Haggard for a sit-down song swap—the first of its kind. Willie and Merle had known each other for years, but they never really spent much time making music together.

The Songwriters' Specials were a big hit. But after ten years somebody finally noticed that not a single female songwriter had ever been included in any of the shows. Actually, that person was singer-songwriter and producer Gail Davies, who was proud of her own major-label debut, and proud to be part of a growing community of women composers and performers that included Emmylou Harris, Rosanne Cash, Lacy J. Dalton, Pam Rose, and Mary Ann Kennedy (known professionally as Kennedy-Rose). And that was exactly who came with her in January 1986 to do one of the finest and most-requested *Austin City Limits* programs ever.

GIRLS GOT GAME (1986)
After years of neglect, the first Women Songwriters' Special featured (left to right): Gail Davies, Rosanne Cash, Emmylou Harris, Lacy J. Dalton, Pam Rose, and Mary Ann Kennedy.

WOMEN IN SONG

GRRRLS WITH GUITARS

CHIRPS. CANARIES. TORCH SINGERS. Divas. Thrushes. Chanteuses. Songbirds. Girl groups. Blues mamas. You know—chick singers.

Also, chick songwriters. And chick guitarists, bass players, drummers, keyboardists, producers, bandleaders, and choreographers. Girls with guitars. On second thought, make that women.

Or, as Wynonna sang in Mary Chapin Carpenter's song of the same name, "She wasn't any debutante. . . . She didn't go out for cheerleading. . . . Boys are kind of nervous 'round . . . Girls with guitars."

In writing a history of women in country music, authors Robert K. Oermann and Mary A. Bufwak penned words that might be applied to the passage of women through all forms of American music in the past century: "The story of women in country music is a window into the world of the majority of American women. It describes poverty, hardship, economic exploitation, sexual subjugation, and limited opportunities. Sometimes it is self-defeating and reactionary, painful and despairing. But it also contains outspoken protest and joyful rebellion, shouts of exaltation and bugle calls of freedom. There is humor as well as sadness here, victory as well as heartache."

While it might not be otherwise illustrative to link, say, Mother Maybelle Carter to Billie Holiday, it is easy to cite common elements that shaped their music: poverty, a certain fatalism, an implicit recognition of powerful unseen forces that shaped human affairs, and a belief in the transfiguring power of love (carnal love, to be sure in Billie's case, versus the spiritual embrace that Mother Maybelle sang about). Both sang, and in singing, opened a window to the world as seen through a woman's eyes.

Today women sing and play from a thousand perspectives. Whatever else can be said of fin de siècle American pop culture, any society that can extend the accolades of stardom to both Mariah Carey and Courtney Love, modatingly broad-minded . . . Ani DiFranco, Riot Grrrls and VH-1 divas, Joni Mitchell and Lauryn Hill and Shania Twain is certainly accommodatingly broad-minded (no pun intended). And speaking of broad-minded . . . Female musicians, songwriters, and vocalists are less and less inclined to have their achievements categorized by gender. Bonnie Raitt, Mary Cutrufello, Queen Ida, Alison Krauss, and Marcia Ball are superb instrumentalists, period. No distaff qualification needed, thanks very much.

TANYA TUCKER (1985)
Tanya Tucker started out as a singing teen sensation and eventually evolved into "country's bad girl." She was one of the first to "cross the line" with her sexy-but-sweet songs.

WYNONNA (1996)
Fiery redhead Wynonna draws as much from rock, blues, and gospel as she does from country music, and in addition to her own platinum-success career, will always be one of the Judds.

BONNIE RAITT (1983)
Long before she became the household name she is now, Bonnie Raitt was an Austin favorite. Deservedly famous for her beautiful voice and smoldering delivery, she's also the best female blues-rock guitarist in the world.

MARY CUTRUFELLO (1996)
Some day you'll say you saw her first on Austin City Limits. From Texas by way of Yale, she rocks!

In a similar vein, Rosanne Cash has said, "My own life inspires me mainly, and the internal landscape and the internal climate—just paying attention to it. Having a kind of constant inner dialogue. Just like my eyes are brown, I am a writer, you know?"

Cash, who has penned such radio-friendly hit singles as "Seven Year Ache" and "Blue Moon With Heartache," has also crafted two darkly lustrous, painfully intimate concept albums, *Interiors* and *The Wheel.* In each case her viewpoint has been uniquely feminine—"Don't give me your life/I have got one of my own," she sings—but in no way limited or compromised by that perspective.

Though she has eschewed it in recent years, Cash came out of the same Nashville womb that yielded country music's greatest female stars. Though those women—Tammy Wynette, Loretta Lynn, Kitty Wells, Patsy Cline, and others—were able to exercise little direct influence over their career direction, production, or choice of material, their sororal offspring were inspired by their empathy and honesty not only to pursue a musical career but to seize control over it.

CARLENE CARTER (1993)
Carlene Carter proves that beauty and power make a powerful combination.

ROSANNE CASH AND SHAWN COLVIN

Rosanne Cash and Shawn Colvin have both played a definite role in shaping *Austin City Limits'* overall musical perspective. I view them as ultimate artists who just happen to be women. Rosanne Cash was the first woman of my generation to make her mark on country music. Her musical pedigree didn't hurt, but it was her lyrics, finesse, and rockin' style that set her apart. Rosanne has real cool. I honestly believe she cleared the way for the leagues of women singer-songwriters who have followed in her footsteps.

Shawn Colvin's first performance is probably my favorite *ACL* performance, ever. Shawn—solo. In a white dress with fishnet hose . . . playing guitar like no woman had ever played guitar on our stage. Those songs were so direct, passionate, and pure. A woman's voice. She blew everyone in the audience away. Shawn's sister, Kay, joined her onstage for a quick rendition of the "Roadrunner" cartoon theme . . . just another day in the life of the Colvin girls, but it gave us a window to her world. Good stuff.

SUSAN CALDWELL, Associate Producer

ROSANNE CASH (1982)

Rosanne is an enchanting and incredibly sexy performer, a gifted songwriter, and a compelling vocalist. She has it all. An Austin City Limits *favorite, she has appeared on the show many times.*

SHAWN COLVIN (1994)

"To have enough notoriety to be asked to be on Austin City Limits *was like a major validation," enthused Shawn Colvin. "ACL is for people who write, sing, and play well . . . country, folk, blues, even jazz . . . there is that kind of melting pot that's come about over the past 25 years."*

NANCI GRIFFITH (1997)
Like all of us, Nanci Griffith got here as fast as she could; only in her case it wasn't by moving from some other place—she was raised in Austin. Nanci transcends labels; more than a folksinger/balladeer, she can rock.

COWBOY JUNKIES WITH MARGO TIMMONS (1990)
With a quiet beauty and voice that sweeps over you like a narcotic, Margo Timmons and Cowboy Junkies weave a magic web of melodies.

"Loretta was the first person that inspired me that I didn't have to play other people's songs, that I could write my own dadgum songs and play my own rhythm guitar," Nanci Griffith told a reporter for *New Texas* in 1983. "Her songs were little incredibly vivid stories that hit their subjects right on the head."

Griffith was the driving force behind one of *Austin City Limits*' most memorable Songwriters' Specials when she helmed an acoustic quorum of women songwriters in Season 17 that included the Indigo Girls, Julie Gold ("From a Distance"), and Mary Chapin Carpenter. "That was my doing," Griffith said proudly. "And it was a very special thing for me in that Terry Lickona allowed me a free hand. The Indigo Girls didn't have a record deal at the time, and they got their record deal following the program. And Mary was only just fixing to happen at the time, and people got to hear what a great songwriter Julie Gold was. Terry has always been great about letting the artists run amok on the show."

SARA HICKMAN (1990)
Dallas native Sara Hickman's spirit pervades her music—and that's why she connects so well with her audiences.

INDIGO GIRLS (1997)
Folk-rock with an edge and a message, the Indigo Girls (Amy Ray and Emily Saliers) met in school in Georgia and have attracted some of the most loyal fans in pop music today.

HORMONAL IMBALANCE

In the first four seasons of *Austin City Limits* (almost fifty programs), a total of only four women were featured (and two of them were Marcia Ball). In Season 24 alone, seven female artists headlined their own segments, from Deana Carter and the Dixie Chicks to Ruth Brown, Lucinda Williams, and Susan Tedeschi, all great song stylists and writers.

So, were we deaf and dumb, sexist pigs, or what? We probably missed some wonderful talent in those early years, but the fact is, women's voices weren't being heard much back then. Not that they didn't have a lot to say. They just didn't have that many outlets. The music world and the world around it have changed. The rise of women to the creative front line of popular music has been one of the great stories of the nineties. Look at the huge success of the Lilith Fair Festivals. There are great new singers-songwriters-stylists emerging every year.

So who's left on the *ACL* wish list? Right up there at the top are Dolly Parton, Aretha Franklin, and Joni Mitchell. Then there is the great norteño diva Lydia Mendoza, and the best of the new talent, like Sarah McLachlan, Lauryn Hill, Cassandra Wilson, Alanis Morisette, and Shania Twain.

TERRY LICKONA, Producer

MARCIA BALL WITH TRACY NELSON AND IRMA THOMAS (1997)

These wonderfully gifted individual performers coalesced into an ad hoc blues supergroup with the release of "Sing It!" Each of them is accomplished in her own right. Austinite Marcia Ball (left) plays a raucous Louisiana blues piano, and has been described as the love child of Jerry Lee Lewis and Miss Manners. Irma Thomas (center) is the queen of New Orleans blues, and Tracy Nelson's (right) big voice defines blues power. Impossibly, in their case, the whole is greater than the sum of the parts.

MICHELLE SHOCKED (1989)
Michelle Shocked writes evocative songs, many having to do with people and memories of another time and place.

LISA LOEB (1996)
Dallas native Lisa Loeb scored a couple of hits on the pop charts with her personal yet direct songs.

LUCINDA WILLIAMS (1991)
Lucinda Williams is seen here in her first ACL appearance.

SUZANNE VEGA (1993)
Suzanne Vega is one of the '90s breed of women singer-songwriters whose songs have more of an edge, both musically and lyrically.

EMMYLOU HARRIS

Emmylou Harris made her third *ACL* appearance one hot Saturday night in August 1988. Given her usual standard of excellence, it is no surprise that the taping went swimmingly. Having watched playback and given her seal of approval, Emmy found herself with the balance of a Saturday night to spend in Austin. As it turned out, she didn't have to go far to find a party.

Just across Guadalupe Street from the KLRU building stands (rather, leans) the Hole In the Wall, a venerated, spit-in-your-eye blue-collar bar and restaurant that pre-dates even *Austin City Limits.* Over the years the joint has served as something of an unofficial *ACL* bullpen; Timbuk 3 ("The Future's So Bright, I Gotta Wear Shades") held forth there for years before being discovered by a major record label, and Nanci Griffith had a weekly gig there almost before she was old enough to go to the movies by herself. More recently, the club served as an incubator for Fastball, Austin's latest pop export. A much-beloved joint in Austin, the Hole In the Wall is nonetheless utterly devoid of pretensions.

On this night the stage was occupied by Rosie Flores, a great singer and songwriter from San Antonio who had become a mainstay of the same SoCal-Bakersfield scene that spawned Dwight Yoakam and others. Emmy and Rosie had crossed paths many times before, and it wasn't long before Harris found herself onstage playing and singing in the small smoky bar, to the manifest delight of the audience. The tequila began flowing, empty shot glasses began to accumulate on guitar amplifiers, and, as Harris ruefully put it years later, "The bottle let me down—the whole bottle! I must say, I'm a pretty puny drinker [but] it *was* the Hole In the Wall."

Everyone was happy, except for one crank with his back to the stage who was trying to focus on the baseball game on TV behind the bar. There he sat, grousing into his beer, as honky-tonk magic transpired behind him ten feet away. There's just no pleasing some people.

JOHN T. DAVIS

EMMYLOU HARRIS (1981)

Emmylou's first ACL appearance in 1981 was one of her first television performances, and she was terrified. The adoring crowd of Austin music fans and the show's easy style brought out the best in Emmy and her "Hot Band."

Led by the example of Dolly Parton, the savvy businesswoman swathed in big hair and rhinestones, modern country performers such as Reba McEntire and Wynonna have established themselves as business as well as artistic powerhouses. Similar events transpired in the pop music arena. Though no women currently head a major label, no one familiar with the pop power structure would argue the point that Madonna, Whitney Houston, Janet Jackson, and Barbra Streisand are powerful corporate entities in their own right. The modern story of women in music is not about competition with men; it's about control of their own destinies.

A sense of destiny is not something that has ever been in short supply in Texas. Whether this contributes to the significant number of female musicians who have either emerged from or migrated to the Lone Star State is open to speculation. But there has been no lack of vibrant, distinctive stylists associated with the region. A cursory glance reveals virtuosos in a number of genres:

KATE WOLF (1985)
Months before her untimely death, Kate Wolf enchanted us with her wonderful folksinging. Scott Newton's photo ended up being the cover of her last, posthumously released album.

- Rock and pop: Janis Joplin, Shawn Colvin, Lisa Loeb, Sara Hickman, Kathy Valentine, Erykah Badu

- Country and country-rock: Dixie Chicks, Holly Dunn, Rosie Flores, Cindy Walker, Laura Lee McBride, Kelly Willis, Chris O'Connell and Cindy Cashdollar (both Asleep at the Wheel alumnae), Tanya Tucker, Barbara and Louise Mandrell

- Blues, jazz, and R&B: "Big Mama" Thornton, Victoria Spivey, Barbara Lynn ("You'll Lose A Good Thing"), Marcia Ball, Sippie "The Texas Nightingale" Wallace, "Little Esther" Phillips, Lou Ann Barton, Angela Strehli, Carmen Bradford

- Conjunto and Tejano: Selena, Lydia Mendoza, Laura Canales, Eva Ybarra

- Folk and Americana: Carolyn Hester, Nanci Griffith, Tish Hinojosa, Lucinda Williams, Eliza Gilkyson, Katy Moffatt, Michelle Shocked, Christine Albert

Not all of these women are native to Texas, but the state has played a formative part in their careers, especially through outlets such as the annual Kerrville Folk Festival. Girls with guitars will always have a home in the Lone Star State.

KELLY WILLIS (1990)
Kelly Willis hopes that she doesn't "fall into the trap of just trying to make things I think people want to hear instead of making something unique and interesting."

LONE STARS

Texas is a State of Mind

THE FIGURATIVE MOTHER OF MUSIC IN TEXAS might be said to have been a woman named Emily Morgan. A twenty-something mulatto servant woman from Harrisburg, she was appropriated by the Mexican general Santa Ana and forced to accompany him on his march to quash the rebellious settlers of Texas in 1836. Some say she was a spy for the Texians, as they were then known, while others maintain that she furnished Santa Ana with a romantic distraction at a crucial moment, thus helping Sam Houston and his fighters to surprise the Mexican forces at the Battle of San Jacinto and win Texas independence. Whatever the truth, she inspired a song, "The Yellow Rose of Texas," which endures to this day.

Music in Texas, of course, has many parents, of all colors and persuasions. By a happy geographic accident, the state sits at the intersection of a host of vibrant races and cultures. German, Czech, and Polish immigrants settled in the Hill Country of Central Texas, bringing with them their traditional polkas, mazurkas, and waltzes. When those accordion-driven melodies drifted south, they were adopted by the Mexican population of the South Texas brush country and transformed into conjunto, corridas, and norteño, the musical leitmotifs of the border.

In the east out past the Piney Woods, zydeco and Cajun music ebbed and flowed with tidal fluidity across the Sabine River marking the border between Texas and Louisiana. The territory between Beaumont and Baton Rouge might be said to be a single musical landscape with two soundtracks. The distinction between zydeco and Cajun music is roughly the same as that between blues and country; zydeco, the more vibrant and percussive of the two, is played mostly by blacks and Creoles, while the traditional-sounding Cajun music is the province of (mostly) white descendants of Acadian settlers. There are plenty of exceptions on both sides of the line, of course. Hey, who cares—let the good times roll, 'chere!

GARY P. NUNN (1988)

Although he's moved back to his native Oklahoma, Gary P. Nunn was an Austinite when it really mattered: the '70s. An original member of Jerry Jeff Walker's band, which later became the Lost Gonzo Band (minus Jerry Jeff), he was onstage at the Armadillo World Headquarters backing up Michael Murphey when Murphey first sang, "I Just Wanna Be a Cosmic Cowboy." Scott Newton marks that as the birth of the "progressive country" movement—a hint that Austin possessed the power to create its own musical art forms. Gary P. wrote "London Homesick Blues," which became the Austin City Limits *theme. Twenty-five years later, it still ties us to our roots.*

JOE ELY (1979)
One of Lloyd Maines's early appearances on the show (on pedal steel, of course), with fellow Lubbock, Texas, native Joe Ely and his band.

JUNIOR BROWN (1997)
Junior Brown is an original, but he makes traditional country music relevant for the '90s.

JOE ELY, JIMMIE DALE GILMORE, BUTCH HANCOCK (1992)

Converging in Austin after the demise of the Flatlanders in the early '70s, this trio of singer-songwriters from Lubbock continues to create great music. Joe Ely, Jimmie Dale Gilmore, and Butch Hancock (left to right) are now independent performers, but as Scott Newton sees it, taken together they define a greater whole. Joe is dynamic and energetic live; Butch is deep and perceptive, the best writer of the group. Jimmie Dale's voice gathers and resonates the penetrating West Texas wind.

GUY CLARK (1989)
Another great Texas singer-songwriter (now in self-imposed exile in Nashville), Guy Clark looks like a preacher in this shot. He's not preaching religion, however; he's spinning tales.

MICHAEL MARTIN MURPHEY (1990)
A veteran of the early years of Austin City Limits and the "Cosmic Cowboy" scene, Michael Martin Murphey today dedicates himself to promoting cowboy history and culture in song.

Out west, in and near the Panhandle, a whole other thing sprang up, just in time to combat the Depression blues. In Fort Worth country string band fiddlers like Bob Wills and Milton Brown and bandleaders like W. Lee "Pappy" O'Daniel threw together a hobo's stew of country blues, West Texas twin fiddles, hot jazz licks, cowboy standards, big-band showmanship (Wills had done some time in a blackface minstrel show), steel guitar rags, and Lone Star moxie. The whole glorious mess was called western swing, and it dead-solid rocked the house for three decades.

Years later, young folk, country, and rock musicians from Buddy Holly to Joe Ely would arise out of the same West Texas dust that gave rise to Bob Wills and start the whole process over again, mixing any influence that came to hand with a bracing disregard for prevailing stylistic boundaries.

There was more: Texarkana-born Scott Joplin sparked a national obsession with ragtime anthems like "Maple Leaf Rag" and "The Entertainer." The country blues of Blind Lemon Jefferson metamorphosed in the crucible of urban life into the electric blues of Albert Collins. In a parallel transition, sentimental cowboy love songs yielded to the cheatin' and drinkin' chronicles of the honky-tonks.

Jazz, with its famous school of "Texas Tenors" saxmen and native musicians like boogie-woogie master Moon Mullican, guitarist Charlie Christian, trombonist Jack Teagarden, pianist Teddy Wilson, and free-form visionary Ornette Coleman, also made its presence felt. Today young artists like Erykah Badu and Roy Hargrove (both proud graduates of Booker T. Washington High School for the Performing and Visual Arts in Dallas) are putting a fresh Texas imprint on jazz and R&B, while Houston is home to one of the hottest rap and hip-hop scenes in the nation.

LEE ROY PARNELL (1992)
"I don't fall into that 'flavor of the month' thing," declares Lee Roy Parnell. "I kind of do what I do, and I'm not competing with anybody else. From there, you begin this journey inward, and that's when your artistry really begins."

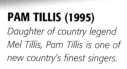

PAM TILLIS (1995)
Daughter of country legend Mel Tillis, Pam Tillis is one of new country's finest singers.

SWEETHEARTS OF THE RODEO
(1990)
One of country's few successful sister acts, Sweethearts of the Rodeo borrowed its name from The Byrds' classic country-rock album of the '60s, but Janice Gill's and Kristine Arnold's harmonies are nothing but original.

The common denominator of all these disparate strains of music, in retrospect, seems to be the desire to pack a dance floor. Be it a Tejano cumbia, a country two-step, or a belly-rubbing blues ballad, dancers, not applause, are how you know your band has gotten over in Texas. To this day, approving audiences out in West Texas may sit eerily silent between numbers, emitting a bare smattering of applause, but packing the dance floor when the band kicks back in.

"If you could play a shuffle, you could work anywhere," says journeyman guitarist-band-leader-producer Stephen Bruton. A shuffle, by the way, makes people dance like the hard-shell Baptists just left town. Bruton, who was born in Fort Worth and went on to work with Delbert McClinton, Kris Kristofferson, Bonnie Raitt, and others too numerous to mention, knew that command of a shuffle—the basic dance track in Texas for decades—could land you work with a black R&B band, a white country band, or a three-set-a-night rock group. It was, and largely remains, one of the Rosetta Stones of Texas music.

"Texas is a state of mind," wrote John Steinbeck in *Travels with Charley,* and it remains true today. Every Texas musician, whether native or immigrant, is heir to the freewheel-ing, assimilist, experimental legacy that is central to the creative vitality of the region. It is that legacy *Austin City Limits* has come to commemorate and celebrate.

Appearing on *Austin City Limits* has a special poignance for Texas-bred artists. Just like fledgling musicians elsewhere, they often grow up watching the show. But unlike viewers elsewhere, they have a personal connection with the program. Some, like Lyle Lovett, Nanci Griffith, Jimmie Vaughan, Jimmie Dale Gilmore, Fastball, W.C. Clark, and Robert Earl Keen, cut their teeth playing at the Cactus Cafe, the Hole In the Wall, emmajoe's, and Antone's—all clubs within a literal stone's throw of the KLRU studio. All of them knew the hometown musicians who appeared on the show. If they didn't share club bills with them, they ran into them buying cigarettes at 7-Eleven or eating migas at Las Manitas.

At times Austin musicians have gnashed their teeth when they and their peers seem slighted by *ACL* in favor of the occasional flavor of the month with a Nashville or Los Angeles area code, whom the show by necessity sometimes had to accommodate to cater to a national television audience.

Some locals feel the show is a natural rite of passage, kind of like a bar mitzvah. One songwriter of some contemporary national renown literally sat in an *ACL* staffer's door one day, lobbying for an appearance on the show. The staffer in question didn't feel like the time was quite right at that moment, but he still had to kind of halfway admire the young guy's sense of entitlement.

LYLE LOVETT (1989)

In Scott Newton's eyes, "Lyle Lovett articulates a side of Texas that virtually no one else approaches artistically. Texas is bigger, if that's possible, because of him. His understated, self-deprecating, dry viewpoint, artfully delivered, conveys the intelligence, wit, and creativity of the Lone Star State." This photo dates from the days of Big Hair Lyle, when he first appeared with His Large Band.

FAVORITE SON (1993)

"The biggest influences on me were the people I got to work with in the clubs," Lyle Lovett recalls. "Of course, great singer-songwriters had their effect—Townes Van Zandt, Willis Alan Ramsey, Guy Clark—but people that I would open for sometimes in Houston and Austin, like Eric Taylor, Uncle Walt's Band, Vince Bell, Don Sanders—those are the people I listen to now."

FIRST *ACL* SHOW (1987)

Lyle Lovett's first Austin City Limits took place in 1987—after a few years of sitting in the audience, then singing back-up for Nanci Griffith in 1984.

DIXIE CHICKS (1998)

One of those "overnight success" stories that took ten years of paying hard dues, the Dixie Chicks became the hottest act in country music in '99, and they're still on a roll.

And then there are two Texas musicians who hand the show down like a family legacy.

Over the course of its twenty-five years, *Austin City Limits* has featured parents and offspring (the Judds, Mel and Pam Tillis, Clifton and C.J. Chenier), brothers (Jimmie and Stevie Ray Vaughan, Flaco and Santiago Jimenez, the Neville Brothers), sisters (Sweethearts of the Rodeo), and husbands and wives (Johnny Cash and June Carter, Waylon Jennings and Jessi Colter). But native Texans Lloyd and Natalie Maines represent a special case. Between the father and the daughter, they span almost the entirety of *ACL*'s history.

At twenty-four, Natalie has hit multi-platinum paydirt as the lead vocalist for the vibrant Dallas-based trio the Dixie Chicks. The Chicks' major-label debut, *Wide Open Spaces,* sprinted to the top of the charts in 1998 and yielded a six-pack of hits, along with enough plaques, Grammys, and other trophies to stock a good-sized pawn shop. The band (which also includes Dallas sisters Martie Seidel and Emily Erwin) had released three other albums with other members, but the addition of the Lubbock-born Natalie, with her full-throttle voice and stage presence of gleeful abandon, provided the final component for hit-making chemistry.

Her forty-seven-year old father, Lloyd, is not as well known to the general public, but to those in the know, he is recognized as one of the pedal steel guitar's premier virtuosos and innovators. Welding a rock sensibility to a country tradition, Lloyd injected a new urgency into an instrument hitherto identified largely with weeping laments. His instrumental duel with guitarist Jesse Taylor on "Boxcars," from Joe Ely's 1978 album *Honky-Tonk Masquerade,* can still take the breath away.

Both Lloyd and Natalie come by their musical heritage honestly. Lloyd's father and uncles formed the original Maines Brothers Band, a popular West Texas dance band operating out of Acuff, a small town near Lubbock out on the windswept Great South Plains. As a boy, Lloyd and his siblings were billed as "The Little Maines Brothers" before succeeding their parents as the second-generation Maines Brothers Band in the 1970s. The group recorded a series of albums and, as the Panhandle Mystery Band, backed up artist-musician Terry Allen before disbanding in the early nineties.

Starting in 1977 Lloyd toured the country as the steel player in the original Joe Ely Band, who set the standard for a blistering hybrid of country and rock that owed nothing to Nashville calculation, and everything to West Texas's three-chords-and-a-cloud-of-dust rock and roll tradition.

The Ely band taped their first *Austin City Limits* episode in 1979, which aired as part of Season 5 the next year. Over time Lloyd would also appear on the show with the Maines Brothers, Terry Allen, Robert Earl Keen, Charlie Robison, and others, making him (with the possible exception of fiddler Johnny Gimble) the most prolific session musician in *ACL*'s history.

NATALIE AND LLOYD MAINES (1998)
Daughter Natalie Maines presents her father, Lloyd, with a homemade trophy in recognition of his many performances on Austin City Limits over twenty-three years.

MAINES BROTHERS BAND (1984)
They blew out of West Texas like a tumbleweed. Lloyd Maines (center) carried on the family musical tradition, as does daughter Natalie today.

RISING STARS

GARTH WHO?

"**H**E NOT BUSY BEING BORN," sang Bob Dylan, "is busy dying." By the same token, the star who is not rising is often in decline. That is the harsh Darwinian reality that the economy of the multimedia entertainment industry has imposed on its most perishable commodity—the talent.

It was not always thus. In country music, for instance, a couple of durable hits often ensured the singer a fan base for life. Now country music, like all the other multifaceted flavors of pop music—and pop culture as a whole—is viewed as a generic, self-sustaining creature, demanding only the periodic infusion of youth, ignorance, and fresh energy to feed the beast.

As dozens of venerable country stars who had given their lives to the cultivation of an audience and an art form have been made suddenly and rudely aware, their legacy has been handed over to callow young hunks-in-hats who take their orders from demographic researchers bowing to the God of Market Share. Just another pop commodity to be bought, sold, or traded in on next year's model.

Pop culture is inherently disposable, or so we're told. The "overnight sensation" generally has a career as truncated as it is incandescent. "I'm an instant star," David Bowie once declared. "Just add water and stir."

And yet, for all the cynicism attached to Bowie's remark, there is something exhilarating in catching a genuinely gifted artist on the cusp of a promising career. Austin's musical history is replete with stories of musicians who played weeknights for free beer and tips, and were abruptly catapulted to national renown. Similarly, touring artists who found small and friendly audiences in Austin might, after winning the karmic lottery, find themselves packing local arenas, their loyal old fans lost in a sea of new converts.

A case in point: One of the first times Jimmy Buffett came to town, he pulled up in front of the old Castle Creek club at Lavaca and 15th Street in a rented station wagon, pulled his guitar out of the back seat, and walked in to play for the people. One of the patrons on the scene later reported that when Buffett took a break, he invited the modestly numbered audience to come with him next door to the Capitol Oyster Bar for a cold beer and a dozen raw.

Today, on his infrequent returns to the city (the Austin market is really too small for the scale of his operation), Mr. Margaritaville routinely sells out the Frank Erwin Center, the giant basketball cathedral on the University of Texas campus. Funny thing, though, Buffett nearly always makes an onstage mention, with undisguised fondness, of the good old days at Castle Creek.

KEB' MO' (1996)
"Blues is an ingredient that made everything else for me more coherent, more legitimate, and mean more," says Keb' Mo'. "The blues is more of a self-awakening than a change of bag, of musical direction."

**JIMMY
BUFFETT (1976)**
*Jimmy Buffett, hangin' out by the bus
before his first show in 1976. Jimmy
says he wrote "Margaritaville" in Austin
in a popular Tex-Mex joint.*

JIMMY BUFFETT (1983)
*Jimmy Buffett has appeared on the
show twice, but during the early and
mid-'70s he was a regular performer
in Austin clubs. His carefree goodtime
upbeat reputation is legendary, and
well deserved, as any Parrot head will
attest. Whenever he puts down his
pen and gets out of his hammock he
packs stadiums.*

The opportunity to watch an artist grow and mature, and test and then transcend his or her own limits is a rare and unceasing pleasure. Often, that pleasure has occurred in the context of an *Austin City Limits* taping.

Of necessity, *ACL* incorporates a certain roll-the-dice fatalism into its operating philosophy. At any given moment during the show's history, there have been entire constellations of hot young stars-in-the-making, incandescent and chomping at the bit. Which is not to say that the phrase "rising star" automatically connotes youth—as a refutation of that concept, just consider Don Walser, the "Pavarotti of the Plains," whose spine-tingling western yodeling has made him an improbable, sixty-something "overnight sensation."

Some of those whom the show featured in their ascendancy—Keb' Mo', Steve Wariner, Dwight Yoakam, Indigo Girls, Vince Gill, and the Neville Brothers come to mind—seemed destined to burn long and bright from the get-go.

STEVE WARINER (1983)
Country Comeback Kid. Always an inside favorite, Garth Brooks helped to bring back Steve centerstage, where his songwriting and picking talents shine.

DON WALSER (1996)
"The Pavarotti of the Plains," Don Walser is one of the last of the true-blue Texas yodelers.

Then there are others for whom an *ACL* appearance perhaps marked an apex in a career arc cut short for any of a host of reasons. Their stars have sputtered and faded and the show's producers and viewers can only look back and say, "What if?" (Where are you today, Will T. Massey, McBride and the Ride, Con Hunley, Lacy J. Dalton, Norton Buffalo?) This is not to say that those stars lost in the firmament were not talented. They might even, in fact, reignite, given the right circumstances. But the vagaries of the artist's temperament and the fickle bottom-line nature of the entertainment industry have cast far more people by the wayside than they've elevated to the Hit Parade.

That being the case, *Austin City Limits* has been uncommonly lucky over the years in advocating for performers who went on to justify that televised leap of faith with careers that have succeeded on multiple levels. Both Nanci Griffith and Garth Brooks, for instance, are successful in widely varying degrees of commercial magnitude today. But the show took a chance on both of them when the ball might have bounced in myriad directions. Who is to say which of their lives was more profoundly affected by the experience?

To budding musicians in Austin and elsewhere, *ACL* was not only part of the fabric of their youth, it had a sort of a hippest-frat-on-campus allure. Deana Carter, who taped the show for the first time on the eve of the release of her second album (following her wildly successful maiden effort, *Did I Shave My Legs For This?*), talked about "an *Austin City Limits* aesthetic." She elaborated, "Well, I was excited the whole time I was here, and I was nervous. . . . It's a kind of televised vibe. You walk in and see the [skyline] backdrop, and it's just the way the look of the show is, the feel that's in the room, and that's cool."

"It was cool," echoed young blues guitarist Kenny Wayne Shepherd. "All the guys in the band, we grew up watching the show. We grew up watching our heroes play on the show."

KENNY WAYNE SHEPHERD (1996)
Kenny Wayne Shepherd came roaring out of the Louisiana bayous with a searing blues guitar sound that attracted immediate credibility from his blues seniors, and will continue to be a force to be reckoned with well beyond his teens.

DEANA CARTER (1998)
"I almost felt like we weren't even filming; it's more about the vibe and what you can share and how you interact with the audience," explains Deana Carter. It's kind of a televised vibe, which is cool."

Nanci Griffith Makes Her Debut

Nanci Griffith had sat in the audience at *Austin City Limits* tapings. She had held down a weekly gig at the Hole In the Wall. She had shared tip jars and happy hour gigs with performers who were appearing on the show. And she felt downright proprietary about a show that finally offered a national forum for her and all the left-of-center poets and pickers with whom she felt allied.

So when she finally got the call to tape an episode in 1984, she was determined to make a splash. She hustled over to the big Woolworth's store on the corner of Congress Avenue and Sixth Street (the same department store that she featured in her hit "Love At the Five and Dime") and bought a Butterick-type dress pattern and a bolt of yellow material in a vividly flowered pattern. And from somewhere she came up with a pair of red shoes that would have had Dorothy exclaiming, "To *die* for!"

Talk about a serene sense of self-confidence. . . . to make your national television debut with a big band (that included as a backup singer the then-unknown Lyle Lovett) and a dress you sewed yourself. Years later, Nanci looked back fondly on her "coming out."

"Yeah, I made that yellow dress. I donated it to Terry [Lickona], along with the red slippers I wore. I received so many comments about that dress over the years. People still come up to me and ask me about that dress! I got the pattern at Woolworth's, the "Love At the Five-and-Dime" Woolworth's in Austin, and sewed it myself. I stuck out like an odd bouquet."

JOHN T. DAVIS

NANCI GRIFFITH (1984)
A hometown favorite who has taken her music to fans around the world, Nanci Griffith "had gone to see so many shows," and she believes that "getting to do Austin City Limits for the first time was a massive event in my career."

To Trisha Yearwood, playing *ACL* was like a step backward and a step forward simultaneously. "I remember watching Willie Nelson on there," the country star recalled. "And now, going back and watching older shows, I see musicians that I know now, and I'm really blown away by it all. Back then, fifteen and twenty years ago when I was watching television, you couldn't find Emmylou Harris on a network."

Miles Zuniga of Fastball, the young Austin pop trio that smoked the charts with "The Way" in the summer of 1998, recalled making the move from Fastball's regular venue at the Hole In the Wall bar to the *ACL* studio across the street. "I'd dreamed about being on the show for years, but I never thought there was much of a possibility," he confessed. "The format has been one that I didn't really think that any bands that I'd been in would fit into; people seem to know it as a country-oriented show. So to actually do the show, it's something else—those pictures on the wall as you're coming in, just thinking about those people who have done the show before, well, it's pretty amazing."

Like Zuniga, other Austin artists have possessive feelings toward the show. They look out from the stage and they don't see cameras and lights, they see family, fans, friends, and fellow musicians. Country-Tejano star Rick Treviño remembers feeling humbled at seeing so many kinfolks in his first audience. Singer-songwriter Robert Earl Keen began dating his future wife, Kathleen, through the show (see sidebar on page 138). The show has had an effect on hometown performers in odd and unanticipated ways.

TRISHA YEARWOOD (1991)
"The first time I did the show," recalled Trisha Yearwood, "there was the awe of coming in and seeing the set that I've watched on TV for years. Fifteen years ago when I was watching television, there wasn't a whole lot of country music on TV. You couldn't find Emmylou Harris on a network."

FASTBALL (1998)
From the Hole In the Wall bar to Austin City Limits— literally across the street, but ten years away in terms of hard dues and hard playin'—Austin's big success story of the '90s burned up the airwaves with their megahit "The Way."

TIMBUK 3 (1989)
Timbuk 3 was an Austin-based duo, best known for their hit "The Future's So Bright I Gotta Wear Shades." They fleshed out their innovative sound with recorded rhythm tracks. Thus, in this off-beat shot, they're not turning their backs to the audience as much as they're centering themselves with their synthesized "band."

ROBERT EARL KEEN

My wife and I knew each other when she was a student at U.T., but we started dating after we went to the Nanci Griffith show in 1984—December 10, 1984. She was sitting with her boyfriend at the time, and he went on home. And we went to the Texas Chili Parlor afterwards, and talked and talked. I guess that's why I like the Chili Parlor. And I said, "Hey, why don't we go out?" And she said, "I gotta get rid of this boyfriend." Well, we finally weeded him out after awhile. I guess *Austin City Limits* made a certain change in my life.

ROBERT EARL KEEN

ROBERT EARL KEEN (1994)
Robert Earl Keen's songs convey the joy of "the Texas condition" better than anyone writing songs today. Scott Newton believes that Keen has a talent for noticing the little details that make a song spring to life. He's a favorite of almost every discernible subgroup of Texans—frat kids, hippies, cowboys, you name it—which may explain the wild audience reaction whenever he plays to a crowd.

ERIC JOHNSON (1996)
Another Austin native, Eric Johnson is at one with his guitar. He's been a cover boy for every guitar magazine many times over, and has won virtually every award a guitarist can. His intensity and precision have left guitar wannabes shaking their heads in wonder.

MONTE MONTGOMERY (1999)
Monte Montgomery is Austin's most recent gift to the musical nation. According to Scott Newton, "He wrings more original sound out of an acoustic guitar, a virtual wall of complex articulate music, than anyone I've ever seen. Right now, he's playing to audiences of 200 in clubs, but if anyone makes it from here to there, it's sure to be this innovative, self-confident performer."

SUBDUDES (1991)
The Subdudes were cousins and childhood neighbors from Louisiana who grew up to form an innovative, original-sounding band. You had to see them for yourself to understand how a single tambourine could do the job of an entire drum kit.

THE FABULOUS THUNDERBIRDS (1986)
The T-Birds were an Austin-based blues band that hit it big in the '80s. Lead singer Kim Wilson and lead guitarist Jimmie Vaughan broadened the music scene by showing that you could be from Austin and make it commercially by doing something other than country music.

An *ACL* appearance, of course, guarantees nothing. Promising bands, including Timbuk 3, the Subdudes, Storyville, the Fabulous Thunderbirds, and Pure Prairie League, performed outstanding sets on the show and then witnessed their ensembles fragment or evaporate for unrelated reasons.

Other performers—k.d. lang, Alison Krauss, George Strait, Shawn Colvin, Lorrie Morgan, and the Mavericks, for instance—seem destined to have become successful whether they ever set foot on the program's stage or not, such was the magnitude of their talent and desire.

And with still others, including Whiskeytown, Lisa Loeb, Son Volt, Vonda Shepard, Gillian Welch, Allison Moorer, and BR5-49, the jury remains out, a hostage to time and circumstance.

It's the circumstance of not knowing that is half of the fun. Somewhere out there tonight, in the backstreets of Austin (or Seattle, or Minneapolis, or New Orleans) is some-one whose name no one knows, but who is set to light up the night. "I saw her back when," we'll tell each other a few years hence. "Oh yeah, I knew right then she had the real thing. I just knew it from the start!"

GILLIAN WELCH (1996)
Her Appalachian-style songs defy her L.A. roots, but Gillian Welch and partner David Rawlings evoke harmonies and images from another era.

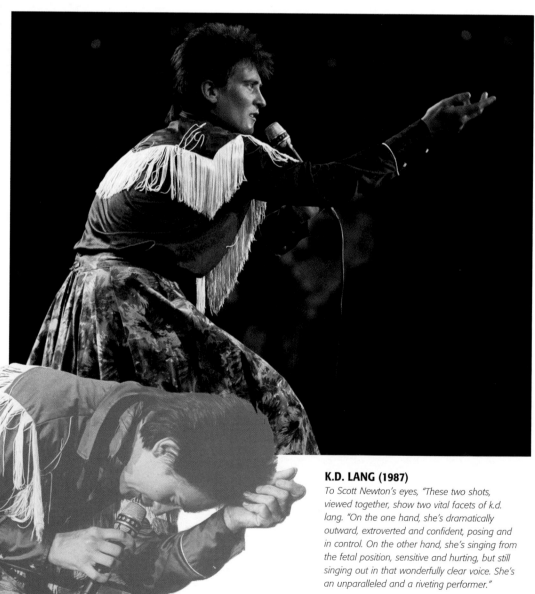

K.D. LANG (1987)
To Scott Newton's eyes, "These two shots, viewed together, show two vital facets of k.d. lang. "On the one hand, she's dramatically outward, extroverted and confident, posing and in control. On the other hand, she's singing from the fetal position, sensitive and hurting, but still singing out in that wonderfully clear voice. She's an unparalleled and a riveting performer."

GARTH BROOKS

Joe Harris was a long-time Nashville booking agent who was always ready with a pitch for "the next big thing" to hit country music. He had called me many times, but this time, in late 1989, he was right on the money. We had heard about Garth Brooks, of course, but still didn't know that much about him: A hunk with a hat and a college degree from Oklahoma who wanted to be a country singer.

Joe was a likable guy, and I trusted his instincts, so we booked the show for January 1990, in Season 15. Within two months, Garth *was* "the next big thing" and he kept getting bigger and bigger, and ten years later, there's still nobody bigger.

His *Austin City Limits* show was pretty laid back compared to his later arena shows—no pyrotechnics or swinging from the rafters (he did jump up on the drum riser, however).

He is a perfect gentleman to work with, and polite in the extreme. He talked about growing up in Oklahoma and watching *Austin City Limits* with his dad, and he was very generous with his praise for the show: "Getting to play on *Austin City Limits,*" he said, "is like getting to play in the World Series."

TERRY LICKONA, Producer

GARTH BROOKS (1990)
Garth Brooks breaks all the records, and does it his way.

SHAWN COLVIN WAS SOUNDING JUST A LITTLE BIT HOT. "Did you see that little blurb that guy in *Rolling Stone* wrote about 'Why did Sheryl Crow do *Austin City Limits*?'" she asked accusingly.

Pausing momentarily to give thanks to the gods that he wasn't the offending scribe in question, the ink-stained wretch on the other end of the telephone line wittily replied, "Um, no, I don't think so."

It Was Never Just About Cowboys

"He was up in arms!" Colvin continued. "He thought it was wrong. He thought the show was for roots artists, and what was *she* doing on it? Either the show was selling out, or it was beneath her. I don't know who he was pissed at.

"But," she went on, "the point of me bringing that up is that *Austin City Limits* is for people who write, sing, and play well. And that crosses over to people like Sheryl and Bruce Hornsby, and not just country players or blues players or folk players. There is that kind of melting pot that's come about over the past twenty-five years. And anyway, I thought Sheryl did a great job."

Colvin's point is well taken. Despite its Stetson-and-boots image, *Austin City Limits* over the years has presented performers who do not fall neatly into preconceived categories. Many of those between-the-cracks artists hail from Louisiana, whose musical heritage and diversity rivals that of Texas. The Neville Brothers, Fats Domino, Marcia Ball, Dr. John, Zachary Richard, the Dirty Dozen Brass Band, Irma Thomas, Pete Fountain, Clifton Chenier and his son C.J., Beausoleil, and many more have given the program heavy, gumbo-scented infusions of Cajun, zydeco, and Big Easy mojo over the years.

Sprinkled throughout the show's history are performers the idle viewer would not normally associate with the show. *A Prairie Home Companion* creator Garrison Keillor performed with Chet Atkins and a gospel quartet; jazz pioneer Lionel Hampton made a landmark appearance in Season 24; Boho singer and actor Tom Waits made one of his only sustained television performances, with a theatrical stage presentation that included a lamp post and a gasoline pump; English folk-rocker Billy Bragg used his episode to perform songs from *Mermaid Avenue,* the album on which Bragg set to music a suite of previously unknown lyrics by Woody Guthrie.

PASSENGER (1981)
Austin's premier jazz band of the early '80s, Passenger showcased the talents of Roscoe Beck (bass) and Mitch Watkins (guitar); in the background is Steve Meador (drums); not seen: Bill Ginn (keyboards) and Paul Ostermayer (saxophone).

THE NEVILLE BROTHERS (1994)

"Our music is a vehicle to get people to understand there's one race, the human race," explains Aaron Neville. "Martin Luther King Jr. said once that we've got to live together as brothers and sisters on this planet or we all die together as fools. We have to keep reminding people that we're all connected in some way."

DR. JOHN (1992)

The living personification of the word funky, *Dr. John lives in his own groove.*

ZACHARY RICHARD (1993)

"There are parts of that Southern Louisiana tradition that are irresistible— the Cajun stuff, the zydeco music," Zachary Richard says. "Someone described it once as being able to make a dead man wiggle his toes."

DIRTY DOZEN BRASS BAND (1993)

This was one of those shows where you can't sit still, a New Orleans tradition that's contagious wherever it goes.

CLIFTON CHENIER (1978)

Only in America—and only in Lousiana—could a music called zydeco be born. The late Clifton Chenier was the king of zydeco—and he took the accordion where no man had gone before.

C. J. CHENIER (1991)

Taking a tradition to a new generation and remaking it as his own, C.J. Chenier (right) and his band follow in the king's footsteps.

BEAUSOLEIL (1989)
Michael Doucet and Beausoleil show the diversity of American music as well as of Austin City Limits. You won't find Cajun music like this anywhere else in the world!

PETE FOUNTAIN (1981)
Bourbon Street came to Austin when Pete Fountain brought his clarinet for a spectacular collaboration with Texas fiddler Johnny Gimble.

DOUG KERSHAW (1978)
The "Ragin' Cajun" Doug Kershaw earns his nickname every night.

GLITTER 'N' TINSEL

I think Tom Waits in Season 4, when he brought in his whole set, with the gasoline pump and the streetlight was one of my favorite episodes. There was so much glitter from the set, they never could get it out of the studio. For years after that, when you came in to play, you'd come out covered with this glitter and wonder, "Where did that come from?"

NANCI GRIFFITH

TOM WAITS (1978)
A rare performance and a bold step out for Austin City Limits. *Twenty years later, fans still call asking for repeats or video copies of this show.*

BILLY BRAGG (1998)

A brilliant British songwriter and political activist, Billy Bragg was picked by Woody Guthrie's family to write the music (with WILCO) for a treasure trove of his newly discovered songs. He not only brought Woody back to life for the '90s, but showed an entirely different dimension to his writing.

DAN HICKS (1991)

Eccentric, quirky—all that and more, Dan Hicks and the Hot Licks brought the '60s back to life for one memorable night in 1991.

LITTLE FEAT (1990)
Legendary rock-and-rollers from the '70s, Little Feat has carried on without missing a beat since the untimely death of singer Lowell George in 1979.

LEO KOTTKE (1987)
Leo Kottke is a one-man show in more ways than one. A brilliant showman on guitar, his stories between songs have left his audience crying with laughter.

GARRISON KEILLOR

Garrison Keillor revolutionized modern radio by heading back to the future. His show, *A Prairie Home Companion,* restored the sense of imagination and wonder that had been so sorely missing from the medium since its golden age in the thirties and forties. For more than two decades, *PHC* has been a public radio weekend tradition, and Keillor's ability to spin tales has enraptured millions of listeners.

That magic never seemed to come across on television, however, in the few attempts to translate *Prairie Home*'s success to the tube. Garrison himself never felt particularly comfortable with the medium, and it seemed to diminish the people and places he talked about with such eloquence—except on *Austin City Limits,* that is.

Garrison staged a very special show in the summer of 1992 while *PHC* was on hiatus, with the Hopeful Gospel Quartet and guests Chet Atkins, Johnny Gimble, and Robin and Linda Williams. Garrison sings a pretty mean gospel bass himself.

Performing on the *Austin City Limits* stage, with a live, breathing audience just a few intimate feet away, and having the freedom to say and do whatever he wanted without the intrusions of TV production no doubt gave Garrison a format as close to his radio show as television can get.

Offstage, Garrison can seem an aloof figure, not easily approachable—not in a hostile or arrogant way, but more in the manner of an absent-minded professor, lost in his thoughts. In reality he has a devilish, sometimes scorching, sense of humor, and he enjoys wisecracking with the crew and poking fun at himself.

He came back a few years later, in 1998, to host a special *Best of Austin City Limits* in honor of his friend Chet Atkins. All he had to do was introduce the various videotape highlights of Chet's performances, and he did it with his usual aplomb.

It's too bad he forgot his socks. He arrived at the studio wearing a slightly rumpled gray suit (which looked suspiciously like the same one he'd worn with red socks in 1992—a good luck totem, maybe?), with Birkenstocks and bare feet. It was an odd ensemble—we had to ask him to pull down his pant legs to cover his shiny shins, but then again, nobody has ever accused Garrison of being a fashion plate, and on radio, who would know?

TERRY LICKONA, Producer

**CHET ATKINS WITH
GARRISON KEILLOR (1992)**

They may seem like an odd couple, but Garrison Keillor's small-town charm and Chet Atkins's easy country style are perfect companions. The two shared a magic moment.

GEORGE THOROGOOD (1981)
George Thorogood expanded the show's reach into hard-driving rock music in the seventh season. The experiment was successful and helped broaden the scope of the show.

SQUEEZEBOX SPECIAL (1986)
Why not? There aren't many virtuosos on any instrument who have made their mark like Ponty Bone, Queen Ida, and Santiago Jimenez, Jr. (left to right). The only thing missing was polka.

8½ SOUVENIRS (1997)
Austin's take on the '90s swing craze, 8½ Souvenirs
updates Django Reinhardt classics with an original
touch, and brings out the best dancers in town.

BETO Y LOS FAIRLANES (1979)
A classic Austin musical gumbo, Beto y Los Fairlanes layers jazz, Latin spice, and plenty of funk, led (more or less) by maestro Beto (Robert "Dude" Skiles).

MANHATTAN TRANSFER (1997)
Texas meets New York when the Manhattan Transfer swings into town.

153

STRENGTH IN NUMBERS (1989)
Five of Nashville's most gifted acoustic musicians came together under the moniker Strength in Numbers (left to right): Bela Fleck, banjo; Edgar Meyer, upright bass; Sam Bush, mandolin; Jerry Douglas, dobro; and Mark O'Connor, fiddle.

HOOTIE & THE BLOWFISH (1999)
They had one of the most popular records of all time, but Hootie & the Blowfish were thrilled to get their own full-hour show on Austin City Limits, where they've been inspired by their favorite artists since college days.

Lionel Hampton's Prayer Book

Despite the small number of personnel, the *ACL* staff goes out of their way to make a personal bond with the artists who come to town to do the show, and tries to accommodate their special requests. When legendary jazz pioneer Lionel Hampton brought in his swing band for Season 24, I went over to his hotel to greet him when he arrived. Even in his nineties, he still had that spark, and was anxious to talk to me.

LIONEL HAMPTON (1998)
One of the pioneers of jazz and arguably the real "King of Swing," Lionel Hampton brought his orchestra and proved he can still pack a punch well into his nineties.

"I wish I could have brought my twenty-piece orchestra," was the first thing he said. Alas, that was too many musicians for our budget.

As he sat there in the lobby looking concerned, he did ask for a special favor. "You name it, Mr. Hampton!" I replied.

The musician had forgotten to bring his Christian Science book of daily prayers, and wondered if one could be found for him in Austin. I didn't have a clue where to begin, but our ace limo driver, Al Adams, knew of a Christian Science reading room just blocks away, which would be closing in five minutes. We hustled over in the limo, roaring up just as they were locking the doors, and wouldn't you know, they had only one copy left of that month's book. When I realized I had only four dollars in cash in my wallet, Al came to the rescue once more. The smile on Lionel's face when I handed him his book of prayers will be forever etched in my memory.

TERRY LICKONA, Producer

LEONARD COHEN

Other than perhaps Stevie Ray Vaughan, the one program that got the biggest reaction of all time was the 1989 debut of Leonard Cohen, the mysterious poet of song who is a real master of the art.

The taping caught everybody by surprise and was almost a religious experience for some people in the audience, given Leonard's enigmatic persona and infrequent concert appearances. Even in person he has a certain spiritual aura about him.

He and his band flew in on the red-eye straight from L.A. after playing a late-night show, and showed up for rehearsal in the afternoon looking like they were still wearing the same clothes.

I was really looking forward to meeting *the* Leonard Cohen. I could tell he was tired, so I asked if there was anything we could get for him. He "hmmmm"-ed a few minutes and then said, "I believe a bottle of tequila would be very nice to have right now."

The bottle did not survive rehearsal, but it must have brought out the Muse in Leonard and his stellar band that night. When the show aired, it got an amazing response. Every Monday morning we could tell from the calls in which city the episode had aired over the weekend. And the calls came from an amazing range of folks: a priest in Cleveland, who said it was not only the best *Austin City Limits* show he'd ever seen, it was the best *television* show he'd ever seen; a self-described Jewish grandmother in Florida said the same thing; and a flabbergasted country music fan from Oklahoma said it was the first time she had ever enjoyed a show that wasn't country!

Oddly enough, the only negative response came from Austin itself, where a man excoriated me for letting "an obvious devil-worshiper" appear on our show "singing satanic messages." It had something to do with the entire band being dressed in black, and Leonard talking about "the voices in the night and the spirits burning in Austin." (He was describing the local live music scene in poetic allegory, as usual.) There is just no way to explain Leonard Cohen to certain people.

TERRY LICKONA, Producer

LEONARD COHEN (1989)

When Scott Newton is asked what his favorite show of all time was, he always answers, "The first Leonard Cohen show. With a large band of incredible musicians, his show was simultaneously understated and spectacular, profound and entertaining. We received more response to his show than any other, with the possible exception of Stevie Ray Vaughan. This shot ended up on the cover of the Leonard Cohen Live *CD."*

SAGEBRUSH SYMPHONY (1995)

The only time in its history that Austin City Limits *left the state of Texas, it didn't go very far—just to the neighbors to the north in Oklahoma City, to present Michael Martin Murphey's "Sagebrush Symphony" with the Oklahoma City Philharmonic (under a* very *starry night).*

WALTER HYATT

After twenty-five years, it's not surprising that so many of the great artists who have appeared on the show have passed from the scene, most after long, legendary careers. The lives suddenly or tragically cut short hit home the hardest: Stevie Ray Vaughan, who died in a helicopter crash, or guitar virtuosos Roy Buchanan and Danny Gatton, who took their own lives.

Walter Hyatt's death had a special meaning and a profound impact. Walter was killed in the ValuJet crash in the Florida swamps in 1996, and when his name showed up on the passenger list that appeared in the Austin newspaper that Sunday, the whole town went into shock. During his tenure in Austin, he had evolved and matured as a musician and found the love of his life, his wife, Heidi.

He was such a genuine person with such genuinely special talent that he touched the hearts and musical minds of thousands of different people, from fans to music biz big-shots. His songs were poetry beyond the norm, and the depth and breadth of his music were extraordinary. Lyle Lovett, Shawn Colvin, Jimmie Dale Gilmore, and David Ball and Champ Hood—his partners in the wonderful acoustic trio Uncle Walt's Band—joined together for a sad but inspired tribute to another fallen comrade.

TERRY LICKONA, Producer

WALTER HYATT (1990)

Walter Hyatt was the Walt in Uncle Walt's Band, a legendary folk-pop trio that moved to Austin in the early '70s. Scott Newton believes, "To know him was to love him. Walter was a nexus, an integrating force and gentle spirit who the muse clearly favored. He was a prolific songwriter who will probably become more well known posthumously than he was in life, as future performers discover his trove of beautiful songs."

WALTER HYATT—
UNCLE WALT'S BAND (1979)

Uncle Walt's Band in 1979 (left to right):
Walter Hyatt, Champ Hood, and David Ball.

LYLE LOVETT WITH
SHAWN COLVIN (1996)

For the tribute to Walter
Hyatt, Lyle Lovett and
Shawn Colvin did a rare
duet, Walter's "Babes in
the Woods."

TRIBUTE TO WALTER HYATT
(1996)

After Walter Hyatt's tragic death in the
ValuJet crash, some of his closest friends
gathered to pay tribute as best they
could—with his own songs (front row,
left to right: David Ball, Champ Hood,
Lyle Lovett, Junior Brown, Willis Alan
Ramsey, Allison Moorer, and Jimmie
Dale Gilmore.

FOR THE SAKE OF THE SONG
A TRIBUTE TO TOWNES VAN ZANDT

On New Year's Day 1997, when Townes Van Zandt died, I knew *ACL* had to pay tribute to one of the seminal Texas songwriters of the generation. It was too late to do anything for that particular season, so it was over a year later when the "Celebration of Townes Van Zandt" actually aired, but it was worth the wait. The finished product was a quintessential *Austin City Limits* episode.

Townes was no household name, but every songwriter, singer, and serious music fan placed him way up there in the pantheon of great writers. The problem was who to invite for a one-hour program when the possibilities were endless? Superstars and the songwriter on the street alike worshipped his work. Names like Bob Dylan, Neil Young, even Bono and Beck kept coming up.

After a few futile inquiries were made, we decided to call up Guy Clark, Townes's best friend. When Guy played at Townes's memorial service in Nashville, he said, in typical fashion, "I booked this gig thirty years ago."

Guy and his wife, songwriter Susanna Clark, helped put together a group of real hardcore Townes-ies—the folks who knew Townes and were directly inspired by him in a personal way. And what a group it turned out to be! Emmylou Harris, Willie Nelson, Steve Earle, Nanci Griffith, Lyle Lovett, Rodney Crowell, Jack Clements (Townes's first producer and a great writer himself), Peter Rowan, and Townes's son, John T., who bears a haunting resemblance to his father. *Austin City Limits* turned into a house of worship that night.

TERRY LICKONA, Producer

**TRIBUTE TO
TOWNES VAN ZANDT (1997)**
One year after his death, the Austin City Limits stage was (literally) filled with Townes's friends performing his songs in tribute (left to right): "Cowboy" Jack Clement (Townes's producer), Lyle Lovett, Rodney Crowell, Emmylou Harris, Willie Nelson, Guy Clark, John T. Van Zandt (Townes's son), Nanci Griffith, Steve Earle, and Peter Rowan.

TOWNES VAN ZANDT (1982)
Townes Van Zandt was Texas's own Dylan Thomas. His view of the human condition was bleak but gracefully poetic. His life was the same.

From the beginning, *ACL* took advantage of the inherent if overlooked diversity of the roots music scene that simmered under the mass media's cultural radar. In Season 1, in addition to emblematic Austin country-rockers such as Asleep at the Wheel, Rusty Wier, Jerry Jeff Walker, Alvin Crow, and Greezy Wheels, Joe Gracey (the radio deejay and newspaper columnist who served as the talent coordinator in the show's first days) also enlisted zydeco master Clifton Chenier, conjunto accordionist Flaco Jimenez, mountain man balladeer Bobby Bridger, and a local vaudeville show band dubbed Balcones Fault, after the city's premier geological feature.

Even the Austin performers upped the ante to break out of their assigned categories. Maverick country-rocker Jerry Jeff Walker performed in 1988 with a fourteen-piece string section recruited from the Austin Symphony and conducted by prodigal composer and performer David Amram, who has himself worked with everyone from Leonard Bernstein to Jack Kerouac. "With anyone else, they would say it was a career move," said Jerry Jeff in retrospect. "With me, they said I was just being idiosyncratic."

Michael Martin Murphey, a onetime Austin resident, used a 1991 appearance to showcase an orchestra of his own, in this case, the Oklahoma City Philharmonic, as part of his "Salute to the Cowboy."

Asleep at the Wheel used a Season 23 appearance to invite not only bluegrass maestro Ricky Skaggs (which you might expect) but also vocalese swing stars the Manhattan Transfer (who'd a thunk it?).

There were also tributes to instruments—the mandolin and the accordion—and a bookended pair of showcases dedicated to Mexican roots music and the modern Tejano sound. And then, of course, there were the indescribably moving all-star tributes to two fallen musical comrades, Walter Hyatt and Townes Van Zandt.

If there is one central observation about *Austin City Limits* to bear in mind, it is this: It was never just about cowboys.

MANDOLIN SPECIAL (1980)

A unique showcase for a unique instrument, "Mandolin Special" brought together (left to right) Johnny Gimble (who temporarily traded his mandolin for his trademark fiddle), David Grisman, Tiny Moore (who invented the electric mandolin when he played with Bob Wills' Texas Playboys), and Jethro Burns (of Homer and Jethro fame).

BACKSTAGE

A DAY IN THE LIFE OF AUSTIN CITY LIMITS

DECEMBER FIFTH, 1998

IRONICALLY, THE TAPING SESSION SELECTED to represent an archetypal "day in the life" of *Austin City Limits* was anything but typical. For one thing, there were to be two artists taped this night, for presentation in 1999 as part of Season 24. Shows are usually taped in one calendar year, usually between July and December, and aired beginning early the next year.

First up was Bruce Hornsby, whose muscular mixture of pop hooks, piano virtuosity, and a fluid mixture of jazz, rock, and even country and bluegrass influences was an instant hit; Hornsby reaped three hit singles and a Grammy with his first album alone. He was on hand to perform songs from a new two-disc set, *Spirit Trail.*

LUCINDA WILLIAMS (CIRCA 1974)

Early on in the process of looking through all the photos in ACL's files for this book, Scott Newton came across this shot of Lucinda Williams playing for tips on the "Drag"—Guadalupe Street, alongside the University of Texas campus and down the street from the ACL studio.

Scheduled to follow Hornsby was evocative southern songwriter Lucinda Williams, whose slow-a-borning fifth album, *Car Wheels On a Gravel Road,* emerged after a six-year gestation to nearly universal critical acclaim. Smoldering with echoes of love, lust, and loss, and filigreed with Dixie-Gothic touches, Williams's best songs paint sharply etched portraits with spare, sensual strokes. A former Austinite, Williams used to busk for tips on the Drag, the main thoroughfare running down the western boundary of U.T., just down the street, ironically, from the building where *ACL* is videotaped.

The idea of taping two artists on the same night was nothing new; the crew calls such back-to-back tapings "double-shoots." But in the past, the ticketholders have stayed for both acts, with an intermission in between. This night, for the first time, the staff and volunteers were going to "turn the house," ushering out one crowd before seating another.

Producer Terry Lickona was convinced such a shuffling of bodies would result in fresher audience reactions, and he professed not to be worried about the potential for logistical gridlock. His opinion on both subjects was not universally shared by the staff or crew.

The evening also marked another first. Lucinda Williams had filmed an episode for Season 24 previously, back in July. But so dissatisfied was she with her performance and the audience reaction that she and her record company contributed money to tape a new episode. This was a first for the show. Artists had sweetened musical tracks or overdubbed vocals or instrumental passages after the fact, but no one had ever reshot an entire appearance.

So while events proceeded with the customary smoothness born of endless repetition on one level, new situations and unanticipated challenges pushed both performers and the *Austin City Limits* crew in unexpected directions.

11:00 A.M.: Members of the *Austin City Limits* staff arrive at the KLRU studios to begin prepping the stage in Studio 6-A for the night's marathon double-shoot. For most, it was the start of a 15- or 16-hour day. At the same time, Lucinda Williams's road crew begins to load the band's equipment into the ground-floor freight elevator and transfer it to the studio on the sixth floor.

11:45 A.M.: Lighting designer Bob Selby is sitting at the back of Studio 6-A trying to settle on a lighting plan for the night's show. Typically it is a compromise between artistic and technical considerations. The performer's production team "will send us one lighting plan, we draw up another, and we'll eventually end up with a third thing altogether," he says philosophically.

2:00 P.M.: Williams ambles onstage to begin her soundcheck. She is closing the show, which means she has to rehearse first; afterward her gear will be moved offstage and Hornsby and his band will rehearse. Their instruments and amps will remain onstage until showtime. As for Lucinda, she was up until three A.M. the night before. She has been touring hard for months, and boasts the motel tan to prove it.

LIGHTING SETUP
Lighting technician Walter Olden fine-tunes his instruments between rehearsals. (Photo by Sung Park © Austin American-Statesman.)

The show has put her up in the glossy Hyatt hotel on the edge of Town Lake, but she is pining for her old digs, the Austin Motel, a funky, downscale joint on South Congress. The Hyatt is nice, she allows, but, "it doesn't have that thang. . . ." The "thang" in question is soul, grit, Southern-fried je ne sais quois.

2:10 P.M.: Mike Archenhold, Michael Emery, Vance Holmes, and Todd Pankey—the camera operators—begin to unlimber the big beasts they will waltz around the stage during the taping. Robert Moorhead, who operates a handheld camera, will make an appearance later.

Off to the side, Susan Caldwell, one of the show's two associate producers, watches patiently. She and her counterpart, Jeff Peterson, usually take turns "handling" an artist—that is, troubleshooting, trying to anticipate demands both large and small, putting out fires wherever necessary. For today's double-shoot, Caldwell is shepherding Lucinda and Peterson is handling Bruce.

2:25 P.M.: Lucinda, staring at some distant spot on the far horizon, runs down "Car Wheels On a Gravel Road." It is a song about dislocation, as seen through the eyes of a small child staring out of a car's back window toward some diminishing dream of home. It is, in the best sense of the word, haunting. She pays no attention to the cameras dipping and swaying around her, searching for angles for shots. The song stops, and the first of many, many technical and electronic adjustments are made.

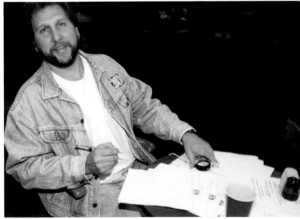

GARY AT REHEARSAL
Director Gary Menotti times every song— every verse, every solo—during rehearsal, then assigns camera shots for each show.

At a table in front of the stage, Gary Menotti, who has been on site since 10:30 this morning, is twisting a stopwatch in his hands and making notes. As the show's longtime director, he must make sure all the microphones and equipment are placed so as not to interfere with the shots he wants. The lighting has to be coordinated, as do the camera locations.

During each song at rehearsal, Menotti will make notes from which he will construct shot sheets for his cameramen to use during the taping. Everything is keyed to his stopwatch, which is why the rehearsal strives to be as much a mirror image of the actual performance as possible. It never really is, of course. Onstage improvisations and happy (and not-so-happy) accidents invariably occur, and Menotti and his crew have had to learn to roll on a moment's notice with the good, the bad, and the ugly.

2:45 P.M.: Williams wants to rehearse another number or two. Terry Lickona does not. A few days previously, Williams's manager had called Lickona to say that his client wanted to rest, conserve her voice, and skip rehearsal. Having taped the show so recently, she knows the routine. Lickona agreed, and the schedule was shortened simply to include a soundcheck for the band. But now Lucinda is here, pining to rehearse after all, and time is slipping away.

**DAVID HOUGH
IN AUDIO CONTROL**

Long-time audio director David Hough brings the music to life, whether through a three-inch TV speaker or a complete stereo surround system.

"Let's get on with it," Lickona says. He is mindful that Hornsby still has to soundcheck and rehearse, and that the doors are opening an hour earlier than usual to accommodate the crowded schedule. "We can't afford to be an hour behind on a day like today."

"We can't make soundcheck happen," says Susan Caldwell, mindful of inevitable technical snafus and artists' peculiar internal clocks.

Though they are disagreeing strenuously, Lickona's and Caldwell's voices are clipped, controlled, and calm. Both have been down this road many times. The added pressure of this unusual day is evident, however.

Onstage, Williams holds up her hands like puppy dog paws and makes playful little doggy begging noises, asking for more time.

Lickona acquiesces, not happy about it. As Williams cues her band and Menotti makes more notes, Lickona mutters under his breath, "We need to go, we need to go, we need to go. . . ."

3:00 P.M.: Jeff Peterson, trying to get ready for the set change, tells the crew, "Let's roll [Bruce Hornsby's] piano in now, and at least that's done." He walks toward the back of the studio, looking distracted. "Is there anyone here I can yell at?" he asks no one in particular.

"You can yell at me," says Bob Selby agreeably, from behind his lighting console.

"Bob!" Peterson bellows, and keeps walking.

Selby smiles. "Ah, that felt good. Getting yelled at makes me feel like part of the team."

LINE-UP OUTSIDE

The line starts early for regulars who know the routine and determined music fans alike. (Photo by Sung Park © Austin American-Statesman.)

3:05 P.M.: Lucinda, sitting in the bleachers now, is trying to finalize her set list from a three-ring binder containing her song lyrics. It is her security blanket. "Nothing worse than forgetting the words to your own songs," she mutters.

"Can we do both 'Lake Charles' and 'Hot Blood'?" she asks. "But where can 'Hot Blood' go?" Her anxiety ratchets up one notch.

Caldwell points to a spot between two songs on the set list. "Here," she says decisively. One question answered.

Another looms. Where, someone asks Lucinda, are she and her beau, bassist Richard Price, going to eat? Williams acts as if she can't believe the question. There are some things she really misses about Texas. "*Mexican* food," she says emphatically.

While she replies, nine or ten guys are groaning and heaving, trying to hoist an enormous Baldwin grand piano onstage for Hornsby's rehearsal.

3:10 P.M.: Downstairs on the plaza that separates the building containing KLRU's studios from the U.T. radio, television, and film department, a half dozen people have hunkered down outside the door. These folks are holding "Space Available" tickets for one of tonight's shows, meaning they will get in only if some of those guaranteed admission turn out to be no-shows. Doors will open at 6:00 P.M.

Since this stand-by admission is on a first-come basis, they have come early, equipped with camp chairs, cushions, laptop computers, ponderously thick novels, crossword puzzles, and cell phones to while away the time. They have done this before.

4:20 P.M.: Bruce Hornsby arrives and takes his place, noodling around on the keyboard while talking to Lickona and Jeff Peterson, throwing off ornate, free-flowing jazz riffs seemingly as an afterthought. Peterson asks for a set list. Hornsby replies he never works with one, but will cobble one up for this occasion. He scribbles down a dozen songs on a piece of paper. "This is real bootleg," he says.

Peterson, knowing Hornsby's propensity for open-ended improvisation, respectfully asks him to condense his songs. Though Bruce and Lucinda will both play over an hour, each set will be edited down to two twenty-six-minute segments to make up a one-hour broadcast. Hornsby has done the show before, in Season 19, and he too knows the drill. He nods.

JOE COOK
Longtime security chief Joe Cook (right) briefs producer Terry Lickona (left) and associate producer Jeff Peterson. (Photo by Sung Park © Austin American-Statesman.)

4:40 P.M.: Hornsby's rehearsal isn't five minutes old before a microphone breaks down. Bruce retreats to the dressing room on the fifth floor to await its repair. "That's it," says Menotti fatalistically. "Rehearsal's over."

He and some of the staff and crew break for a catered supper of jambalaya and Caesar salad, served at the back of the studio. One crewman who is not so fortunate tells him, "We just want you to know, Gary, that the crew will be happy to work straight through without a dinner break." He's kidding. Sort of.

4:50 P.M.: Happily the recalcitrant microphone is quickly repaired, and Bruce is soon onstage romping through "The End of the Innocence," the hit song he penned with Don Henley. The stage, dominated by the huge piano, is cluttered with gear and musicians. Getting clean shots, as Menotti is coming to realize, is going to be a bitch.

Hornsby is trying to loosen up, slipping between meters and keys as he sings. "Look," he crows as his bass player cracks up, "I'm really a jazz singer!"

5:14 P.M.: Hornsby runs through "The Road Not Taken" and "Look Out Any Window" as the overhead lights are being configured for his band. It is a tedious process, and not nearly finished. "Gary will have to shoot from the hip tonight," observes Jeff Peterson. The doors are scheduled to open to the public in forty-five minutes.

6:00 P.M.: In the foyer outside Studio 6-A, volunteers fold *ACL* T-shirts and pour many cups of cold ZiegenBock draft beer (provided free by one of the show's underwriters), in anticipation of the first elevator loads of fans who will momentarily ascend to the sixth floor. The volunteers work tirelessly, directing traffic and juggling seating, for little more than an opportunity to see the show. Some have been on hand for years.

Many of the 450 seats are reserved for bigwigs, guests of the artists, sponsors who trade out hotel rooms, food, and airline tickets to the show, volunteers, media representatives, and big contributors to KLRU. But enough of the general public gets in to keep a populist spirit in the air. On most nights, even the "Space Available" hopefuls can be accommodated, and their delight at being on the fabled set is palpable and contagious.

GARY IN CONTROL ROOM

Director Gary Menotti (left) calls the shots during the show, with technical director Ed Fuentes at the helm. (Photo by Sung Park © Austin American-Statesman.)

6:50 P.M.: Gary Menotti enters the video control room. He takes his place in the pilot's seat on the left side of the big control board facing a wall of monitors. Terry Lickona takes another chair at the board, flanking Ed Fuentes, the show's longtime technical director. The video control room is surprisingly small, about the size of an apartment living room, but the myriad views of the studio on the monitors make it seem vast. The audio side of the production is controlled by David Hough from an even smaller, more cluttered room across the hall.

7:10 P.M.: Terry Lickona emerges onstage and engages in his ritualistic audience warm-up: "Good evening, welcome to *Austin City Limits.* We hope you're happy to be here. . . . How many are here for the first time? . . . Let's take a moment to thank our sponsors, without whom . . . And our volunteers, who . . . We hope you don't have to use the facilities downstairs, but if nature calls, please try to leave between songs. . . . Please turn off your cell phones. . . . The only real rule is to have a great time." He has done this a thousand times.

"You can't really classify Bruce," he says by way of introducing Hornsby. "The best that can be said is that he represents the best of original forms of American music."

In the artists' bullpen at stage right, one of Hornsby's bandmates makes a satirical salaaming bow towards the boss. "Have fun," Peterson tells him as he strides onstage.

7:35 P.M.: As Hornsby cranks out "Resting Place" and "King of the Hill," Gary Menotti is directing in the control room, on his feet, rocking from side to side.

As he calls the shots to his cameramen, who are working off their own shot sheets, he is in constant motion. Asking for a dissolve or a dolly or a lingering close-up, he sweeps his arms in balletic fashion. From the back, lit by the monitors, he looks as though he is doing a sort of cybernetic tai chi.

"I'm not conscious of doing that, but people point it out all the time," he explained earlier, when someone mentioned it. After a particularly nice pick-up, he says over his headset, "Thanks, guys, that will look real nice in the edit." Menotti knows the shots he wants and, as director since 1981, his on-the-fly shot selections often form the final cut of the show.

BRUCE HORNSBY (1998)

For Bruce Hornsby and the band, it's always a musical exploration and adventure, and it's an adventure just trying to keep up with him.

7:50 P.M.: The band dead-solid nails "Rainbow's Cadillac," a Hornsby-penned paean to a street basketball legend. The music is pouring off the stage like water, and Hornsby's quicksilver piano runs float atop the funky, tongue-in-groove rhythm section like cream. The song earns a standing ovation.

8:07 P.M.: Hornsby comes offstage, looking perturbed, after his last number. Jeff Peterson asks him if there is anything he'd like to do over. "I'm hearing a lot of out-of-tune shit," he tells his musicians, although no one onstage or in the control room appears to have noticed such a gaffe.

After the show, Hornsby will take the audio tapes home with him and remix them to his satisfaction. Although the staff will frequently let an artist take the tapes to overdub an individual part, it is a rare privilege to let a performer remix his or her entire show. "He's one of the ones we trust," says Peterson simply.

8:20 P.M.: Hornsby comes offstage after his encore. In the heat of the moment, he is not happy with his performance. "The audience was kinder toward us than we deserved," he says.

9:50 P.M.: The house has been turned, and a new crowd is at the tables and in the bleachers. Bruce's gear has been struck and replaced by Lucinda's backline. Things are about ready to proceed, but as the moment of truth approaches, Lucinda is coiling herself tighter and tighter, until she resembles (however improbable the picture) a cat walking on eggshells in a room full of rocking chairs.

In some ways, this is standard operating procedure. Those who have known Williams for years know that she moves in accordance with her own internal rhythms. They joke about living on "Lucinda Standard Time" when they are in her vicinity. But she trusts her internal barometer absolutely, and whenever that mechanism is jostled by outside forces, her sense of well-being is compromised. She is, in her left-of-center way, very decisive and goal-oriented, with a powerful work ethic. She doesn't understand why people become impatient with her equivocation. As she has said before, you can't praise the work and criticize the process.

At this moment the process includes a cowboy hat. When she last did the show in July, Williams left behind a beloved straw cowboy hat. Though the item in question looked as if it had been used as a carwash chamois, it had a certain mojo that its owner found comforting.

She is delighted to learn that Terry Lickona rescued it from the dressing room and saved it for her. She is less delighted to learn that Lickona and Menotti would prefer she not wear it onstage because of the shadow it casts over her eyes and face (and in Lucinda's case, her large and luminous blue eyes are indeed the windows to her soul).

Now there is a seesawing tension. Wear the hat if it helps you nail the performance, her manager, Frank Callari, tells her. Susan Caldwell, the *ACL* staffer on hand, is being very solicitous and affirming, without quite encouraging her to wear the totem on camera. No one on the show is going to tell her she can't do something she feels strongly about, but all the same. . . .

I want a personal assistant, Williams is saying to Callari in a low, terse voice. "I don't want to have to fuck with the guitar or anything else. I don't want to have to fuck with shit. . . I just want to get dressed and show up. I already wrote the songs and made the

CAMERA GANG
The unlikely gang behind the cameras (left to right): Mike Archenhold, Doug Robb, Robert Moorhead, Dusty Sexton, Todd Pankey, director Gary Menotti, Caesar Jaceldo, Michael Emery. Their skill at creating dramatic images by pushing around 300-pound studio cameras or lugging 50-pound portables on their shoulders requires more art than heft.

JOHN T. DAVIS WITH LUCINDA WILLIAMS
Author John T. Davis (right) with Lucinda Williams and the famous (infamous?) hat.

LUCINDA WILLIAMS'S STAGE SETUP

album. . . . That's the hard part, isn't it?" It's nothing personal; this is merely the sound of tension being vented.

A young woman has gone down to the bus and returned with three new straw cowboy hats, one of which Lucinda purchased today. She tries them on, feeling as though she has painted herself into a corner. At the last minute, she flings one hat away from her in disgust. It's showtime.

9:57 P.M.: Lucinda is onstage, bare-headed, singing "Pineola," a fatalistic tale of suicide and fresh graves. On the monitors in the control room, she seems rigid, looking out over the audience's heads. Her hands fall into the familiar patterns on the guitar. Her plaintive, yearning voice sways, swoops, and keens. "Metal Firecracker" follows, then "Car Wheels On a Gravel Road" and a lovely, gently rocking love song, "Right In Time." She is in the musical pocket, and it is magic to watch.

10:25 P.M.: A lighting snafu in the control room—Williams is left in shadow as a song kicks off—elicits a gotcha! smile from her. That was the fault of *you* guys, the grin says, and the mood both onstage and in the control room seems to lighten perceptibly.

10:42 P.M.: Gremlins invade Williams's set as clams—the musicians' word for mistakes and miscues—pile atop clams. The band tries four takes of "Hot Blood" and then "Can't Let Go," and it's nothing doing. Lucinda switches to "Change the Locks," makes it most of the way through, flubs a line . . . and goes ahead anyway, pushing the lyric harder, almost snarling. In response, Kenny Vaughn, her guitarist, uncorks a chainsaw solo that teeters on the edge of distortion.

"Joy," the song that follows, is even more intense and abandoned. "You got no right to take my joy—I want it back!" she growls, exorcising the tensions and second-guesses. It is a riveting performance. Sometimes, Callari is saying in the control room, when she gets really pissed off, it makes a better show.

11:15 P.M.: Williams has switched to an array of Howlin' Wolf songs and ancient Delta blues. The show has run long and there is enough in the can to extract a thirty-minute episode, easy. "She's asking how long she can play," says Menotti, relaying a question over his headset. "We've got less than ten minutes of tape left, but we have runover [tape] available."

"Tell them to tell her ten minutes," says Lickona.

Menotti thumbs the intercom switch and speaks into his headset to the floor manager. "Terry says she can go as long as she wants to," he says sweetly.

11:35 P.M.: Williams does go precisely as long as she wants to. Which is long indeed. "Jackson" precedes "Sweet Old World," which is followed by "Passionate Kisses," "Something About What Happens When We Talk," and more vintage blues. Past midnight, the audience dwindles. She doesn't care. She plays and sings as though she is hunting prey.

Later, after the last of the crowd has departed, Lucinda will stay and watch playback until almost three in the morning. Caldwell hands her a release form and explains how the deal works: She can stop the tape and ask questions; she can note details she wants to tweak in each song; she can have a VHS copy of the show to view on the bus for later feedback. The audio track will be mixed separately for maximum clarity. Musicians never get this stuff on other TV shows. Ever.

Out in an empty Studio 6-A, the stage is bare, the tables and chairs stacked. A few empty beer cups and concert programs litter the bleachers. The place feels abandoned.

The day finally ends, closer to dawn than dusk. She likes it, Lucinda tells an exhausted Susan Caldwell.

And with that simple declaration, *Austin City Limits* has captured lightning in a bottle once more.

Postscript: On January 21, 1999, Bruce Hornsby and Jeff Peterson talked about Hornsby's performance for the *Austin City Limits* cameras. Despite his initial reservations at the time about some "out-of-tune shit" in the wake of the performance, time had lent Hornsby some perspective, and in retrospect, he told Peterson, he was very pleased with the segment—he even expressed a wish to make an hour-length episode out of the performance. In the end, Hornsby and his engineer merely remixed, and did not rerecord, about an hour's worth of what Bruce described as "monster stuff."

"The tone of the entire conversation was friendly and informal," Peterson reported. "Bruce felt that we had captured a particularly good performance."

LUCINDA WILLIAMS (1998)

*From busking for tips with her guitar on the street
two blocks from the ACL studio in the mid-'70s to headlining her
own show, Lucinda has arrived. With her insightful lyrics and
unique artistic voice, this native of Arkansas, Texas, and Louisiana
is a home-grown success story, no matter where she lives.*

FREQUENTLY ASKED QUESTIONS

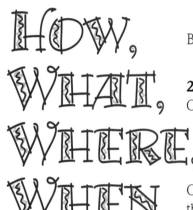

1. How do I get in touch with *Austin City Limits*?

By mail:

    Austin City Limits
    P.O. Box 7158
    Austin, TX 78713

By phone:

    (512) 471-4811 (KLRU main line)
    (512) 475-9077 (*ACL* hotline, for taping information)

By e-mail:

    Visit the *Austin City Limits* website at *www.austincitylimits.com*

2. When is *Austin City Limits* taped?

Our taping schedule varies from year to year, but generally we are in production for a seven-month period between the months of July and January, depending on the artists' availability. Call our hotline number (see above) for details.

3. Where is *Austin City Limits* taped?

Contrary to appearances, *Austin City Limits* is not taped outdoors on a hillside overlooking the city, but in a television studio located on the University of Texas campus. The famous skyline set, based on a photograph of the city taken from South Austin, debuted in 1982 for our seventh season, and has remained the series' backdrop ever since.

4. How do I get tickets to an *ACL* taping?

Unfortunately, due to our limited audience capacity and the heavy demand for tickets, we are no longer able to make special arrangements for our out-of-town fans. If you live in Austin or have plans to visit, call our hotline number to find out more about our schedule and for information on how to obtain tickets. Generally an announcement of a ticket give-away is made on one or more local radio stations, and tickets are handed out two per person on a first-come, first-served basis. They're free, if you can get 'em!

5. Can I visit the studio?

Sure! KLRU has welcomed people from all over the world into the *Austin City Limits* studio, from South Korea, Canada, and Mexico, to Argentina, England, and Russia. (Lots of folks come from across the U.S. and Canada, too.) Bring your camera and we'll take your picture on the stage. Please call (512) 471-4811 to set up an appointment.

6. How does an artist or band get booked on *Austin City Limits*?

The producers and executives behind *Austin City Limits* book a wide range of American roots music artists, ranging from country, blues, swing, and folk, to rock and roll, as well as regional sounds like western swing, Tejano, zydeco, and bluegrass. They're especially interested in singer-songwriters, and originality is a key criterion. Most performers (but not all) who appear on the show have a fair amount of live performing and recording experience, with either independent or major recording labels. These days we generally do not book artists who do not already have some national exposure. But we'll listen to anything that comes in, so managers, publicists, or artists are welcome to send samples to the producers at the address above.

7. Are videotapes, CDs, or cassettes of *Austin City Limits* programs available?

This is a tricky question to answer. There are several "Best of *Austin City Limits*" CD compilations available in record stores (two country, one blues, and a "Stevie Ray Vaughan Retrospective" home video). As this book goes to press, we are negotiating with various international distributors to make it possible to purchase additional *ACL* programs in these formats—hopefully in time for our twenty-fifth anniversary. The best advice is to call the *Austin City Limits* office for information.

8. Why isn't *Austin City Limits* on my local PBS station?

Every PBS station decides independently which programs it will air. As of this writing, some stations only schedule the series at certain times of the year. You should contact your local station for more information, or to receive a copy of their program guide. Most PBS stations publish a monthly guide in print and on their website listing all the programming for the month. PBS station addresses and phone numbers and stations with websites are listed on *PBS Online.*

9. When will a certain program air in my area?

For your reference, national airdates for *Austin City Limits* are listed on the *ACL* website. Again, check with your local station for the exact time and date of particular episodes.

10. Will you ever repeat the program featuring (insert your favorite artist here)?

Every *Austin City Limits* program is available for broadcast a maximum of four times within a three-year period following the original airdate. After that, the program will not be rebroadcast, unless the producers make special arrangements to renew the broadcast rights. If it is not listed in our national schedule on the *Austin City Limits* website, that means it is not available for broadcast at this time.

11. How do I contact an artist who has appeared on the show?

Send your letter to the artist by name, c/o *Austin City Limits* (see address opposite page), and we'll forward the letter to the artist's representative.

12. Are artists paid to perform on *Austin City Limits*?

You bet, but that's not the reason they do it! Every performer who appears on the show receives scale wages as set by the American Federation of Musicians (usually a few hundred dollars per person). Artists do the show because they love a format where they can do anything they want, and because it's a great exposure to a national television audience.

13. Is there a line of *Austin City Limits* merchandise?

Yes, indeed! You can buy *Austin City Limits* T-shirts, hats, jackets, and any number of other commemorative items. Check our website for details, or if you're coming to Austin, visit the *Austin City Limits* store in the new Austin Bergstrom airport.

14. What the hell is the name of that dad-gum armadillo song?

"London Homesick Blues," by Gary P. Nunn, has been the theme song of *Austin City Limits* since Season 2. You can hear the original version, sung by Gary P., on Jerry Jeff Walker's 1973 album, *Viva Terlingua.* The version you hear at the end of the program was recorded during the very first season of *Austin City Limits,* during a taping by the Lost Gonzo Band. Gary P. himself recorded a live album, *Home with the Armadillo,* at his own *ACL* appearance in 1983, and that album features yet another version of "London Homesick Blues."

15. Where can I see good live music in Austin?

They call it the "Live Music Capital of the World," you know, and *Austin City Limits* is the product of Austin's own thriving music scene. There are dozens of venues throughout the city that regularly host the same and similar performers that appear on *Austin City Limits*, as well as outlets for almost every describable type of music. If you're in Austin, consult the listings of the *Austin Chronicle* and the *Austin American-Statesman*. These listings can also be accessed via the web at *www.auschron.com* and *www.Austin360.com*. Have fun!

AFTERWORD

ALMOST SINCE THE BEGINNING, the question has been asked, "How long can *Austin City Limits* go on?" We were thrilled to celebrate our fifth season, and after some bumpy years, our tenth anniversary seemed like a really big deal. We wondered then if we could make it to Season 15, but make it we did, with a little help from friends like Stevie Ray Vaughan, Garth Brooks, Lyle Lovett, Mary Chapin Carpenter, and John Denver, among many others.

Season 20 was another major milestone, and for the first time we realized that with a little more luck, we might just make it to our grand twenty-fifth anniversary in 2000.

So now what? Nothing lasts forever, but *Austin City Limits* has become an institution: it's the longest-running showcase for popular music on American television today. More importantly, it has become a treasured chronicle of original American roots music for the past quarter-century.

We have every intention of continuing—and expanding—that tradition. With public television as our natural "home," we are expanding *Austin City Limits* to reach the rest of the world through foreign syndication. A companion series of radio specials is also in the works.

With an estimated six hundred-plus artist performances (and something like ten thousand-plus individual songs!), we hope to be able to offer video and/or CD copies of many of these programs one day soon. Within a few years you may be able to go to the *Austin City Limits* website *(www.austincitylimits.com)* and download your favorite program from our catalog.

Austin City Limits has always thrived on its simplicity. As long as we offer an uncluttered showcase for good, original music, we believe the artists and audience will come. As long as people enjoy the opportunity to see and hear their favorite music in concert brought into their own homes, we believe that *Austin City Limits* will celebrate many more anniversaries in the years to come. After all, *Austin City Limits* is where American music lives.

TERRY LICKONA, Producer

CHRONOLOGY OF PROGRAMS AND SONGS

No book about *Austin City Limits* would be complete without acknowledging the songs that have graced the airwaves for the last quarter century, so here is a complete listing starting from the very beginning. Note: Most of the shows included "London Homesick Blues," by Gary P. Nunn, as the theme song.

PILOT (1975)

WILLIE NELSON
Whiskey River; Stay All Night; Bloody Mary Morning; Redneck Mother; Okie from Muskogee; Ain't It Funny/Crazy; Headed Home to Austin; Phases and Stages; It's Not Supposed to Be That Way; Good Hearted Woman; Pick Up the Tempo; Will the Circle Be Unbroken; When the Roll Is Called Up Yonder; Mountain Dew; Song for You; Turn Out the Lights; Rollin' in My Sweet Baby's Arms

SEASON 1 (1976)

ASLEEP AT THE WHEEL / BOB WILLS' ORIGINAL TEXAS PLAYBOYS
Asleep at the Wheel: Take Me Back to Tulsa; Bump Bounce Boogie; The Letter that Johnny Walker Read; Nothing Takes the Place of You; Let Me Go Home, Whiskey
Bob Wills' Original Texas Playboys: San Antonio Rose; Steel Guitar Rag; Milk Cow Blues; Keith's Waltz; Faded Love

RUSTY WIER
One More Time; I Heard You Been Layin' My Old Lady; Cheryl Doreen; Blue Haze; Jeremiah Black; Relief; Stoned Slow Rugged; Sofia; Agua Dulce; Sally Mae; Don't It Make You Wanna Dance

TOWNES VAN ZANDT / CLIFTON CHENIER
Townes Van Zandt: Dollar Bill Blues; Ballad of Ira Hayes; If I Needed You; Talkin' Fraternity Blues; White Freight Liner; Don't Take It Too Bad; Talkin' Karate Blues; Shrimp Song; My Starter Won't Start
Clifton Chenier: Every Once in a While; You Don't Have to Go; Calenda; Trouble in Mind; No Salt in Your Snap Beans; What'd I Say

FLACO JIMENEZ WITH RY COODER AND AUGIE MEYERS
La Cumbia; La Polaka; La Nueva Senida; He'll Have to Go; My Arms Wait for You; Morenita Mia; La Estrella; Cajun Song; Pass Me By; Medley: Viva Sequin/Rancho Grande/Turkey in the Straw/San Antonio Rose; La Bamba

DOUG SAHM
Is Anybody Going to San Antone?; Hoedown; Rain; Papa Ain't Salty No More; Stormy Monday; At the Crossroads; Laredo; Dynamite Woman; Medley: Crazy Crazy Baby/One Night with You/Sometimes I Cry When I'm Lonely/Tutti Frutti; Mendocino; It's Gonna Be Easy; She's About a Mover

ALVIN CROW AND THE PLEASANT VALLEY BOYS
Wine Me Up; Louisiana Man; Fiddler's Lady; Rear View Mirror; I Just Dropped By to See the Show; Nyquil Blues;

Dynamite Diana; When I Stop Loving You; That's a Touch I Like; All Night Long; Cotton Eyed Joe; The Texas Kid; Milk Cow Blues; Faded Love; Six Pack to Go; Boil Them Cabbage Down

STEVE FROMHOLZ
Ain't It Nice to Be Alone; Neon Shadows; Texas Trilogy; Bear Song; Stoned Again; She's a Lady; Lucky Touch; Knockin' on Wood; Dear Darcy; Redneck Mother

B.W. STEVENSON / BOBBY BRIDGER
Bobby Bridger: Just Fompin' Around; The Sculpture; Altitude; Our Spirits Will Abide; People Carry On; Free My Spirit
B.W. Stevenson: Temper, Temper; Kokomo; Cold, Cold Winter; Hold On; On My Own; Train Song

WHEATFIELD
Last Train to Pontchartrain; Reason for Leaving; Cruzan Time; From Winter; The Lady Has No Heart; Drifting Along; Cardinal; Flapjack Blues; Canadian Bluegrass; Waxahachie Woman; Conversation; Mother Earth

BALCONES FAULT
Cartagenera; Shop Around; Up in the Air; You Can Do It; 42nd Street; Will Power; El Pescador; Darlin'; Fats Waller Medley; Pa Todo El Ano; Leave Your Hat On; Jesus Christ Was a Teenager Too

MARCIA BALL / GREEZY WHEELS
Greezy Wheels: Rollin' in My Sweet Baby's Arms; Cotton Eyed Joe; Sad, What a Dilemma; Romance; Sideman's Party; Everybody Knows; Right Now Rag
Marcia Ball: Freight Train Boogie; Saturday Night Fish Fry; When You Were Here; Make Me A Pallet; I'm Not Blind; In the Night; All Night Long; Good Girl's Gonna Go Bad; Done Got Over; Cowboy's Sweetheart; Burnin' Love; Standin' on This Corner

THE CHARLIE DANIELS BAND
Whiskey; New York City/Kingsize Rosewood Bed; Trudy; Saddle Tramp; Long Haired Country Boy; Franklin Limestone; It's My Life; Texas; Orange Blossom Special

LOST GONZO BAND / JERRY JEFF WALKER
Lost Gonzo Band: Dead Armadillo; Railroad Man; The Last Thing I Needed; London Homesick Blues
Jerry Jeff Walker: Redneck Mother; Backslider's Wine; I Like To Sleep Late in the Mornin'; L.A. Freeway; Mr. Bojangles; My Old Man; Gettin' By; Will the Circle Be Unbroken

SEASON 2 (1977)

WILLIE NELSON / TRACY NELSON
Willie Nelson: Time of the Preacher; I Couldn't Believe It Was True; Time of the Preacher Theme; Blue Rock

Montana/Red-Headed Stranger; Blue Eyes Crying in the Rain; Time Of the Preacher Theme; Just As I Am; Denver; O'er the Waves; Down Yonder; Down Yonder (Reprise); Can I Sleep in Your Arms?; Remember Me; Hands on the Wheel; Bandera
Tracy Nelson: After the Fire Is Gone; It's a Sad Situation; I Couldn't Stay Here If I Wanted; I Could Have Been Your Best Friend; Down So Low

AMAZING RHYTHM ACES / GOVE SCRIVENOR
Amazing Rhythm Aces: Hit the Nail on the Head; Anything You Want; Who Will Be the Next Fool?; Emma Jean; These Dreams of Losing You; I'll Be Gone; Dancing the Night Away; A Fool for the Woman; The End Is Not in Sight; Typical American Boy; Third Rate Romance
Gove Scrivenor: Makes My Love Come Rolling Down; Jesu, Joy of Man's Desiring; All I Want To Do Is See You Again; Pigeon River Breakdown

EARL SCRUGGS REVUE
Nashville Skyline Rag; I Shall Be Released; Lady in the First Degree; Sally Gooding; Black Mountain Blues; I Just Can't Seem To Care; Every Man Has Had His Own Price; Earl's Breakdown; Freight Train; Flint Hill Special; Stay All Night, Stay A Little Longer; Orange Blossom Special; Everybody Wants to Go to Heaven; Wooden Nickels; Foggy Mountain Breakdown; Carolina Boogie; Bugle Call Rag

JIMMY BUFFETT / RUSTY WIER
Jimmy Buffett: Wino and I Know; Dallas; Trying to Reason with the Hurricanes; Havana Daydreaming; Banana Republic; Got a Caribbean Soul I Can Barely Control . . .
Rusty Wier: Queen of My Dreams; Pass the Buck; Coast of Colorado; The Devil Lives in Dallas; Whiskey Still; I Don't Wanna Lay This Guitar Down; Tell Me Truly, Julie

GATEMOUTH BROWN / DELBERT McCLINTON
Gatemouth Brown: Okie Dokie Stomp; Blackjack; When My Blue Moon Turns to Gold; Up Jumped the Devil; Chicken Shift; Gate Walks the Board; Orange Blossom Special
Delbert McClinton: Back to Louisiana; Bad Luck; Part-Time Love; Honky Tonkin'; Ruby Louise; Pledging My Love

FIREFALL / DENIM
Firefall: Do What You Want; Cinderella; Even Steven; You Are the Woman; Sad Ol' Love Song; No Way Out; Livin' Ain't Livin'; Mexico
Denim: I'll Get Along; I'd Be Lost without You; Panhandle Memory; Let's Keep this Thing Going

GUY CLARK / STEVE FROMHOLZ
Guy Clark: Texas 1947; Virginia's Real; The Ballad of Laverne and Captain Flint; It's about Time; The Last

Gunfighter; Desperadoes Waiting for a Train; Texas Cookin'
Steve Fromholz: Fool's Paradise; Buzzard Blues; Road to Kentucky; Sweet Janey; I'd Have to Be Crazy

THE DIRT BAND / KIWI

The Nitty Gritty Dirt Band: Hony Tonkin'; Every Day Pays; Dismal Swamp; Rocky Top; Harmonica Dust; Randy Lynn Rag; Classical Banjo; Mr. Bojangles; Bayou Jubilee; Battle of New Orleans; Diggy Diggy Lo; Will the Circle Be Unbroken
Kiwi: Ain't Nobody Knocking at My Door; Early Morning Riser; I Am a Walrus

LARRY GATLIN / ALEX HARVEY

Larry Gatlin: Broken Lady; Delta Dirt; The Heart; Ode to the Road; I Just Can't Get Her Out of My Mind; Help Me; Hallelujah; Broken Lady
Alex Harvey: Some One Who Cares; Catfish Bates; Sleep All Mornin'; Tell It All Brother; Rings; Tulsa Turnaround; Makin' Music for Money; Delta Dawn

WILLIS ALAN RAMSEY / ROY BUCHANAN

Willis Alan Ramsey: Ballad of Spider Jones; Painted Lady; Geraldine and the Honey Bee; Northeast Texas Women; Watermelon Man; Muskrat Love
Roy Buchanan: Woman, You Must Be Crazy; Roy's Bluz; Sweet Dreams; Hey Joe; The Messiah Will Come Again

SEASON 3 (1978)

MICHAEL MURPHEY

Texas Morning; Mind Your Own Business; Wandering Minstrel; Boy from the Country; Carolina in the Pines; Medicine Man; Nothing's Your Own; Paradise; Loners; Wildfire; Holy Roller

STEVE GOODMAN

If Your Life Was on Videotape; Men Who Love Women Who Love Men; Banana Republic; The 20th Century Is Almost Over; Old Fashioned Girl; City of New Orleans; Chicken Cordon Blues/This Hotel Room; Can't Go Back; The Dutchman; You Never Even Called Me by My Name; My Old Man; I'll Fly Away

JOHN PRINE

Spanish Pipe Dream; Six O'clock News; Fish & Whistle; Illegal Smile; That's the Way the World Goes 'Round; Hello in There; Bottomless Lake; Bruised Orange; Saboo Visits the Twin Cities Alone; Pretty Good; Paradise; There She Goes; Saddles in the Rain

BOB WILLS' ORIGINAL TEXAS PLAYBOYS / ERNEST TUBB AND THE TEXAS TROUBADORS

Bob Wills' Original Texas Playboys: San Antonio Rose; Miss Molly; Steel Guitar Rag; Big Balls in Cowtown; You're OK; That's What I Like about the South; Right or Wrong; Texas Playboys Theme; Stay All Night
Ernest Tubb: Thanks a Lot; In the Jailhouse Now; Waltz Across Texas; If You Don't Quit Checking on Me; There's a Little Bit of Everything in Texas; Walking the Floor Over You; Tomorrow Never Comes

CHET ATKINS / MERLE TRAVIS

Chet Atkins: Autumn Leaves; Recuerdos de Alhambra; Black Mountain Rag; You'd Be So Nice to Come Home To; Frog Kissing; Until It's Time for You to Go; Snowbird; Wildwood Flower/Freight Train; Yakety Sax
Merle Travis: Nine Pound Hammer; Detour; Hominy Grits; Sixteen Tons; Smoke Smoke Smoke That Cigarette; Cannonball Rag; White Heat

DOC WATSON / GOVE

Doc and Merle Watson: Way Downtown; Lonesome Road; Mole in the Ground; Summertime; Sweet Georgia Brown; Peach Pickin' Time; Will the Circle Be Unbroken; Rain Crow Bill; Tennessee Stud
Gove Scrivenor: Poor Howard; Autoharp; Change Partners; Good Time Lady; Pigeon River Breakdown

JOHNNY RODRIGUEZ / LINDA HARGROVE

Johnny Rodriguez: Ridin' My Thumb To Mexico; There'll Always Be Honky Tonks in Texas; Tell All Your Troubles to Me; Rodeo Rider; Eres Tu; Desperado; Savin' This Love Song For You; Remember Me; We're Over
Johnny Rodriguez (with Willie Nelson): Jambalaya; Stay All Night
Linda Hargrove: Blue Jean Country Queen; Love Was; All Alone in Austin; Music Is Your Mistress; Love, You're the Teacher; Let It Shine; Mexican Love Song

JOHN HARTFORD / THE DILLARDS

John Hartford: One Wart; The Julia Belle Swaim; Don't Leave Your Records in the Sun; Would Not Be Here; Boogie; Little Cabin on the Hill; Rollin' in My Sweet Baby's Arms
The Dillards: Walkin' in Jerusalem; Daddy Was a Mover; Charlotte Breakdown; Dueling Banjos; Somebody Touched Me; Boil Them Cabbage Down; Orange Blossom Special; Old Joe Clark

JESSE WINCHESTER / MOTHER OF PEARL

Jesse Winchester: Midnight Bus; Nothing But a Breeze; Let the Rough Side Drag; Mississippi, You're on My Mind; Rhumba Man; Yankee Lady; Can't Stand Up Alone; Brand New Tennessee Waltz; Jambalaya
Mother of Pearl: Carmen Wear Your Red Dress; Cryin' Time; Rainy Day; Levi's Night Tonight; Sweet Melissa

ASLEEP AT THE WHEEL / BOBBY BRIDGER

Asleep at the Wheel: Nobody Here But Us Chickens; When Love Goes Wrong; Jumping at the Woodside; Jole Blon; Big Mamou; Louisiana; Choo Choo Ch' Boogie; Take Me Back to Tulsa; Boil Them Cabbage Down
Bobby Bridger: The Call; Breakaway; Red Cloud; Buffalo; Blackfoot

VASSAR CLEMENTS / GATEMOUTH BROWN

Gatemouth Brown: Heavy Juice; Gate's Salty Blues; Gate's Tune; Dark End of the Highway; Ag's Groove; One O'clock Jump
Vassar Clements: Mixed Melody; Peking Fling; Mocking Bird; Barnyard Boogie; Vassar's Boogie; Will the Circle Be Unbroken

MERLE HAGGARD AND THE STRANGERS

A Workin' Man Can't Get Nowhere Today; Silver Wings; Ramblin' Fever; Lonesome Fugitive; Sing Me Back Home; Orange Blossom Special; Old-Fashioned Love; Cherokee Maiden; San Antonio Rose; Fiddle Segment Jumping; Misery; Cowboy Sweetheart; Farmer's Daughter; Brain Cloudy Blues; Long Black Limousine

KILLOUGH & ECKLEY / THE LOST GONZO BAND

Killough & Eckley: Grinnin' My Blues Away; Absentee Fathers; Deep River Blues; Who Do You Know in Idaho?; Billy, Oh Billy; Back on the Road Again
Lost Gonzo Band: Take Advantage of Your Chances; Sweet Little Lilly; Daddy's Money; Life in the Pines; Honky Tonk Man; Public Domain; London Homesick Blues

SEASON 4 (1979)

NORTON BUFFALO

Where Has She Gone; High Tide in Wingo; Another Day; Gepetto; Ghetto Hotel; One Kiss to Say Goodbye; Thinkin' 'Bout You Babe; Wasn't It Bad Enough; Eugene; Hangin' Tree; Eighteen Wheels

JOHN McEUEN WITH VASSAR CLEMENTS, BYRON BERLINE, AND SPECIAL GUEST ELIZABETH COTTEN

John McEuen: Soldier's Joy; The Mountain Whipoorwill; I Am A Pilgrim
Vassar Clements: Listen To the Mockingbird; There'll Be No Teardrops Tonight
B. Savage: Fugue in C
Byron Berline: Tom and Jerry
John McEuen (with Marty Stuart, Vassar Clements, Byron Berline, B. Savage): Dixie Hoedown; Randy Lynn Rag
Elizabeth Cotten: Baby Ain't No Lie; Freight Train; Ol' Rattler; Old Georgee Buck

DAN DEL SANTO / TAJ MAHAL

Dan Del Santo: White Feathers in the Coop; Go on Back To Mama/Get Right; Whatever Way You Want It/On Higher Ground; Timmy Duran the Mandolin Man; Gonna Blow My Top
Taj Mahal: Queen Bee; Mail Box Blues; You're My Destiny; Slave Driver; Whistlin' Dixie

THE NEVILLE BROTHERS / ROBERT SHAW / LIGHTNIN' HOPKINS

The Neville Brothers Band: Sittin' in Limbo; Fire on the Bayou; Greatest Love; Fever; Hey Pocky Way/Down By the Riverside
Robert Shaw: Piggly Wiggly; Low Down Shame; Haddie Green
Lightnin' Hopkins: Mojo Hand; She Ain't No Cadillac; Black and Evil; Rock Me Baby

NASHVILLE SUPER PICKERS / TOM T. HALL

Chas. McCoy: Rollin' in My Sweet Baby's Arms; Shenandoah; Wabash Canonball
H. Robbins: Sweet Dreams
Phil Baugh: Shadow of Your Smile
Buddy Emmons: New Road
Johnny Gimble: Faded Love/San Antonio Rose; Fiddlin' Around
Tom T. Hall: Country Is; Ballad of 40 Dollars; Clayton Delaney; Foggy Mt. Breakdown; I Know You're Still Married; What Have You Got to Lose?; Old Dogs, Children and Watermelon Wine

LEON REDBONE / STEVE FROMHOLZ

Leon Redbone: Champagne Charlie; Alabama Jubilee; Diddy Wa Diddy; Walking Stick; The One Rose That's Left My Heart; Desert Blues
Steven Fromholz: Everybody's Goin' on the Road; Dear Darcy; The Bear Song; Yellow Cat; A Little More Holy Than I Am; I'd Have to Be Crazy

TOM WAITS

Summertime/Burma Shave; Annie's Back in Town/I Wish I Was in New Orleans; On the Nickel; Romeo Is Bleeding; Medley: Silent Night/Christmas Carol from a Hooker in Minneapolis; Small Change

DELBERT McCLINTON / CATE BROTHERS

Delbert McClinton: Maybe Some Day Baby; Night Life; Linda Lou; I Received a Letter; Object of My Affection; Take It Easy; Victim of Life's Circumstances
The Cate Brothers: I Won't Wait; Union Man; I Don't Know Why; Time Is a Thief; Where Can We Go?

PURE PRAIRIE LEAGUE / BOBBY BARE

Pure Prairie League: Kansas City Southern; Place in the Middle; Amie; Pickin' to Beat the Devil; Just Fly; Two Lane Highway

Bobby Bare: Arizona Desert; On a Real Good Night; Detroit City; Drop Kick Me Jesus; Feel a Whole Lot Better; *Sleeptight* Good Night Man; Marie Laveau

ALVIN CROW / MARCIA BALL

Alvin Crow: Yes She Do, No She Don't; Sands of Texas; Fiddler's Lady; Turkey, Texas; Bon Temps Roulet; Crazy Little Mama; You Send Me; Nyquil Blues; Cotton-Eyed Joe

Marcia Ball: Big River; Two-Timer; Leavin' Louisiana; Circuit Queen; In the Night; Goin' Back to Louisiana; Good Time Saturday Night

HOYT AXTON

Will the Circle Be Unbroken; An Old Greyhound; Lion in the Winter; Flash of Fire; Maybelline; Geronimo's Cadillac; Shoplifting One; Shoplifting Two; Gypsy Moth; The Devil; When Morning Comes; Evangelina; Them Downers; Never Been to Spain; Joy to the World

LITTLE JOE Y LA FAMILIA / ESTEBAN JORDAN

Little Joe y La Familia: Cumbachero; Las Nubes; Chain Smoker; Cuando Salgo a Los Campos; Can't Help Myself; El Merto Vivo

Esteban Jordan: Raw Can-Can; Canto al Pueblo; La Mucura; Bionic Box; La Camelia/Squeezebox Man

DOUG KERSHAW / CLIFTON CHENIER

Doug Kershaw: Diggy Diggy Lo; Mama's Got the Know-How; Marie; Louisiana Sun; Jambalaya; Cajun Stripper; Louisiana Man

Clifton Chenier: Just Like A Woman; No Salt in Your Snap Beans; Jolé Blon; Flip, Flop and Fly; Goin' Home Tomorrow; Rock House

SEASON 5 (1980)

ROY CLARK AND GATEMOUTH BROWN

Roy Clark and Gatemouth Brown: A Train; Caledonia; One O'clock Jump

Roy Clark: Great Pretender; Talk 'Bout a Party; Folsom Prison; Double Eagle; Born To Lose

Gatemouth Brown: The Drifter; Chicken Shift

DON WILLIAMS / JANIE FRICKE

Don Williams: We Should Be Together; Amanda; Say It Again; Atta Way To Go; Tulsa Time; 'Til the Rivers All Run Dry; It Must Be Love; My Best Friend; Gypsy Woman

Janie Fricke: Texas Proud; One of These Days; Gonna Love Me 'Til the Cows Come Home; But Love Me; Love Away Your Troubles; Medley: The Night They Drove Old Dixie Down/St. James Infirmary/American Trilogy; Crazy Arms/Pass Me By; Gone at Last

SONGWRITERS' SPECIAL

Hank Cochran: Make the World Go Away; Don't Do Windows; You Comb Her Hair

Willie Nelson: What Can You Do to Me Now; Night Life; Angel Flying Too Close to the Ground; Ain't It Funny How Time Slips Away

Whitey Shafer: That's the Way Love Goes; I'll Break Out Again Tonight; You Are a Liar

Red Lane: Black Jack County; I Must Have Done Something Wrong

Floyd Tillman: It Makes No Difference; A Song of Music; Slippin' Around

Sonny Throckmorton: Friday Night Blues

Ray Price: I'm Still Not Over You

RAY CHARLES AND HIS ORCHESTRA

Georgia (Vamp); Oh What a Beautiful Morning; Georgia; Busted; Born to Lose; Some Enchanted Evening; Hit the Road Jack; Can't Stop Loving You; I Can See Clearly Now; Classical/Steel Guitar Rag/Yodel; Deep in the Heart of Texas

RALPH STANLEY AND THE CLINCH MOUNTAIN BOYS / UNCLE WALT'S BAND

Ralph Stanley and the Clinch Mt. Boys: How Mountain Girls Can Love; Rocky Island; Nobody's Love Like Mine; Clinch Mountain Back Step; Little Maggie; Lost Train Blues; This Old Town; Glory Land; Henry Brown

Uncle Walt's Band: Keep on Working; Honest Pappas; Don't Ya Know; Seat of Logic; Green Tree; Getaway; For the First Time; Snowin' Me Under; Sittin' on Top of the World

JOE ELY / JERRY JEFF WALKER

Joe Ely: I Got My Hopes Up High; She Never Spoke Spanish to Me; I'll Be Your Fool; Boxcars; Standin' in a Big Hotel; Down on the Drag; Annie's Been Workin' on the Midnight Shift; Suckin' on a Big Bottle of Gin

Jerry Jeff Walker: L.A. Freeway; Contrary to Ordinary; Jaded Lover; Comfort and Crazy; Pick Up the Tempo

HANK WILLIAMS JR. / SHAKE RUSSELL BAND

Hank Williams Jr.: Move It on Over; Whiskey Bent and Hell Bound; Hank; Outlaw Women; White Lightnin'; Cheatin' Heart; Women I've Never Had; Come and Go Blues; Family Tradition

Shake Russell: You Wouldn't Know Me; Deep in the West

Dana Cooper: Fade Away

Shake Russell and Dana Cooper: Rollin' My Blues; Lover, Baby Friend; Troubles

JOHNNY GIMBLE / TEXAS SWING PIONEERS

Johnny Gimble and Bosque Bandits: Bob Wills' Medley; Panhandle Rag; Estrellita; End of the Line; Pretty Palomino

Texas Swing Pioneers: Washington & Lee Swing; Right Or Wrong; Truck Driver's Blues; Bells of St. Mary's; J.R. Blues; Muskrat Rambler; Jessie; Please Don't Talk about Me When I'm Gone; Just Because

JOHNNY PAYCHECK / BILLY JOE SHAVER

Johnny Paycheck: Ragged But Right; I'm the Only Hell My Mama Ever Raised; Friend Lover Wife; Trials and Tribulations; Cocaine Train; Slide Off of Your Satin Sheets; Me and the IRS; Take This Job and Shove It

Billy Joe Shaver: Sweet Mama; Ride Me Down Easy; Willie the Wandering Gypsy and Me; Black Rose; Honky Tonk Heroes; I've Been to Georgia on a Fast Train; Ragged Old Truck; I'm Just an Old Chunk of Coal; You Asked Me To

FLACO JIMENEZ / BETO Y LOS FAIRLANES

Flaco Jimenez: Abre El Corazon; Cielito Lindo; Spanish Eyes; Teresa La Pandera; Mexico; Hasta La Vista

Beto y Los Fairlanes: El Cartero; Piddlin'; Shize N Rine; Fat Boy in the Water; Chalupa Supreme; Corazon De Algodon

MOE BANDY AND JOE STAMPLEY / MARTY ROBBINS

Moe Bandy and Joe Stampley: Honky Tonk Man; Partners in Rhyme; Holding the Bag; Good 'Ole Boys

Joe Stampley: Roll on Big Mama; Ten Minutes; Do You Ever Fool Around?; Here I Am, Drunk Again

Moe Bandy: I Cheated the Right Out of You; It's A Cheatin' Situation; Tell 'Ole I Ain't Here

Marty Robbins: Big Iron; Laredo; Buenos Dias Argentina; Washed My Hand in Muddy Water; My Woman, My Woman, My Wife; You Gave Me a Mountain; All Around Cowboy; El Paso

CARL PERKINS / JOE SUN

Carl Perkins: Matchbox; Boppin' the Blues; That's Alright Mama; Fifties Medley: Tutti Frutti/I'm Walkin'/Whole Lotta Shakin'/Hound Dog; Turnaround; Honey Don't; Miss Understood; Blue Suede Shoes; I Got a Woman

Joe Sun: Ready for Times; Gettin' Bombed, Boozed & Busted; Old Flames Can't Hold a Candle to Me; I'll Find It Where I Can; Born Too Late

MEL TILLIS / GAIL DAVIES

Mel Tillis: Stay All Night; Burning Memories; Good Woman Blues/I Got the Hoss; Coca Cola Cowboy; Ruby; Orange Blossom Special; Medley: One More Drink/I Wanna Go Stateside/I Ain't Never Seen Nobody Like You

Gail Davies: Blue Heartache; Bucket to the South; Grandma's Song; Someone Is Looking; Good Lovin' Man; Like Strangers; Need Your Lovin'

SEASON 6 (1981)

THE CHARLIE DANIELS BAND

Funky Junky; Damn Good Cowboy; In America; Legend of Wooly Swamp; Johnny B. Goode; Can't You See; Carolina; Long-Haired Country Boy; Texas; The Devil Went Down to Georgia; The South's Gonna Do It Again; Amazing Grace/Will the Circle Be Unbroken

BOBBY BARE / LACY J. DALTON

Bobby Bare: Drunk and Crazy; Numbers; Detroit City; Drinkin' and Druggin'; The Credit Card Song; Ugly Woman; Tequila Sheila; I Gotta Get Rid of This Band

Lacy J. Dalton: Ain't Nobody Like; Tennessee Waltz; Are There Any Cowboys Left in the Good Ole USA?; Crazy Blue Eyes; Hard Times; Losin' Kind of Love; Blues; Carolina Come On

GEORGE JONES WITH HANK THOMPSON

George Jones: The Race Is On; Bartender's Blues; Once You've Had the Best; Jambalaya; Picture of Me Without You; Ida Red; Her Name Is . . .; Some Day My Day Will Come; Take Me Back to Tulsa; The Wild Side of Life; Hey Mr. Bartender; White Lightnin'; I'm Not Ready Yet; Me and Jesus; Milk Cow Blues; Maiden's Prayer; He Stopped Loving Her Today; Medley: Walk Through This World with Me/The Window Up Above/She Thinks I Still Care

RAY PRICE AND THE CHEROKEE COWBOYS / ASLEEP AT THE WHEEL

Ray Price: Crazy Arms/Heartaches By the Number; Another Woman; Don't You Ever Get Tired of Hurting Me; San Antonio Rose; Night Life; I Love You Because; For the Good Times; Faded Love

Asleep at the Wheel: Devil's Dream; Miles and Miles of Texas; Cool as the Breeze; Sugar Foot Rag; Walkin' After Midnight; Up, Up, Up; Roll 'Em; Am I High?; Cotton-Eyed Joe

JOHNNY RODRIGUEZ / ALABAMA

Johnny Rodriguez: Streetwalker; Ridin' My Thumb; First To Fall; Love Put a Song in My Heart; Happy Endings; Head over Heels; That's the Way Love Goes; Rio Grande; North of the Border; Stagger Lee

Alabama: Tennessee River; Why Lady Why; Fantasy; Salty Dog/Going Down the Road Feelin' Bad; Keep on Dreamin'; My Home's in Alabama

DAVID GRISMAN QUINTET / MANDOLIN SPECIAL

The David Grisman Quintet: E.M.D.; Opus 38; Dawgma; Naima; Dawg's Rag

David Grisman (with Tiny Moore, Johnny Gimble, Eldon Shamblin, Jethro Burns): Groovin' High; Tiny's Rag;

Jethro's Tune; Blues in G; Swing 39; Tom and Jerry Medley; How High the Moon

BILL MONROE AND THE BLUEGRASS BOYS / RIDERS IN THE SKY
Bill Monroe: Muleskinner Blues; Blue Moon of Kentucky; Bluegrass Breakdown; Uncle Pen; Goodbye Old Pal; In the Pines; Panhandle Country; The Old Crossroads; John Henry/Y'all Come; Watermelon on the Vine
Riders in the Sky: Riders in the Sky; That's How the Yodel Was Born; Bluebonnet Lady; Cielito Lindo; Cattle Call; Rabbit Dance; Pecos Bill; So Long, Saddle Pals

TONY JOE WHITE / GARY STEWART
Tony Joe White: Mamas, Don't Let Your Cowboys Grow Up to Be Babies; Redneck Woman; Rainy Night in Georgia; Polk Salad Annie; Willie and Laura Mae Jones; Billy; Lustful Earl and the Married Woman; I Came Here to Party; I Get Off on It
Gary Stewart: Honky-Tonkin'; I've Got This Drinkin' Thing; She's Actin' Single, I'm Drinkin' Doubles; L'il Junior; Your Place or Mine?

SONGWRITERS' ENCORE
Red Lane: Uncle Harvey's Plane; They Don't Make Love Like They Used To; I've Been All Night Goin' Home; I'll Just Keep on Falling in Love
Hank Cochran: Little Bitty Tear; I Fall to Pieces
Willie Nelson: Healing Hands of Time; Angel Flying Too Close to the Ground; Good Hearted Woman
Floyd Tillman: Gotta Have My Baby Back; Some Other World; I Love You So Much It Hurts
Whitey Shafer: Cold Fort Worth Beer; Whitey Shafer Story: 'Dem Boots; Where Are All the Girls I Used to Cheat With?; Bandy the Rodeo Clown
Sonny Throckmorton: The Way I Am; Middle-Age Crazy
Hank Thompson: Don't You Ever Get Tired of Hurting Me?

CHARLEY PRIDE / RAZZY BAILEY
Charley Pride: Is Anybody Goin' to San Antone?; Kiss an Angel; Kaw-Liga; Missing You; You Almost Slipped My Mind; Jailhouse Rock; Mississippi Cotton-Pickin' Delta Town; Roll On, Mississippi; Honky Tonk Blues; Oldies Medley: Snakes Crawl at Night/Just Between You and Me/Crazy Part's Over Now/Does My Ring Hurt Your Finger?/Baby It's Gonna Take a Little Bit Longer/I'm Just Me; Cotton Fields; When I Stop Leavin' I'll Be Gone
Razzy Bailey: Ain't Got No Business Doing Business Today; Good Hearted Woman; What's a Little Love between Friends?; 9,999,999 Tears; T for Texas; I Keep Coming Back; Lovin' Up a Storm; True Life Country Music

MICHAEL MURPHEY / ED BRUCE
Michael Murphey: Still Taking Chances; Cowboy Cadillac; Once a Drifter; Cherokee Fiddle; Hard Country; Hard Partyin' Country Darlin'; Cosmic Cowboy
Ed Bruce: Medley: Tennessee Cowboy Band/The Man That Turned Mama On/Streets of Laredo; 39 and Holding; Girls, Women and Ladies; Mamas, Don't Let Your Babies Grow Up To Be. . .; Texas

LEO KOTTKE / PASSENGER
Leo Kottke: June Bug; Pamela Brown; Orange Room; Louise; Eight Miles High; "Chicken Story"/Jack Fig
Passenger: Ocho Rios; Windsor Dreams; Just Like You Said; Flight 121

JOE "KING" CARRASCO / THE SIR DOUGLAS QUINTET
Joe "King" Carrasco: Party Weekend; Party Doll; 96 Tears; One More Time; Caca De Vaca; Betty's World; Let's Get Pretty; Rock Este Noche; Please Mr. Sandman; Love Me, Love Me/Susan Friendly; Don't Bug Me Baby

The Sir Douglas Quintet: Who'll Be the Next in Line?; Down on the Border; Who Were You Thinking Of?; Is Anybody Goin' to San Antone/Texas Tornado; She's About a Mover

SEASON 7 (1982)

EMMYLOU HARRIS / RODNEY CROWELL
Emmylou Harris: Two More Bottles of Wine; San Antonio Rose; Millworker; Las Vegas; If I Needed You; Born to Run; Shop Around/He's a Rebel/Too Tired to Run/Saturday Nite
Rodney Crowell: Stars on the Water; Queen of Hearts; Leavin' Louisiana in the Broad Daylight; Ain't No Money; All You've Got to Do; Ain't Livin' Long Like This

KRIS KRISTOFFERSON
Do I Have to Draw a Picture; Lover Please; I Can Help; Me & Bobby McGee; Star-Crossed Lovers; The Bandits of Beverly Hills; Magdeline; Sugarman; Nobody Loves Anybody Anymore; If It's All the Same to You; Borderland; The Pilgrim; Lovin' Her Was Easier; Sunday Morning/Silver Tongued Devil/Smile at Me Again; Why Me Lord

JERRY REED / CHET ATKINS
Jerry Reed: Give Me Back My Blues; Amos Moses; Sugarfoot Rag; Guitar Man; Foggy Mountain Breakdown; Patches; When You're Hot You're Hot; East Bound and Down
Chet Atkins: Orange Blossom Special; Dance with Me; Stars and Stripes; Gallopin' Guitars; Muskrat Ramble; Maidens Prayer/Faded Love/San Antonio Rose; Yankee Doodle/Dixie

JOHNNY LEE / CHARLY McCLAIN
Johnny Lee: Highways Run Forever; One in a Million; Rode Hard and Put Up Wet; Red Sails in the Sunset; Pickin' Up Strangers; Stand By Me; Bet Your Heart on Me; Lookin' for Love
Charly McClain: He's Back; Women Get Lonely; Men; Love in Motion; You and Me; When Love Ain't Right; Sweet and Easy; Sleepin' with the Radio On; Who's Cheatin' Who

WILLIE NELSON / GUY CLARK
Willie Nelson: Whiskey River; Bloody Mary Morning; She's Not for You; I Never Cared for You; Old Flames Can't Hold a Candle to You; Shotgun Willie; Milk Cow Blues
Guy Clark: L.A. Freeway; Who Do You Think You Are?; Partner Nobody Chose; Rita Ballew; The Last Gunfighter; The South Coast of Texas; Texas Cookin'

MERLE HAGGARD AND THE STRANGERS
Big City; I Think I'll Just Stay Here and Drink; My Favorite Memory; Back to the Barrooms; You Don't Have Very Far to Go; Silver Wings; Sing Me Back Home; Faded Blue Jeans; Misery and Gin; Miss the Mississippi; The Way I Am; I'm Almost Ready; Are the Good Times Really Over for Good; Okie from Muskogee

THE BELLAMY BROTHERS / JOHN ANDERSON
Bellamy Brothers: Let Your Love Flow; Sugar Daddy; Dancin' Cowboys; Honey We Don't Know; Number Two; You're My Favorite Star; Beautiful Body
John Anderson: I'm Just an Old Chunk of Coal; She Just Started Liking Cheatin' Songs; 1959; Working Man Blues; Four or Five Times; I Love You a Thousand Ways; Chicken Truck; Your Lyin' Blue Eyes; You Can't Judge a Book by Looking at the Cover

LARRY GATLIN / RICKY SKAGGS
Larry Gatlin: Broken Lady; I Don't Want to Cry; Sweet Becky Walker; Take Me to Your Lovin' Place; Takin' Somebody with Me When I Fall; The Midnight Choir;

What Are We Doin' Lonesome; The Last Love Song; She Used to Sing on Sunday; All the Gold in California
Ricky Skaggs: Heartbroke; Sweet Temptation; Don't Get Above Your Raisin; Sally Goodin'; Talk about Sufferin'; Sweetheart of Mine; You Can See Me Walkin'

TOMPALL AND THE GLASER BROTHERS / GEORGE STRAIT
Tompall and the Glaser Brothers: Just One Time; T for Texas; The Last Thing on My Mind; California Girl and the Tennessee Square; Ring Ring; Sweet City Woman
George Strait: Unwound; Driving Nails in My Coffin; Her Goodbye Hit Me in the Heart; Down and Out; The New Never Wore Off; Miss Molly; Fool Hearted Memory; If You're Thinkin' You Want a Stranger; If You Think I'm Crazy Now

DON McLEAN / TERRI GIBBS
Don McLean: Cryin'; Isn't It Strange; Prime Time; American Pie; Vincent; Jerusalem
Terri Gibbs: Mis'ry River; I Wanna Be Around; Ashes to Ashes; It's True; Georgia; Somebody's Knockin'; What'd I Say?

ROY CLARK / THE GEEZINSLAWS
Roy Clark: A Bottle of the Way I Feel; Foggy Mountain Breakdown; Saturday Night; Ghost Riders in the Sky; Under the Double Eagle; Tumblin' Tumbleweeds; Duelin' Banjos; Come Live with Me; Paradise Knife and Gun Club; Malaguena
The Geezinslaws: Put Another Log on the Fire; Jukebox; My Ol' Buddy; When I Die; Somewhere over the Rainbow; Redneck

PETE FOUNTAIN / JAZZMANIAN DEVIL
Pete Fountain: Walkin' the Floor over You; High Society; Tin Roof Blues; When the Saints Go Marching In
Jazzmanian Devil: Mamacate; Quintana; Alicia; Jihi; Fromunda

GEORGE THOROGOOD AND THE DESTROYERS / DAVE OLNEY AND THE X-RAYS
George Thorogood: House of Blue Lights; House from Philly; Wanted All Over the World; Who Do You Love?; I'll Change My Style; No Particular Place to Go
David Olney: Frankie and Johnnie; She's Bound to Go; Steal My Thunder; Love Is Illegal; Love and Money; Wait Here for the Cops; Contender

SEASON 8 (1983)

MICKEY GILLEY / T.G. SHEPPARD
Mickey Gilley: The Girls Get Prettier at Closing Time; Put Your Dreams Away; Stand by Me; Sweet Honky Tonk Wine; True Love Ways; You Don't Know Me; Object of My Affection; Diggy Liggy Lo
T.G. Sheppard: Do You Want To Go To Heaven; War Is Hell on the Homefront; Finally; Party Time; Crazy in the Dark; I Loved 'Em Every One; Only One You

DON WILLIAMS / WEST TEXAS SONGWRITERS' SPECIAL
Don Williams: Mistakes; Listen to the Radio; I Believe in Love; Some Broken Hearts Never Mend; Good Ole Boys Like Me; Ridin' Sideways; Tulsa Time; Lord I Hope this Day Is Good
Butch Hancock: The Wind's Dominion
Townes Van Zandt: Pancho & Lefty; If I Needed You
David Halley: Hard Livin'; Rain Just Falls
Butch Hancock and Jimmie Gilmore: If You Were a Bluebird
Jimmie Gilmore: Dallas

ROY ORBISON

Only the Lonely; Dream Baby; In Dreams; Mean Woman; Blue Angel; Lana; Blue Bayou; Leah; Candy Man; Crying; Ooby Dooby; Hound Dog; Working for the Man; Down the Line; It's Over; Pretty Woman; Running Scared

SONGWRITERS' SHOWCASE

John Prine: There She Goes; Grandpa Was a Carpenter; Aimless Love
Billy Joe Shaver: I've Been to Georgia on a Fast Train; I'm Just an Old Chunk of Coal; Ride Me Down Easy
Rodney Crowell: 'Till I Can Control Again; No Memories Hanging 'Round; Shame on the Moon
Guy Clark: The Carpenter; Home Grown Tomatoes; L.A. Freeway
Keith Sykes: Coast of Marseilles; I'm Not Strange; One True Love
Bill Caswell: Sodbuster; Don't Tell Mama

B.B. KING

Everyday I Have the Blues; Night Life; Everybody I Know Sings the Blues; Since I Met You Baby; Love Me Tender; Some Help I Don't Really Need; When It All Comes Down; One of Those Nights; You and Me/Me and You; Someone Really Loves You (Guess Who); The Thrill Is Gone

JANIE FRICKE / B.J. THOMAS

Janie Fricke: He's a Heartache; Don't Worry 'Bout Me Baby; Down to My Last Broken Heart/Do Me with Love; Please Help Me I'm Falling; I'll Need Someone to Hold Me When I Cry; Fox on the Run; You Don't Know Love; It Ain't Easy Bein' Easy; Lovin' You Is Too Hard on My Heart; Closing Band Vamp
B.J. Thomas: Raindrops Keep Fallin' on My Head; Somebody Done Somebody Wrong Song; So Lonesome I Could Cry; Amazing Grace; Hooked on a Feelin'; Old-Fashioned Love; Mighty Clouds of Joy; Brickyard Blues

FRIZZELL AND WEST / CON HUNLEY

Frizzell and West: Another Honky Tonk Night on Broadway; I Just Came Here to Dance (The Gold); I'm Gonna Hire a Wino; Texas State of Mind; Steppin' Out; Wishing Room; Will You Marry Me Again?; You're the Reason God Made Oklahoma
Con Hunley: He Don't Love You; Confidential; Livin' on the Funky Side; Since I Fell; I Got the Rhythm from My Daddy. . .; No Relief; Oh! Girl; Never Had It Laid on Me

MICHAEL MURPHEY / GARY P. NUNN

Michael Murphey: Still Takin' Chances; Cherokee Fiddle; Alleys of Austin; Calico Silver; Dancin' in the Meadow; What's Forever For?
Gary P. Nunn: Nights Never Get Lonely; Last Thing I Needed the First Thing This Morning; Public Domain; Tennessee Road; What I Like About Texas; London Homesick Blues

ROSANNE CASH / STEVE WARINER

Rosanne Cash: Seven Year Ache; My Baby Thinks He's a Train; I Wonder; Ain't No Money; Blue Moon with Heartache; Oh Yes I Can; No Memories; Right or Wrong
Steve Wariner: It's Your Move; I Can Hear Kentucky Callin' Me; By Now; Your Memory; Kansas City Lights; Don't Plan on Sleeping Tonight; Here We Are; All Roads Lead to You

RANK AND FILE / DELBERT McCLINTON

Rank and File: Coyote; Ring of Fire; Wabash Cannonball; Klansman; Lucky Day; Amanda Ruth; Rank and File
Delbert McClinton: Fool in Love; Lipstick, Powder and Paint; Back to Louisiana; Jealous Kind; Let Love Come Between Us; Givin' It Up for Your Love; Turn on Your Love Light

TAMMY WYNETTE / JOHN CONLEE

Tammy Wynette: Medley: Your Good Girl's Gonna Go Bad/Apt. #9/I Don't Wanna Play House/ D·I·V·O·R·C·E/Singing My Song; A Good Night's Love; Another Chance; 'Til I Can Make It on My Own; Boil Them Cabbage Down; Crying in the Rain; Gospel Medley: I'll Fly Away/Will the Circle Be Unbroken/I Saw The Light; Stand by Your Man
John Conlee: A Little of You; Friday Night Blues; Busted; Hits Medley: Before My Time/Lay Lady Lay/She Can't Say That Anymore; Ain't No Way to Make a Bad Love Grow; The Backside of Thirty; Rose Colored Glasses

ROGER MILLER / EARL THOMAS CONLEY

Roger Miller: Me and Bobby McGee; Dang Me; Can't Roller Skate in a Buffalo Herd/Chug A Lug; England Swings; Husbands and Wives; King of the Road; Can't Go on this Way; Invitation to the Blues; Old Friends; Milk Cow Blues
Earl Thomas Conley: Somewhere Between Right and Wrong; Silent Treatment; Fire and Smoke; Tell Me Why; Stranded on a Dead End Street; This Ain't No Way to Be; Highway Home; Heavenly Bodies

LORETTA LYNN

Running Naked in the Rain; You're Looking at Country; Silver Threads and Golden Needles; I Lie; Don't Come Home a Drinkin'; Love Is a Foundation; You Ain't Woman Enough to Take My Man; They Don't Make 'Em Like My Daddy; Thank God I'm a Country Girl; One's on the Way/The Pill; You Can't Be a Beacon (If Your Light Don't Shine); Rocky Top; Two Dollars in the Juke Box; Honky Tonk Girl; Patsy Cline Medley: I Fall to Pieces/ Walkin' After Midnight/He's Got You/Back in Baby's Arms/Crazy; Makin' Love from Memory; God Bless America Again; Coal Miner's Daughter

SEASON 9 (1984)

RAY CHARLES / LEE GREENWOOD

Ray Charles: Ridin' Thumb; Georgia; I'm Busted; I'll Be Over You/I Can't Stop Loving You; 3/4 Time/Born to Love Me; What'd I Say?
Lee Greenwood: Somebody's Gonna Love You; Ring on Her Finger; Gonna Have a Party; It Turns Me Inside Out; The Love Song; C'mon Back; I.O.U.; She's Lyin'

JERRY LEE LEWIS

Keep My Motor Runnin'; Somewhere over the Rainbow; You Win Again; Sweet Little 16; 39 and Holding; Teenage Queen; Boogie Woogie Country Man; Cee Cee Rider; Chantilly Lace; I'll Find It Where I Can; In the Garden; No Headstone on My Grave; Shake That Thing; Great Balls of Fire; Whole Lotta Shakin' Goin On

FREDDIE POWERS WITH WILLIE NELSON AND MERLE HAGGARD

Freddie Powers (with Willie Nelson and Merle Haggard): I Had a Beautiful Time; Natural High; Daddy's Honky Tonk; Little Hotel Room; Lady Be Good; Gotta Have My Baby; After You've Gone
Freddie Powers: Silver Eagle
Freddie Powers (with Merle Haggard): All I Want To Do Is Sing My Song
Merle Haggard: I've Got the Money; Cold Cold War
Willie Nelson: It Makes No Difference Now
Willie Nelson (with Merle Haggard): Half a Man

GARY MORRIS / GAIL DAVIES

Gary Morris: Velvet Chains; Dreams Die Hard; Fire Going Out; Wind Beneath My Wings; The Love She Found in Me; Headed for a Heartache/Don't Look Back

Gail Davies: Settin' Me Up; Round the Clock Lovin'; Following You Around; Lovely World; Grandma's Song; You Turn Me On, I'm a Radio; Hard Dog to Keep Under the Porch; Singing the Blues

THE WHITES / NEW GRASS REVIVAL

The Whites: When the New Wears Off of Our Love; You Put the Blue in Me; Black Mountain Rag; Pipeliner Blues; I Wonder Who's Holding My Baby Tonight; Hanging Around; Don't You Believe; A House of Gold; There's a Higher Power
New Grass Revival: When the Storm Is Over; White Freightliner Blues; Reach a Little Bit Higher; In the Middle of the Night; I Saw You Running; You Don't Have to Knock; County Clare

JIMMY BUFFETT

Son of a Son of a Sailor; Distantly in Love; Migration; Pencil Thin Moustache; Margaritaville; One Particular Harbour; Changes in Latitude, Changes in Attitude; Come Monday; Stars on the Water; The Pirate Looks at 40; Brown-Eyed Girl; Land Shark; Cheeseburger in Paradise

JOHNNY RODRIGUEZ / DAVID ALLEN COE

Johnny Rodriguez: How Could I Love Her; Foolin'; Love Me with All Your Heart; Victim or a Fool; Paralyzed; That's the Way Love Goes; Back on Her Mind; We Believe in Happy Endings; Take It Easy; We're Over
David Allan Coe: Willie, Waylon and Me; Boston; Fire and Rain/Would You Lay with Me?; Take This Job and Shove It; Cripple Creek; My Girl; Serve Somebody; The Ride; You Never Even Call Me by My Name

DOTTIE WEST / FLOYD CRAMER

Dottie West: Love Cruise; Lesson in Leavin'; Country Sunshine; We've Got Tonight; It's High Time; Leaving Is for Unbelievers; You Pick Me Up (and Put Me Down); Are You Happy, Baby?; You Needed Me
Floyd Cramer: On the Rebound; San Antonio Rose; Always on My Mind; Last Date; Flip Flop Bop; Georgia; Yellow Rose of Texas/Deep in the Heart of Texas; Blue Eyes Crying in the Rain; Morning has Broken; William Tell Overture

BONNIE RAITT / THE LE ROI BROTHERS WITH RAY CAMPI AND SLEEPY LA BEEF

Bonnie Raitt: Green Lights; Can't Get Enough; Love Has No Pride; Love Me Like a Man; Will Ya Won't Ya; Think
Le Roi Brothers: Are You with Me Baby/Say Yeah!!!; Pretty Little Lights of Town; Dance with Me Tonight; DWI; Check This Action
Ray Campi (with Le Roi Brothers): Hollywood Cats; Rockin' at the Ritz
Sleepy La Beef (with Le Roi Brothers): Honey Hush; Tore Up

JOHN ANDERSON / ELIZA GILKYSON

John Anderson: Swingin'; I'm Just an Old Chunk of Coal; Let Somebody Else Drive; I Love You a Thousand Ways; Haunted House; Wild & Blue; Goin' Downhill; Black Sheep
Eliza Gilkyson: Love Will Come True; Wheel of Fortune; American Boys; Gift of Love; Party Monster; The Contender; Red Rose

GEORGE STRAIT / THE KENDALLS

George Strait: Right or Wrong; I Can't See Texas from Here; Amarillo by Morning; Fool Hearted Memory; I'm Satisfied with You; You Look So Good in Love; Corrina, Corrina; Our Paths May Never Cross; The Fire I Can't Put Out; Cherokee Maiden
The Kendalls: If You're Waitin' on Me; Thank God for the Radio; Movin' Train; Already Blue; Making Believe; I Had a Lovely Time; Pittsburgh Stealers; Heaven's Just a Sin Away; Teach Me to Cheat

COUNTRY LEGENDS

Sons of the Pioneers: When the Payday Falls Around; San Antonio Rose; Don't Fence Me In; Cool Water; Tumblin' Tumbleweeds

Faron Young: Wine Me Up; Sweet Dreams; Live Fast, Love Hard, Die Young; Hello Walls

Joe and Rose Maphis: Uncle Joe's Boogie; Dim Lights, Thick Smoke & Loud Music; Five Pound Hammer

Pee Wee King: Bonaparte's Retreat

Redd Stewart: Tennessee Waltz

Collins Sisters: Chattanooga Shoeshine Boy

Johnny Wright: Ashes of Love

Kitty Wells: I Can't Help Wondering; Honky Tonk Angels; Dust on the Bible; I Saw the Light

STEVIE RAY VAUGHAN AND DOUBLE TROUBLE / THE FABULOUS THUNDERBIRDS

Stevie Ray Vaughan: Pride and Joy; Texas Flood; Rude Mood; Voodoo Child; Love Struck Baby

The Fabulous Thunderbirds: Can't Tear It Up Enough; She's Tough; The Crawl; Full Time Lover; One's Too Many; I Believe I'm in Love

SEASON 10 (1985)

OAK RIDGE BOYS / BOB WILLS' ORIGINAL TEXAS PLAYBOYS

Oak Ridge Boys: You're the One; American Made; Love Song; Ozark Mountain Jubilee; Dancin'; Every Day; Elvira; Bobbie Sue; Make My Life

Bob Wills' Original Texas Playboys: Take Me Back to Tulsa; Milk Cow Blues; San Antonio Rose; Steel Guitar Rag; Faded Love; Right or Wrong; Stay All Night; Texas Playboys Theme Song

NEIL YOUNG AND THE INTERNATIONAL HARVESTERS

Are You Ready for the Country?; Field of Opportunity; Are There Any More Real Cowboys?; Let Your Fingers Do the Walkin'; Heart of Gold; Amber Jean; Roll Another Number; Comes a Time; Needle and the Damage Done; Helpless; California Sunset; Old Man; Get Back to the Country; Down by the River

EXILE / THE MAINES BROTHERS BAND WITH TERRY ALLEN

Exile: Give Me One More Chance; Coming Apart at the Seams; Woke Up in Love This Morning; Crazy for Your Love; Take Me Down; The Closer You Get; It Ain't Easy Being Easy; Kiss You All Over; Take Me to the River

The Maines Brothers Band: Crazy Wind; Chevy Van; Little Broken Pieces; Dixieland Rock; Amarillo Highway

Terry Allen: New Delhi Freight Train

WAYLON JENNINGS / BILLY JOE SHAVER

Waylon Jennings: Are You Ready for the Country?; Honky Tonk Heroes; Tongue-in-Mouth Song; People in Texas; Bob Wills Is Still the King; It's Not Supposed to Be That Way; Outlaw Bit; Long Ago & Far Away; Luckenbach, Texas; Storms Never Last; Good-Hearted Woman; Ain't Livin' Long Like This

Billy Joe Shaver: Ride Me Down Easy; Georgia on a Fast Train; Willie the Wandering Gypsy & Me; I'm Gonna Love You 'Til the Cows Come Home; Woman Is the Wonder of the World; Street Walkin' Woman; Bottom Dollar; I'm Just an Old Chunk of Coal

EDDIE RABBITT / TAMMY WYNETTE

Eddie Rabbitt: Driving My Life Away; Rocky Mountain Music; Drinkin'/Two Dollars; Step by Step; Burnin' Up; Best Year of My Life; Big Bertha; You & I; I Love a Rainy Night

Tammy Wynette: Welcome to My World; Another

Chance; Hits Medley: Apt. #9/I Don't Wanna Play House/D·I·V·O·R·C·E/Singing My Song; Rocky Top; Love the World Away; Gospel Medley: Amazing Grace/I'll Fly Away/Will the Circle Be Unbroken/I Saw The Light; Stand by Your Man

RICKY SKAGGS / THE JUDDS

Ricky Skaggs: Uncle Pen; Something in My Heart; Don't Cheat in Our Hometown; Heartbroke; You've Got a Lover; Honey Don't You Open That Door; Forked Dear; Beautiful Life; Highway 40 Blues

The Judds: Girls' Night Out; Had a Dream; Why Not Me?; A Mother's Smile; Mr. Pain; Drops of Water; Mama He's Crazy

GLEN CAMPBELL / EDDY RAVEN

Glen Campbell: Gentle on My Mind; Wichita Lineman; Galveston/Country Boy; By the Time I Get to Phoenix; Have a Little Faith; I Want to Be Wanted; Southern Nights; William Tell Overture

Eddy Raven: Another You; I Should've Called; Thank God for Kids; Sweet Mother Texas; Solo; Hard to Forget; California; She's Gonna Win Your Heart; Mexico/I Could Use Another You

JOE ELY / ERIC JOHNSON

Joe Ely: I Got My Hopes Up High; Cool Rockin' Loretta; Hard Livin'; Dallas; Lipstick; Musta Notta Gotta Lotta; Fingernails

Eric Johnson: Soulful Terrain; Bristol Shores; Tribute to Jerry Reed; I'm Finding You; Manhattan; Cliffs of Dover

THE DIRT BAND / STEVE GOODMAN TRIBUTE

The Nitty Gritty Dirt Band: High Horse; Shot Full of Love; Way Downtown; Face on the Cuttin' Room Floor; Long Hard Road; Bayou Jubilee/Battle of New Orleans

Pinkard and Bowden (with the Nitty Gritty Dirt Band): Don't Pet the Dog

Steve Goodman Tribute: John Prine Intro. #1; Talk Backwards; Elvis Imitators; City of New Orleans; Men Who Love Women Who Love Men; Banana Republic; My Old Man; If Your Life Was on Videotape

JUICE NEWTON / MARK GRAY

Juice Newton: Heartache; Angel of Morning; Love's Been a Little Bit Hard on Me; Little Love; Sweetest Thing I've Ever Known Is Loving You; Queen of Hearts

Mark Gray: Poor Boy; It Ain't Real; Medley: It Ain't Easy/The Closer You Get/Take Me Down/Second Hand Heart; Left Side of the Bed; Smooth Sailin'; This Ole Piano; Diamond in the Dust

LARRY GATLIN / NANCI GRIFFITH

Larry Gatlin and the Gatlin Brothers: Broken Lady; Nightime Magic; Love Is Just a Game; ABC; Houston; I've Done Enough Dying; Lady Takes the Cowboy; All the Gold; Hallelujah

Nanci Griffith: Robin Winter-Smith; There's a Light Beyond These Woods; Roseville Fair; Once in a Very Blue Moon; Last of the True Believers; West Texas Sun; Spin on a Red Brick Floor

FREDDIE POWERS WITH WILLIE NELSON AND MERLE HAGGARD / WHITEY SHAFER

Freddie Powers: Exactly Like You; Deed I Do

Merle Haggard: I Think I'll Just Stay Here and Drink; When Your Baby Starts Steppin'

Willie Nelson: Have I Stayed Away Too Long?; Why Do I Have to Choose

Willie Nelson and Merle Haggard: Columbus Stockade Blues

Whitey Shafer: Cool Ole Fool; That's the Way Love Goes; Where Are All the Girls I Used to Cheat With?; I Love

You Darlin' #4; When Things Are Good I'm Gonna Leave You; Guitar Pickin' Man; What Did You Expect Me to Do?; Does Fort Worth Ever Cross Your Mind?

EARL THOMAS CONLEY / VINCE GILL

Earl Thomas Conley: Your Love's on the Line; Fire & Smoke; Tell Me Why; Angel in Disguise; Heavenly Bodies; Holdin' Her and Lovin' You; Highway Home/Somewhere Between Right & Wrong

Vince Gill: True Love; Never Alone; Savannah; 'Til the Best Comes Along; Colder than Winter; Victim of Life's Circumstances

SEASON 11 (1986)

GARY MORRIS / SYLVIA

Gary Morris: Lasso the Moon; Draggin' the Lake for the Moon; I'll Never Stop Loving You; Anything Goes; Heaven's Hell Without You; Why Lady Why

Sylvia: Give 'Em Rhythm; Tumbleweed Medley; Snapshot; I Can't Help the Way I Feel /Cry Just a Little Bit; Falling in Love; Nobody

MEL TILLIS / THE GEEZINSLAWS

Mel Tillis: Stay All Night; New Patches; California Road; Texas on a Saturday Night; Good Woman Blues/I Got the Hoss; Who's Julie?; Detroit City

The Geezinslaws: Cheatin'; If You Think I'm Crazy Now. . .; Cryin'; Uncloudy Day; Dinosaur; Somewhere Over the Rainbow

GEORGE JONES / VERN GOSDIN

George Jones: No Show Jones; Once You've Had the Best; The Race Is On; Who's Gonna Fill Their Shoes?; Tennessee Whiskey; White Lightnin'; She's the Rock

Vern Gosdin: I Can Tell by the Way You Dance; Dream of Me; Dim Lights, Thick Smoke and Loud Music; Medley: Hangin' On/Yesterday's Gone/Mother Country Music/It Started All Over Again/Break My Mind; Gonna Be Movin' One of These Days; If You're Gonna Do Me Wrong (Do It Right); Way Down Deep

JOHN SCHNEIDER / SOUTHERN PACIFIC

John Schneider: Hollywood Heroes; Country Girls; I Don't Feel Much Like a Cowboy Tonight; I'm Gonna Leave You Tomorrow; One More Night; Who Cares; Just a Good Ole Boy; I've Been around Enough to Know; Trouble

Southern Pacific: Reno Bound; Thing about You; Someone's Gonna Love You Tonight; Perfect Stranger; Heroes; Pink Cadillac

TANYA TUCKER / SAWYER BROWN

Tanya Tucker: San Antonio Stroll; Make You Feel Alright; Rodeo Girls Don't Cry; Changes; Pecos Promenade; Delta Dawn; What's Your Mama's Name

Sawyer Brown: When Your Heart Goes Woo Woo Woo; Leona; Feel Like Me; Broken Candy; Betty's Being Bad; Used to Blue; Step That Step; Smokin' in the Rockies

MERLE HAGGARD AND THE STRANGERS WITH SPECIAL GUEST FREDDIE POWERS

Merle Haggard: Mama Tried; Friend in California; I Can't Believe I Ever Let You Go; Cold War; I Had a Beautiful Time; Silverthorn Mountain; My Mama's Prayers; The Okie from Muskogee's Goin' Home; There's a Pair of Blue Eyes Down in Texas; This Song Is for You; Take Me Back to Tulsa; I Knew the Moment I Lost You; Sally Let Your Bangs Hang Down; Fat Boy Rag; Gone with the Wind (The Big Picture Show); Looking for a Place to Fall Apart; Amber Waves; Okie from Muskogee

Freddie Powers: Texas and Oklahoma; I Don't Care Anymore; I Can't Wait 'Til I Get Home to My San Antonio Rose

ROCKIN' SIDNEY / THE NEVILLE BROTHERS

Rockin' Sidney: Let Me Take You to the Zydeco; Joe Pete Is in the Bed; Zydeco Shoes; No Good Woman; Jalapeño Lena; Dance and Show Off; Toot Toot
Neville Brothers: Midnight Key to the City; Shek-a-Na-Na; Money Back; Wake Up; Never Needed; Big Chief

ROGER McGUINN / KATE WOLF

Roger McGuinn: You Ain't Going Nowhere; I Wanna Grow Up to Be a Politician; Chestnut Mare; Mr. Spaceman; Mister Tambourine Man; Turn, Turn, Turn; Eight Miles High; So You Want to Be a Rock 'N' Roll Star
Kate Wolf: Friend of Mine; Carolina Pines; Love Still Remains; Like a River; Give Yourself to Love; One More Song

LOUISE MANDRELL / MEL McDANIEL

Louise Mandrell: Turn Me Loose; I'm Not Through Lovin' You Yet; Some Girls Have All the Luck; Maybe My Baby; Loving Proof; Saints/I Saw the Light/This Little Light; I Want to Say Yes; Dance 84 Medley; That's When the Music Takes Me
Mel McDaniel: Preachin'; Louisiana Saturday Night; Baby's Got Her Blue Jeans On; Let It Roll; Make It with the Blues; Big Ole Brew; Doctor's Orders; Mississippi, Roll on Forever; Nashville; Stand Up

GEORGE STRAIT / DWIGHT YOAKAM

George Strait: The Fireman; Does Fort Worth Ever Cross Your Mind; The Last Time, the First Time; Amarillo by Morning; Lefty's Gone; One Six Pack to Go; Marina Del Rey; You're Something Special to Me; The Chair; Dance Time in Texas
Dwight Yoakam: Hear Me Callin'; Guitars and Cadillacs; I'll Be Gone; It Won't Hurt; Miner's Prayer; Down the Road; Ring of Fire; Since I Started Drinkin' Again

LEGENDS OF BLUEGRASS

Jim and Jesse and the Virginia Boys: Blue Bonnet Lane; Then I'll Stop Going for You; East Bound Freight Train; North Wind
Mac Wiseman: Wabash Cannonball/I Wonder How the Old Folks Are; Jimmy Brown the Newsboy; Fat Boy Rag; Gone with the Wind (The Big Picture Show); Looking for a Place to Fall Apart; Amber Waves; Okie from Muskogee; 'Tis Sweet to Be Remembered
Ralph Stanley and the Clinch Mountain Boys: Swingin' the 9 Lb. Hammer; Sally Goodin'; I'm Willing to Try; If I Lose/The Kitten and the Cat
Bill Monroe and The Bluegrass Boys: Uncle Pen; The Old Brown County Jamboree Barn
Bill Monroe (with Jim and Jesse): I'm on My Way Back to the Old Home
Bill Monroe (with Mac Wiseman): Travelin' the Lonesome Road
Bill Monroe (with Ralph Stanley): Can't You Hear Me Callin'
Bill Monroe (with Ralph Stanley, Mac Wiseman, Jim and Jesse): Swing Low Sweet Chariot/I'll Fly Away/I Saw the Light

SONGWRITERS' SPECIAL

Gail Davies: Walls Comin' Down; I Will Never Cross That Line; Grandma's Song
Rosanne Cash: Seven Year Ache; Halfway House; My Old Man
Emmylou Harris: When I Was Yours; Diamond in My Crown
Emmylou Harris (with Pam Rose and Mary Ann Kennedy, Lacy J. Dalton, Gail Davies, Rosanne Cash): Sweetheart of the Rodeo
Lacy J. Dalton: Crazy Blue Eyes; Everybody Makes

Mistakes; Adios and Run
Mary Ann Kennedy and Pam Rose: Somebody Else's Fire; Love Like This

AUSTIN CITY LIMITS REUNION SPECIAL

Steve Fromholz: Late Night Neon Shadows
Asleep at the Wheel: Miles and Miles of Texas; You Ain't Livin'
Tracy Nelson: Drowning in Memories
St. Greezy's Wheel: Sideman's Party
Marcia Ball: That's Enough of That Stuff; Eugene
Rusty Wier: Don't It Make You Wanna Dance?
Jerry Jeff Walker: Redneck Mother; Stoney
Gary P. Nunn: London Homesick Blues
Gary P. Nunn, Jerry Jeff Walker, Rusty Wier, Marcia Ball, Tracy Nelson, Asleep at the Wheel, Steve Fromholz, St. Greezy's Wheel: Will the Circle Be Unbroken
The Lost Gonzo Band appeared with all of the above

SEASON 12 (1987)

RONNIE MILSAP

Don't You Know How Much I Love You; Any Day Now; Hits Medley: What a Difference You've Made/Daydreams/Back on My Mind Again/I Wouldn't Have Missed It for the World/It Was Almost Like a Song/Stand by My Woman Man/Pure Love/There Ain't No Gettin' Over Me/What a Difference You've Made; In Love; Heart of Rock 'n' Roll; Happy Birthday, Baby; Stranger in My House; Smokey Mountain Rain; Lost in the Fifties Tonight; Fifties Medley: Come Go with Me/Little Bitty Pretty One/Goodnight Sweetheart/Pa-Pa-Oo-Mow-Mow/Lucille

STEVE WARINER / RESTLESS HEART

Steve Wariner: Crazy; Lynda; There's Always a First Time; Crazy World; Life's Highway; Some Fools Never Learn; Lonely Women; Feels So Right
Restless Heart: She's Coming Home; That Rock Won't Roll; Boy's on a Roll; Till I Loved You; Heartbreak Kid; Let the Heartache Ride; We Owned This Town

BRENDA LEE / SWEETHEARTS OF THE RODEO

Brenda Lee: I'm So Hurt; Hits Medley: Fool #1/Too Many Rivers/Sweet Nothings; Kansas City; Yesterday Once More; Rock 'n' Roll Medley: Tutti Frutti/Johnny B. Goode/Only You/Rip It Up/Great Balls of Fire/Rockin' Robin/Can't Help Falling in Love with You; I'm Sorry; I'll Fly Away; Requests Medley: Cowgirl and the Dandy/Four Poster Bed/Break It to Me Gently
Sweethearts of the Rodeo: Midnight Girl; Since I Found You; Hey Doll Baby; Chains of Gold; I Can't Resist; Gotta Get Away; Paralyzed

LEON RUSSELL / STEVE EARLE

Leon Russell: Key to the Highway; I Believe to My Soul; Tightrope; Mystery Train; Lady Blue; Dixie Lullabye/Honky Tonk; A Song for You
Edgar Winter: Masquerade
Steve Earle: Guitar Town; Hillbilly Highway; Good Ol' Boy; My Old Friend the Blues; Some Day; Fearless Heart; Love You Too Much

FATS DOMINO

I'm Walkin'; Blueberry Hill; My Blue Heaven; Blue Monday; My Girl Josephine; I Want to Walk You Home; It Keeps Rainin' & Rainin'; I'm Ready; Poor Me; Walkin' to New Orleans; Shake, Rattle and Roll; I'm Gonna Be a Wheel; Ain't That a Shame; I Hear You Knockin'; Swanee River; Your Cheatin' Heart; When the Saints Go Marching In/Sentimental Journey

CHET ATKINS AND FRIENDS

Chet Atkins: Kentucky

Chet Atkins and Larry Carlton: Quiet Eyes; Untitled; Knucklebusters
Thom Bresh: Guitar Rag; Farewell My Bluebell; Guitar Breakdown/Change Your Way of Livin'; I'll See You in My Dreams
Chet Atkins, Johnny Gimble, and the Prairie Home Companion *Band:* Black & White Rag
Peter Ostroushko (with Johnny Gimble): Horizontal Hold; Mandopolin'
Butch Thompson: Charleston Rag; Alice Blue Gown
Chet Atkins, Johnny Gimble, Peter Ostroushko: Liberty/Pretty Palomino

RANDY TRAVIS / KATHY MATTEA

Randy Travis: My Heart Cracked; There's No Place Like Home; Diggin' Up Bones; 1982; Ain't No Use to Talk to You About Love; That's the Way Love Goes; Good-Hearted Woman; On the Other Hand; I Saw the Light
Kathy Mattea: Train of Memories; Walk the Way the Wind Blows; You're the Power; Little Bit; Leavin' West Virginia; Love at the Five & Dime; Evenin'

JOHNNY CASH WITH JUNE CARTER AND THE CARTER FAMILY

Johnny Cash: Folsom Prison Blues; Ring of Fire; Sunday Morning Coming Down; I Walk the Line; The Wall; Long Black Veil; Big River; Go Somewhere and Sing My Songs Again; Heavy Metal Don't Mean Rock 'N Roll To Me; Let 'Em Roll; The Ballad of Barbara; She's Not a Bad Woman
Johnny and Tommy Cash: Silver-Haired Daddy of Mine
Johnny Cash and June Carter: Where Did We Go Right?
Johnny Cash (with Carter Family): The Big Light; Wonderful Time Up There; I Walk the Line

SQUEEZEBOX SPECIAL

Ponty Bone and The Squeezetones: Galveston Island; Jumbo Shrimp; Frio City Polka; Papa Was Magic; Easy As Pie
Santiago Jimenez Jr.: Polka; Borracheras De Los Rayas; Viva Austin Polka
Queen Ida and The Bon Temps Band: Every Now and Then; Oh Negress; Cher Dulone; Willie on the Washboard; Tayo Zydeco; Tell Me
Queen Ida and The Bon Temps Band, Santiago Jimenez Jr., Ponty Bone and The Squeezetones,: Jambalaya

THE FABULOUS THUNDERBIRDS / OMAR AND THE HOWLERS

The Fabulous Thunderbirds: Look at That; Why Get Up?; Amnesia; How Do You Spell Love?; Wrap It Up; Tell Me; Tuff Enuff
Omar and the Howlers: Don't You Know?; Mississippi Hoodoo Man; You Ain't Foolin' Nobody; Border Girl; Hard Times in the Land of Plenty; Don't Rock Me the Wrong Way; She's a Woman; Call Me Rockin'

LYLE LOVETT / JUDY RODMAN

Lyle Lovett: Cowboy Man; God Will; This Old Porch; If I Were the Man; Wedding Song; She's No Lady; She's Hot to Go; Closing Time
Judy Rodman: I've Been Had by Love Before; Girls Ride Horses, Too; Until I Met You; I'll Be Your Baby Tonight; You're Gonna Miss Me When I'm Gone; She Thinks She'll Marry, But She Never Will; Sure Need Your Lovin'

RIDERS IN THE SKY / HOT RIZE

Riders in the Sky: Cowboy Jubilee; Back in the Saddle Again; Bobcat Bounce; Northern Lights; Here Comes the Santa Fe; Soon As the Round-Up's Through; I'm Going to Leave Old Texas Now; So Long, Saddle Pals
Hot Rize: Blue Night; Radio Boogie; Martha White Flour Theme; Nellie Kane; Your Light; Apache; Red Remembers; Always Late; Ole Dan Tucker; John Henry

MICHAEL MARTIN MURPHEY / MARTY STUART

Michael Martin Murphey: Rollin' Nowhere; Face in the Crowd; Long Line of Love; You're History; Worlds Apart; What's Forever For?; Texas Morning
Marty Stuart: Only Daddy That'll Walk the Line; Midnight Moonlight; The Shape I'm In; Busy Bee Cafe; Walkin' in Jerusalem; Arlene; If You Want My Love; Honky-Tonker

SEASON 13 (1988)

THE O'KANES / HIGHWAY 101

The O'Kanes: That's All Right, Mama; Can't Stop My Heart from Loving You; Oh Lonesome You; Bluegrass Blues; Daddies Need to Grow Up, Too; Tired of the Runnin'; One True Love
Highway 101: The Bed You Made for Me; One Step Closer; What Am I Worth Here on Earth?; Someday; Somewhere Tonight; Whiskey, If You Were a Woman; Good Goodbye

THE FORESTER SISTERS / THOM BRESH AND LANE BRODY

The Forester Sisters: Mama's Never Seen Those Eyes; That's What Your Love Does To Me; You Again; Say You Lied; I Fell in Love Again Last Night; Lonely Alone; Boogie Woogie Bugle Boy; Sometimes I Feel Like a Motherless Child; Just in Case
Thom Bresh and Lane Brody: Whatever Blows Your Dress Up; Medley: Chopin's Waltz No. 10/Malagueña/ The Entertainer/Cannonball Rag/Dueling Banjos; Not Your Heart; I'm Not Over You; Medley: I Walk the Line/Dang Me/Here You Come Again; The Yellow Rose of Texas

ROSANNE CASH / DESERT ROSE BAND

Rosanne Cash: Hold On; Runaway Train; Tennessee Flat Top Box; The Way We Make a Broken Heart; Rosie Strike Back; The Real Me; Green, Yellow, Red; I Don't Know Why
Desert Rose Band: Tell Me Baby; One Step Forward; Love Reunited; Time Between; He's Back and I'm Blue; Hello Trouble; Ashes of Love; Price of Love

REBA McENTIRE

Reba McEntire: Let the Music Lift You Up; Love Will Find Its Way; Have I Got a Deal for You; How Blue; Somebody Should Leave; Lookin' for a New Love Story; What Am I Gonna Do about You; I Don't Want to Mention Any Names; Mind Your Own Business; The Last One to Know; One Promise Too Late; Little Rock; Medley: I Will Sing Hallelujah/Reach Up; Whoever's in New England; Sweet Dreams

LARRY GATLIN AND THE GATLIN BROTHERS / HOLLY DUNN

Larry Gatlin: Alive and Well; Broken Lady; God Knows It Would Be You; Love of a Lifetime; Talkin' to the Moon; Houston; Swing Down; All the Gold in California; She Used to Be My Baby
Holly Dunn: Only When I Love; Burnin' Wheel; Love Someone Like Me; Why Wyoming?; Daddy's Hands; Strangers Again; Down in Louisiana

JOHN PRINE / ASLEEP AT THE WHEEL

John Prine: Let's Talk Dirty in Hawaiian; Grandpa Was a Carpenter; Aw, Heck; The Oldest Baby in the World; Blow Up Your TV; Souvenirs; Illegal Smile; Paradise
Asleep at the Wheel: Route 66; Blowin' Like a Bandit; I Want a New Drug; Choo Choo Ch' Boogie; Ain't Nobody Here But Us Chickens; The House of Blue Lights; Boogie Back to Texas

K.D. LANG AND THE RECLINES / FOSTER & LLOYD

k.d. lang: Don't Ever Leave Me Again; There You Go; Detour; I Never Promised You a Rose Garden; Hanky Panky; In Care of the Blues; Turn Me 'Round; Three Cigarettes
Foster and Lloyd: Turn Around; What Do You Want From Me This Time?; Crazy Over You; Sure Thing; Texas in 1880; Since I Found You; Hard to Say No

JERRY JEFF WALKER / LOUDON WAINWRIGHT III

Jerry Jeff Walker: Layin' My Life on the Line; Old Pick-Up Truck; I Found a Woman in Texas; The Dutchman; Last Night I Fell in Love; My Buddy; Contrary to Ordinary
Loudon Wainwright III: I'm Alright Without You; Your Mother and I; Mr. Guilty; Baby in the House; Dead Skunk; Hard Day on the Planet; Lullaby

LEO KOTTKE / SCHUYLER, KNOBLOCK AND BICKHARDT

Leo Kottke: Airproofing; Taxco Steps; You Can't Resist It; Julie's House; Pamela Brown; Skinflint
Schuyler, Knoblock and Bickhardt: Baby's Got a New Baby; How Can I Get to Her Heart; Long Line of Love; You Take Me Home; Feels Like Mississippi; Trenches of Love

RICKY VAN SHELTON / DARDEN SMITH

Ricky Van Shelton: Wild-Eyed Dream; Crime of Passion; Life Turned Her That Way; Somebody Lied; Baby I'm Ready; Don't We All Have the Right?; Gold Watch and Chain; Ultimately Fine
Darden Smith: Want You By My Side; Little Maggie; Love Me Like a Soldier; Day After Tomorrow; Talk to Me; God's Will; Clatter and Roll

RICKY SKAGGS / THE WHITES

Ricky Skaggs: San Antonio Rose; Crying My Heart Out Over You; I've Got a New Heartache; Cajun Moon; Uncle Pen; Love Can't Ever Get Better Than This; I'm Tired of Living This Old Way; Walkin' in Jerusalem; Country Boy
The Whites: Pins and Needles; Making Believe; Down in Louisana; You Put the Blue in Me; Hangin' Around; Follow the Leader; If It Ain't Love

THE DIRT BAND / NEW GRASS REVIVAL

The Dirt Band: Oh What a Love; We Have to Stand a Little Rain; Workin' Man; Fishin' in the Dark; Baby's Got a Hold on Me; American Dream; Rave On; Mr. Bojangles
New Grass Revival: Looking Past You; Love Someone Like Me; Revival; 7 x 7; Hold on to a Dream; Ain't That Peculiar; Metric Lips

GENE WATSON / MOE BANDY

Gene Watson: Speak Softly; Got No Reason For Going Home; 14-Karat Mind; You're Out Doing (What I'm Doin' Without); Raising Cain in Texas; Love in the Hot Afternoon; Memories to Burn; Everybody Needs a Hero; Farewell Party
Moe Bandy: You Can't Straddle the Fence Anymore; Bandy the Rodeo Clown; Too Old to Die Young; Hey Joe; Someday Soon; I'm Drunk Again; Cheatin' Situation; Americana; You Haven't Heard the Last of Me

BELLAMY BROTHERS / THE WAGONEERS

Bellamy Brothers: Old Hippie; Too Much Is Not Enough; Santa Fe; Kids of the Baby Boom; Redneck Girl; If I Said You Had a Beautiful Body (Would You Hold It Against Me); Let Your Love Flow
The Wagoneers: I Confess; Help Me Get Over Her; Please Don't Think I'm Guilty; I Want to Know Her Again; Stout and High; It'll Take Some Time; Lie and Say You Love Me Again; I Can't Stay; All Night

SEASON 14 (1989)

GEORGE STRAIT

Am I Blue?; Nobody in His Right Mind; The Fireman; Bigger Man Than Me; If You Ain't Lovin' You Ain't Livin'; Let's Fall to Pieces Together; My Heart Won't Wander Very Far from You; Take Me Back to Tulsa; Milk Cow Blues; All My Exes Live in Texas; Ocean-Front Property; Honky-Tonk Downstairs; Baby Blue; Amarillo by Morning; I Can't See Texas from Here; Lovesick Blues; You Look So Good in Love; Unwound

K.T. OSLIN / RODNEY CROWELL

K. T. Oslin: I'll Always Come Back; 'Round the Clock Lovin'; Hold Me; 80's Ladies; Younger Men; Do Ya?
Rodney Crowell: Stars on the Water; She's Crazy for Leavin'; Till I Can Gain Control Again; Above and Beyond; Highway 17; I Couldn't Leave You If I Tried; Old Pipeliner Blues

THE CHARLIE DANIELS BAND / GARY P. NUNN

The Charlie Daniels Band: Boogie Woogie Man; Ill Wind; Boogie Woogie Fiddle; Fiddle Jam; Waltz Across Texas; Texas; The South's Gonna Do It Again
Gary P. Nunn: London Homesick Blues; Pickup Truck Texas; Too Many Nights in a Roadhouse; What I Like about Texas; The Chili Song; London Homesick Blues (Reggae Version)

STANLEY JORDAN

Tropical Storm; All Blues; The Lady in My Life; Flying Home; Fundance; Angel; Swing Blues; Stairway to Heaven

EMMYLOU HARRIS / NANCI GRIFFITH AND THE BLUE MOON ORCHESTRA

Emmylou Harris: How High the Moon?; Who Will Sing for Me?; Coat of Many Colors; White Line; Wheels; Restless; Boulder to Birmingham; Jambalaya
Nanci Griffith: I Wish It Would Rain; From a Distance; Love Wore a Halo; Gulf Coast Highway; Listen to the Radio; Ford Econoline; Love at the Five and Dime

DELBERT McCLINTON / THE CRICKETS

Delbert McClinton: Shaky Ground; Lipstick Traces; Sandy Beaches; Let Me Be Your Lover; B-Movie; I Want to Love You; Givin' It Up for Your Love
The Crickets: Oh Boy; Three Piece; Your M-M-Memory; Early in the Morning; Well All Right; Brown-Eyed Handsome Man; Real Wild Child; T-Shirt; Peggy Sue; That'll Be the Day

DWIGHT YOAKAM / PATTY LOVELESS

Dwight Yoakam: Guitars, Cadillacs; What I Don't Know; Home of the Blues; A Thousand Miles; Little Ways; Red Dresses; Please, Please, Baby
Dwight Yoakam (with Buck Owens, Flaco Jimenez): Streets of Bakersfield
Patty Loveless: Timber, I'm Falling in Love; Lonely Side of Love; Don't Toss Us Away; I Won't Gamble With Your Love; The Blue Side of Town; If My Heart Had Windows; A Little Bit in Love

SONGWRITERS' SPECIAL

Harlan Howard: Bar Talk; I Wish I Felt This Way at Home; Forever and Ever, Amen; Somewhere Tonight
Don Schlitz: The Gambler; Dig Another Well
Kye Fleming: Don't Rush the River; She Must Be Beautiful
Mark Wright: Nobody Falls Like a Fool; Sunday Sundown
Mike Reid: Stranger in My House; Call Home; Old Folks

BUCK OWENS / THE GEEZINSLAWS

Buck Owens: Act Naturally; Together Again; Love's Gonna Live Here Again; Cryin' Time; I've Got a Tiger by the Tail; A-11; Hot Dog; Put a Quarter in the Jukebox; Johnny B. Goode
Buck Owens (with Dwight Yoakam): Under Your Spell Again
The Geezinslaws: Dr. Jake; On the Street Where You Live; Wedding Bells; Song for the Life; Take It to the Limit; Think About Livin'

TEXAS SHOWCASE WITH ROBERT EARL KEEN JR., ROSIE FLORES, TONY PEREZ, AND JIMMIE DALE GILMORE

Robert Earl Keen: This Old Porch; Mariano; Goin' Down in Style; I Would Change
Tony Perez: Bridge to Burn; Oh How I Love You; I Was Wrong and You Were Right; Things Will Get Better
Rosie Flores: Woman, Walk out the Door; You're the Reason; Drugstore Rock and Roll
Jimmie Dale Gilmore: Movin' On; Ramblin' Man; Don't Look for a Heartache

LEONARD COHEN

Manhattan; Tower of Song; Everybody Knows; Ain't No Cure; The Partisan; Joan of Arc; Jazz Police; If It Be Your Will; Take This Waltz

KEITH WHITLEY / SKIP EWING

Keith Whitley: Miami; Honky-Tonk Heart; Birmingham Turn-Around; I Never Go Around Mirrors; Quittin' Time; When You Say Nothing at All; Don't Close Your Eyes
Skip Ewing: Burnin' a Hole in My Heart; I Don't Have Far to Fall; Don't Mind If I Do; The Gospel According to Luke; It's You Again; The Coast of Colorado; The Door; That's the Way It Always Ends

TIMBUK 3 / ERIC JOHNSON

Timbuk 3: Dance Fever; Life Is Hard; The Future's So Bright I Gotta Wear Shades; Looking For Work; Sample the Dog; Wheel of Fortune; Will You Still Love Me When I'm Dead?; I Need You
Eric Johnson: Cliffs of Dover; Love or Confusion; Righteous; CW; Steve's Boogie; Desert Rose; Zap

JOHN HIATT AND THE GONERS / LOS LOBOS

John Hiatt: Memphis in the Meantime; Drive South; Paper Thin; Slow Turning; Have a Little Faith; This Thing Called Love
Los Lobos: Iguana; La Guacamaya; El Gusto; Carbina 30/30; Que Nadia Sepa Mi Sufrir; San Antonio; Estoy Sentado Aqui; Amarillas; La Pistola y El Corazon

SEASON 15 (1990)

GEORGE JONES / CARL PERKINS

George Jones: The Race Is On; Once You've Had the Best; I'm a One Woman Man; Tennessee Whiskey; The Right Left Hand; The Corvette Song; Who's Gonna Fill Their Shoes?; Yabba Dabba Doo; He Stopped Loving Her Today
Carl Perkins: Matchbox; Boppin' the Blues; Honey, Don't; Born to Rock; Gone, Gone, Gone; Birth of Rock & Roll; Blue Suede Shoes

MARCIA BALL / BEAUSOLEIL

Marcia Ball: Red Hot; La Ti Da; The Power of Love; Mobile; Mama's Cooking; Find Another Fool; How You Carry On
Beausoleil: Jungle a Moi; Hey, Baby Que Paso?; The Coffee Song; Johnny Can't Dance; KLFY Waltz; Cajun Groove; Reel de Dennis McGee

GARY MORRIS / MARY CHAPIN CARPENTER

Gary Morris: Bread and Water; Bring Him Home; Jaws of a Modern Romance; Chrome Plated Heart; These Days; Time Will Tell
Mary Chapin Carpenter: How Do; Down in Mary's Land; Something of a Dreamer; I Never Had It So Good; Slow Country Dance; This Shirt; Too Tired; The Twist and Shout

KATHY MATTEA / TISH HINOJOSA

Kathy Mattea: Burnin' Old Memories; Going, Gone; Life As We Knew It; Untold Stories; Where've You Been?; It's All Over Now; Timber; 18 Wheels
Tish Hinojosa: In the Night; The Voice of the Big Guitar; Till You Love Me Again; The Real West; Donde Voy; The West Side of Town; Love Is on Our Side

WAYLON JENNINGS / MARTY STUART

Waylon Jennings: I'm a Ramblin' Man; I May Be Used; Me and Bobbie McGee; Trouble Man; Mamas, Don't Let Your Babies Grow Up to Be Cowboys; You Asked Me To; Are You Sure Hank Done It This Way; Luckenbach, Texas; I've Always Been Crazy
Marty Stuart: Hillbilly Rock; Don't Leave Her Lonely Too Long; The Wild One; Cry, Cry, Cry; When the Sun Goes Down, I Go Crazy; I Want a Woman; Paint the Town

STEVIE RAY VAUGHAN AND DOUBLE TROUBLE / W.C. CLARK BLUES REVUE

Stevie Ray Vaughan: The House Is Rockin'; Leave My Little Girl Alone; Cold Shot; Crossfire; Riviera Paradise
W.C. Clark Blues Revue (with Stevie Ray Vaughan): Ad Lib Jam
W.C. Clark (with Jimmie Vaughan and Kim Wilson): Make My Guitar Talk
W.C. Clark (with Angela Strehli, Jimmie Vaughan, Kim Wilson, Denny Freeman): Big Town Playboy
W.C. Clark: Lover's Plea; Funny How Time Slips Away
W.C. Clark (with Angela Strehli, Jimmie Vaughan, Kim Wilson, Denny Freeman, Stevie Ray Vaughan, Lou Ann Barton): Take Me to the River

"WILL THE CIRCLE BE UNBROKEN"

The Nitty Gritty Dirt Band: You Ain't Goin' Nowhere; When It's Gone; The Bayou Jubilee
Dirt Band (with Helen and Anita Carter): Keep on the Sunny Side
New Grass Revival: Don't You Hear Jerusalem Moan?
Michael Martin Murphey: Lost River
Paulette Carlson: Lovin' on the Side
Vassar Clements: Bluesberry Hill
Vassar Clements (with Jimmy Martin): Grand Ole Opry Song; Sittin' on Top of the World
John Denver: So It Goes; Take Me Home Country Roads
Dirt Band (with John Denver, Vassar Clements, Jimmy Martin, Paulette Carlson, Michaell Martin Murphy, New Grass Revival, Randy Scruggs, Helen and Anita Carter): Will the Circle Be Unbroken

LYLE LOVETT AND HIS LARGE BAND

Cookin' at the Continental; Here I Am; Cryin' Shame; I Know You Know; Good Intentions; If I Had a Boat; L.A. County; Skinny Legs; Nobody Knows Me; The Wedding Song; What Do You Do?; Wild Women Don't Have the Blues; M·O·N·E·Y; Hot to Go

MICHELLE SHOCKED / STRENGTH IN NUMBERS

Michelle Shocked: Memories of East Texas; The L & N Don't Stop Here Anymore; Penny Evans; Grafitti Limbo; Anchorage; Titanic; Strawberry Jam
Strength in Numbers: Duke and Cookie; One Winter's Night; Slopes; Blue Men of the Sahara

LUCINDA WILLIAMS / GUY CLARK

Lucinda Williams: I Just Want to See You So Bad; Passionate Kisses; Changed the Locks; Crescent City; Price to Pay; Disgusted; Am I Too Blue?; Big Red Sun Blues
Guy Clark: Texas 1947; Old Friends; Come from the Heart; Desperados Waiting for a Train; Doctor, Good Doctor; Better Days; Home-Grown Tomatoes

GARTH BROOKS / SHENANDOAH

Garth Brooks: Not Counting You; Much Too Young (To Feel This Damn Old); Alabama Clay; If Tomorrow Never Comes; Nobody Gets Off in This Town; Every Time That It Rains; The Dance
Shenandoah: Sunday in the South; Two Dozen Roses; She Doesn't Cry Anymore; Huggin' the Shoulder; See If I Care; Mama Knows; The Church on Cumberland Road

JAMES McMURTRY / SWEETHEARTS OF THE RODEO

James McMurtry: Painting by Numbers; Terry; Dancing in Starlight; I'm Not from Here; Too Long in the Wasteland; Talkin' at the Texaco
Sweethearts of the Rodeo: Don't Wake Me Up; Blue to the Bone; What It Does to Me; Uphill All the Way; You Look at Love; This Heart; Como Se Dice?; Satisfy You

LORRIE MORGAN / STEVE WARINER

Lorrie Morgan: Love of Another Kind; Out of Your Shoes; Lone Star State of Mind; He Talks to Me; Five Minutes; Don't Close Your Eyes; Faithfully
Steve Wariner: I Got Dreams; Domino Theory of Love; Arkansas; L·O·V·E, Love; While I'm Holding You Tonight; Your Love Is a Precious Thing; Midnight Fire; Life's Highway

SEASON 16 (1991)

RICKY VAN SHELTON / KELLY WILLIS

Ricky Van Shelton: I've Cried My Last Tear for You; Somebody Lied; Hole in My Pocket; Statue of a Fool; Crime of Passion; I Meant Every Word He Said; Rock Around with Ollie Vee; True Love Ways; Pretty Woman
Kelly Willis: River of Love; Hearts in Trouble; Letter of Love; Everybody's Talking; Standin' by the River; Looking for Someone Like You; You Won't Have Me; Too Much to Ask; Well-Traveled Love

SARA HICKMAN / KENNEDY-ROSE

Sara Hickman: Last Night Was a Big Rain; I Couldn't Help Myself; The Very Thing; Train Song; Simply
Kennedy-Rose: Love Like This; The Only Chain; Love Is the Healer; Leavin' Line; Western Fires

SHELBY LYNNE / WILLIE NELSON

Shelby Lynne: Lonely Weekends; Tough All Over; I Walk the Line; I'm Confessin'; He Stopped Loving Her Today; The Hurtin' Side; Night Life
Willie Nelson: On the Road Again; Medley: Funny How Time Slips Away/Crazy/Night Life; There's Nothing I Can Do About It Now; Blue Eyes Crying in the Rain; Always on My Mind; Medley: Will the Circle Be Unbroken/I'll Fly Away; Amnesia; Valentine; Milk Cow Blues

ALAN JACKSON / MARK COLLIE

Alan Jackson: Dog River Blues; Home; Blue-Blooded Woman; Midnight in Montgomery; Just Playin' Possum; Wanted; Chasin' That Neon Rainbow; Here in the Real World
Mark Collie: Bound to Ramble; Good News and the Bad News; Where There's Smoke You'll Find My Old Flame; Something with a Ring to It; Let Her Go; What I Wouldn't Give; Another Old Soldier; Hardin County Line

COWBOY JUNKIES / WALTER HYATT

Cowboy Junkies: Blue Moon Revisited; Cause Cheap Is How I Feel; Rock and Bird; To Love Is to Bury; Shining Moon; Misguided Angel
Walter Hyatt: This Time Lucille; Tell Me, Baby; King Tears; Blind Love Blues; Outside Looking Out; Que Reste-T-Il De Nos Amours; In November

TEXAS TORNADOS / McBRIDE AND THE RIDE

Texas Tornados: (Hey Baby) Que Paso?; A Man Can Cry; Viva Seguin; San Antonio; Who Were You Thinking Of?; Before the Next Teardrop Falls; She's About a Mover; 96 Tears
McBride and the Ride: Turn to Blue; Nobody's Fool; Ain't No Big Deal; Don't Be Mean to Me If You Don't Mean to Be; Clyde; Felicia; Burnin' Up the Road

MERLE HAGGARD / MASTERS OF BLUEGRASS

Merle Haggard: Honky-Tonk Nightime Man; Big City; That's the Way Love Goes; Stingaree; Under the Bridge; Sometimes I Dream; Workingman Blues; Are the Good Times Really Over for Good; Just Between the Two of Us; If We Make It Through December; Ida Red
Masters of Bluegrass: Night Runner; Dance with Me, Kenny; Lickety-Split; The Saturday Night Fish Fry; Fireball

CHET ATKINS WITH JOHNNY GIMBLE AND THE CLUSTER PLUCKERS

Folsom Prison Blues; Sunrise; Yakety Sax; Mr. Bojangles; Blue Angel; Tahitian Skies; Cascade; I Still Can't Say Good Bye; Steel Guitar Rag
Cluster Pluckers: Before I'm Fool Enough; Nagasaki; Indian Springs; My Home's Across the Blue Ridge Mountains; As Long As There's You; Ain't Misbehavin'; Wayfarin' Stranger; The Next Time I'm in Town

THE ROBERT CRAY BAND / BUDDY GUY

Robert Cray: The Forecast; Bouncin' Back; Right Next Door Because of Me; Consequences; Walk Around Time; Labour of Love
Buddy Guy: Sweet Home Chicago; Mary Had a Little Lamb; Leave My Girl Alone
Stevie Ray Vaughan (Tribute): Tight Rope; Tick Tock

SHAWN COLVIN / JOHN HAMMOND

Shawn Colvin: Another Long One; Riding Shotgun Down the Avalanche; Steady On; Cry Like an Angel; Roadrunner Theme Song; Diamond in the Rough; The Dead of the Night
John Hammond: Ride Till I Die; Dreamy-Eyed Gal; Walking Blues; Come on in My Kitchen; Mother-in-Law Blues; Kind-Hearted Woman

LITTLE FEAT

Hate to Lose Your Lovin'; Medley: That's Her, She's Mine/Fat Man in the Bathtub; Down on the Farm; Sailin' Shoes; 44; Rad Gumbo; Oh, Atlanta; Willin'; Old Folks; Texas Twister; Let It Roll

JOE ELY / FOSTER AND LLOYD

Joe Ely: My Eyes Got Lucky; Rich Man, Poor Man; Honky-Tonk Masquerade; Row of Dominoes; For Your Love; Settle for Love
Foster and Lloyd: Is It Love?; Fair Share; She Knows What She Wants; Faster & Louder; Texas in 1880; Suzette; Crazy Over You; Whole Lotta Love

A SALUTE TO THE COWBOY

Michael Martin Murphey: Cowboy Logic; Medley: I Ride An Old Paint/Whoopee-Ti-Yi-Yo; Tyin' Knots; Red River Valley; Streets of Laredo; Goodbye Ol' Paint; The Yellow Rose of Texas
Riders in the Sky: Back on Those Texas Plains; Jingle, Jangle, Jingle; What Would I Do Without You?; Ride, Cowboy, Ride; When Payday Rolls Around
Waddie Mitchell: Poem: A Story with a Moral
Don Edwards: The Cowboy's Song
Sons of the San Joaquin: Medley: Save That Bay for Me/When the Prairie Sun Climbs Out of the Hay; The Great American Cowboy

SEASON 17 (1992)

SONGWRITERS' SPECIAL

Nanci Griffith: It's a Hard Life Wherever You Go; Late Night Grande Hotel; Listen to the Radio
Mary Chapin Carpenter: Never Had It So Good; I Am a Town; I Feel Lucky
Julie Gold: From a Distance; Heaven Is in Your Eyes; Temporary Worker
Indigo Girls: Fare Thee Well; Jonas Ezekial
Nanci Griffith (with Mary Chapin Carpenter, Julie Gold, Indigo Girls): Got No Expectations

LOS LOBOS / C.J. CHENIER

Los Lobos: One Time, One Night; Emily; I Walk Alone; Can't Understand; Angel Dance; Mexican Americano; Don't Worry Baby
C. J. Chenier: Just Like a Woman; I'm Coming Home; Bo-Legged Woman; Louisiana Two-Step; She's My Woman; My Negress

DAN HICKS AND THE HOT LICKS REVISITED PLUS THE ACOUSTIC WARRIORS

Dan Hicks and the Hot Licks: Canned Music; Where's the Money?; I Feel Like Singing; Milk-Shakin' Mama; I Scare Myself; Along Come a Viper; Payday Blues; Evenin' Breeze
Dan Hicks' Acoustic Warriors: Up, Up, Up; Shootin' Straight; Willie; Doin' It

VINCE GILL / ALISON KRAUSS AND UNION STATION

Vince Gill: Rita Ballou; Never Knew Lonely; Liza Jane; Look at Us; Ridin' the Rodeo; A Sight for Sore Eyes; Oklahoma Borderline
Alison Krauss and Union Station: Steel Rails; Another Night; The Carroll County Blues; I've Got That Old Feelin'; Cluck, Old Hen; Lose Again; It Won't Work This Time; Heartstrings; Dark Skies

ALBERT COLLINS / DANNY GATTON

Albert Collins: Iceman; Lights Are On, Nobody's Home; Head Rag; Travelin' South
Danny Gatton: Funky Mama; Medley: Mystery Train/My Baby Left Me/That's All Right Mama; Red Label; Honky-Tonkin' Country Girl

K.T. OSLIN

I'll Always Come Back; This Woman; Come Next Monday; Mary & Willie; New Way Home; Cornell Crawford; Get Back in the Saddle One More Time; 80's Ladies; Hold Me; Younger Men; Do Ya?

TRAVIS TRITT / HOLLY DUNN

Travis Tritt: I'm Gonna Be Somebody; The Whiskey Ain't Working Anymore; Anymore; Rambler; Help Me Hold On; Here's a Quarter; Put Some Drive in Your Country
Holly Dunn: Heart Full of Love; Let Go; Love Someone Like Me; There Goes My Heart Again; Daddy's Hands; Walkin' After Midnight; No One Takes the Train Anymore; You Really Had Me Going

THE SUBDUDES / BELA FLECK AND THE FLECKTONES

The Subdudes: Push and Shove; Light in Your Eyes; Tell Me What's Wrong; Late at Night; Bye, Bye
Bela Fleck and the Flecktones: Blu-Bop; True North; The Yee-Haw Factor; Flight of the Cosmic Hippo; Tell It to the Governor

TRISHA YEARWOOD / HAL KETCHUM

Trisha Yearwood: That's What I Like About You; Going to Work; Victim of the Game; You Say You Will, But You Never Do; Like We Never Had a Broken Heart; She's in Love with the Boy; Lonesome Dove
Hal Ketchum: I Know Where Love Lives; Small Town Saturday Night; Old Soldiers; The Love or the Wine; I Miss Mary; Past the Point of Rescue; Baby I'm Blue

ROSANNE CASH WITH SPECIAL GUESTS

Rosanne Cash: Halfway House; What We Really Want; Seven Year Ache; Lonely Hearts Brigade
Rosanne Cash (with Bruce Cockburn, Lucinda Williams): Don't Think Twice, It's Alright
Bruce Cockburn: See How I Miss You; Rocket Launcher; Kit Carson; A Dream Like Mine
Lucinda Williams: Something About What Happens When We Talk; Little Angel, Little Brother; Hot Blood; Happy Woman Blues

KEVIN WELCH / WILL T. MASSEY

Kevin Welch: Happy Ever After; I Look For You; True Love Never Dies; Lost Highway; Early Summer Rain; Me and Billy the Kid
Will T. Massey: You Take the Town; Lose Control; Midnight All Night Long; I Ain't Here; Barbed Wire Town; Bravery to Weep; Send Up the Smoke

DOUG STONE / MAURA O'CONNELL

Doug Stone: Jukebox; These Lips Don't Know How to Say Goodbye; We Always Agree on Love; Different Light; Overnight Male; I Thought It Was You; Right to Remain Silent; Pine Box
Maura O'Connell: Summer Fly; When Your Heart Is Weak; Western Highway; Helpless Heart; An Irish Blues; Crazy Dreams

JOHN PRINE / JIMMIE DALE GILMORE

John Prine: You Got Gold; Daddy's Little Pumpkin; Big Old Goofy World; My Old Man; Jesus: The Missing Years; Everything Is Cool
Jimmie Dale Gilmore: These Blues; My Mind Has a Mind of Its Own; Story of You; You've Got to Go to Sleep Alone; After Awhile; Wishin' for You; Midnight Train

SEASON 18 (1993)

MICHAEL NESMITH / EMMYLOU HARRIS AND THE NASH RAMBLERS

Michael Nesmith: Joanne; Laugh Kills Lonesome; Yellow Butterfly; Twilight on the Trail; Rio
Emmylou Harris: Roses in the Snow; Hello, Stranger; Sweet Dreams; Walls of Time; Get Up, John; Making Believe; Luxury Liner

MARC COHN / LEO KOTTKE

Marc Cohn: Walking in Memphis; Ghost Train; Dig Down Deep; Fever; Things We've Handed Down
Leo Kottke: Medley: Available Space/June Bug; Lying in the Arms of Mary; Oddball; Woody Woodpecker; Jesus Maria; Jack Gets Up; Times 12

ASLEEP AT THE WHEEL / RIDERS IN THE SKY

Asleep at the Wheel: Boogie Back to Texas; Boot Scootin' Boogie; Route 66; Fat Boy Rag; Corrine Corrina; Misery; Roly Poly
Riders in the Sky: (There's a) Blue Sky Way Out Yonder; How Does He Yodel?; Palindrome; Miss Molly; Ridin'

Down the Canyon; Buffalo Gals; The Linerider; Surfin' U.S.A.; Sky Ball Paint; So Long, Saddle Pals

PAM TILLIS / MIKE REID

Pam Tillis: Rough and Tumble Heart; Do You Know Where Your Man Is?; Melancholy Child; Shake the Sugar Tree; Let That Pony Run; Cleopatra; Maybe It Was Memphis
Mike Reid: Walk on Faith; This Road; I Can't Make You Love Me; Call Home; It Still Rains in Memphis

LYLE LOVETT AND HIS LARGE BAND / DR. JOHN

Lyle Lovett: Church; She Makes Me Feel Good; She's Leaving Me; All My Love Is Gone; Since the Last Time
Dr. John: Goin' Back to New Orleans; Milneburg Joys; Since I Fell for You; Save the Bones for Henry Jones, 'Cause Henry Don't Eat No Meat; Such a Night; Cupucine

DELBERT McCLINTON / LEE ROY PARNELL

Delbert McClinton: I'm with You; Never Been Rocked Enough; Can I Change My Mind?; Why Me?; Stir It Up; Have a Little Faith in Me; Roll the Dice
Lee Roy Parnell: What Kind of Fool?; Love Without Mercy; 50/50; I'm Broke Again; The Rock; Road Scholar

MARY CHAPIN CARPENTER

You Never Had It So Good; You Win Again; Going Out Tonight; How Do; Rhythm of the Blues; Passionate Kisses; Read My Lips; Only a Dream; Come On Come On; Twist & Shout; He Thinks He'll Keep Her; Moon & St. Christopher; I Feel Lucky

GARRISON KEILLOR AND THE HOPEFUL GOSPEL QUARTET WITH CHET ATKINS AND JOHNNY GIMBLE

Garrison Keillor and the Hopeful Gospel Quartet: Move to the Top of the Mountain; He Knows; Brownie and Pete; Sweet, Sweet Corn; Rollin' & Ramblin'; Stay on the Right Side; Jessie Polka; The Lord Will Make a Way Somehow; That's the Way Love Goes; Sweet Hour of Prayer/His Eye Is on the Sparrow; Now the Day Is Over/Let the Light from the Lighthouse Shine on Me; Couldn't Keep It to Myself

TRACY LAWRENCE / SUZY BOGGUSS

Tracy Lawrence: Honky-Tonk Till My Heart's Content; Runnin' Behind; Somebody Paints the Wall; Honky-Tonk Heart; Paris, Tennessee; Today's Lonely Fool; Heaven Has a Honky-Tonk; Sticks and Stones
Suzy Bogguss: Someday Soon; Aces; Save Yourself; Other Side of the Hill; Outbound Plane; Letting Go; Drive South

KATHY MATTEA / GREAT PLAINS

Kathy Mattea: Listen to the Radio; Time Passes By; Lonesome Standard Time; Knee Deep in a River; Lonely at the Bottom; Amarillo; Seeds
Great Plains: Faster Gun; Southern Belle; Down on Broadway; Take Me to Topeka; Rodeo Drive; Tobacco Road

JOHN GORKA / STEVE FORBERT

John Gorka: Where the Bottles Break; Good; The Gypsy Life; Houses in the Fields; Branching Out; Gravyland
Steve Forbert: Get Well Soon; Mexico; American in Me; Complications; Change in the Weather; Romeo's Tune; You Cannot Win If You Do Not Play

TAJ MAHAL / TISH HINOJOSA

Taj Mahal: Mailbox Blues; Queen Bee; Blues with a Feelin'; Fishin' Blues; Freight Train
Tish Hinojosa: Bandera Del Sol; Something in the Rain; Every Word; Saying You Will; Frida; Cumbia, Polka y Mas

---

SEASON 19 (1994)

ROSANNE CASH / CARLENE CARTER

Rosanne Cash: The Wheel; Seventh Avenue; I'll Change for You; Crescent City; Sleeping in Paris; Man Smart, Woman Smarter
Carlene Carter: Come On Back; Love You Because I Want To; Me and the Wildwood Rose; Cry; Every Little Thing; I Fell in Love

HAL KETCHUM / KELLY WILLIS

Hal Ketchum: Sure Love; 'Til the Coast Is Clear; Walk Away; The Morning Sun; That's What I Get; I Miss My Mary Tonight; She's a Woman
Kelly Willis: Whatever Way the Wind Blows; Take It Out on You; Little Honey; Get Real; Heaven's Just a Sin Away; World Without You; Fist City

ZACHARY RICHARD / DIRTY DOZEN BRASS BAND

Zachary Richard: Who Stole My Monkey?; Come on Sheila; Zydeco Jump; Sunset on Louisianne; Crawfish; Dancing at Double D's
Dirty Dozen Brass Band: Voodoo; Use Your Brain; Sidewalk Blues; Kansas City Stomp; My Feet Can't Fail Me Now

BRUCE HORNSBY / JOHN MAYALL AND THE BLUESBREAKERS

Bruce Hornsby: Long Tall Cool One; Valley Road; Fields of Gray; Another Day
John Mayall: Wake Up Call; The Bear; I Could Cry; Mail Order Mystics

JOHN ANDERSON / BILLY DEAN

John Anderson: Money in the Bank; I Fell in the Water; When It Comes to You; Straight Tequila Night; I've Got It Made; Wild and Blue; Swingin'; Seminole Wind
Billy Dean: Fire in the Dark; Somewhere in My Broken Heart; We Just Disagree; Wanna Take Care of You; If There Hadn't Been You; Billy the Kid

PATTY LOVELESS / MONTE WARDEN

Patty Loveless: Blue Side of Town; Can't Stop Myself from Loving You; You Will; Love Builds the Bridges; How Can I Help You Say Goodbye?; Nothin' But the Wheel; Blame It on Your Heart
Monte Warden: All I Want Is You; Give My Heart a Break; Just to Hear Your Voice; Ain't It Just Like Me; Feel Better; Car Seat
Monte Warden (with Kelly Willis): The Only One

THE BEST OF MERLE HAGGARD: A RETROSPECTIVE

Silver Wings; A Workin' Man Can't Get Nowhere Today; The Fugitive; Sing Me Back Home; San Antonio Rose; The Way I Am; Okie from Muskogee; Misery and Gin; I Think I'll Just Stay Here and Drink; Half a Man; Mama Tried; Cold War; Gone with the Wind; Are the Good Times Really Over?; Big City; If We Make It Through December; Workingman's Blues

SONGWRITERS' SPECIAL

Willie Nelson: Pick Up the Tempo; Sad Songs and Waltzes; I Never Cared for You; Crazy; Worse Things Than Being Alone; Till I Gain Control Again
Willie Nelson (with Lyle Lovett, Rodney Crowell): Stay All Night, Stay a Little Longer
Rodney Crowell: She's Crazy for Leaving; Long, Hard Road; Stuff That Works; I Still Can't Believe You're Gone
Lyle Lovett: Sonja; That's Right, You're Not from Texas; Come On, Baby; Nobody Knows Me

---

JOAN BAEZ / RORY BLOCK

Joan Baez: Love Is Just a Four-Letter Word; Isaac and Abraham; House of the Rising Sun; Forever Young; Welcome Me; I'm with You
Rory Block: Hawkins Blues; Big Road Blues; Terraplane Blues; Got to Shine; Lovin' Whiskey; Silver Wings; Mama's Blues

DIAMOND RIO / JOHN MICHAEL MONTGOMERY

Diamond Rio: Nowhere Bound; Mama, Don't Forget to Pray for Me; Medley: Cattle Call/El Paso/Tumblin' Tumbleweed/They Call the Wind Mariah; Way Out There; Norma Jean Riley; Lyin' Eyes
John Michael Montgomery: Friday at Five; Beers and Bones; I Love the Way You Love Me; Kick It Up; Be My Baby Tonight; I Swear; Life's a Dance

SUZANNE VEGA / DARDEN SMITH

Suzanne Vega: Fat Man and Dancing Girl; If You Were in My Movie; Blood Sings; Luka; Men in a War; Gypsy
Darden Smith: Little Victories; Dream's a Dream; Precious Time; Hole in the River; The Levee Song; Loving Arms

LEONARD COHEN / CHRISTINE ALBERT WITH PAUL GLASSE

Leonard Cohen: The Future; Democracy; Sisters of Mercy; There Is a War
Christine Albert: Boat Starts Rockin'; Take It to the Heart
Christine Albert (with Jimmy La Fave): Come Away with Me
Paul Glasse: Paper Bag Rag; Until a Better Moment; Air Mail Special

JOHN HIATT AND THE GUILTY DOGS / RADNEY FOSTER WITH MARY CHAPIN CARPENTER

John Hiatt: Icy Blue Heart; Loving a Hurricane; Buffalo River Home; Tennessee Plates; Slow Turning; Perfectly Good Guitar
Radney Foster: Just Call Me Lonesome; Running Kind; Closing Time; Hammer and Nails
Radney Foster (with Mary Chapin Carpenter): Nobody Wins

SEASON 20 (1995)

VINCE GILL / JUNIOR BROWN

Vince Gill: Victim of Life's Circumstances; Tryin to Get Over You; What the Cowgirls Do; Whenever You Come Around; Take Your Memory with You When You Go; I Still Believe in You; Last Chance
Junior Brown: Too Many Nights in a Roadhouse; Party Lights; Highway Patrol; The Gal from Oklahoma; Sugar Foot Rag

NANCI GRIFFITH / IRIS DeMENT

Nanci Griffith: Say It Isn't So; Flyer; Time of Inconvenience; These Days; Nobody's Angel; It's a Hard Life Wherever You Go; This Heart
Iris DeMent: Sweet Is the Melody; Mama's Opry; Our Town; Hotter than Mojave in My Heart; God May Forgive You; My Life

BLUEGRASS SPECIAL WITH RICKY SKAGGS, RALPH STANLEY, AND LARRY SPARKS

Larry Sparks: Takin' a Slow Train; Blue Virginia Blues; Kentucky Chimes; Dark Hollow
Ralph Stanley: John Henry; I Only Exist; I'll Answer the Call; Medley: Mule to Ride/Rocky Island/Shout Little Luly
Ralph Stanley (with Ricky Skaggs and Larry Sparks): Lonesome River; Angels Are Singin'; I'm Ready to Go

Ricky Skaggs: How Mountain Girls Can Love; Little Girl of Mine; Cry, Cry, Darlin'; Wheel Hoss

ALAN JACKSON
Don't Rock the Jukebox; Neon Rainbow; Mind Your Own Business; Living on Love; Trying Not to Love You; Summertime Blues; What Kind of Man; Good Year for the Roses; I'm in Love with You Baby and I Don't Even Know Your Name; She's Got the Rhythm; Midnight in Montgomery; Chattahoochee; Mercury Blues

THE NEVILLE BROTHERS / JIMMIE VAUGHAN AND THE TILT-A-WHIRL BAND
The Neville Brothers: Yellow Moon; Sands of Time; The Grand Tour; Medley: Brother John/Iko Iko/Jambalaya; Congo Square
Jimmie Vaughan: Just Like Putty; Flamenco Dancer; Six Strings Down; Boom Bapa Boom

THE MAVERICKS / ROBERT EARL KEEN
The Mavericks: There Goes My Heart; The Things You Said to Me; I Should Have Been True; Pretend; All That Heaven Will Allow; What a Cryin' Shame
Robert Earl Keen: Whenever Kindness Fails; Corpus Christi Bay; Merry Christmas from the Family; I'm Comin' Home; So I Can Take My Rest; The Road Goes on Forever

TEJANO MUSIC SPECIAL
Freddy Fender (with Flaco Jimenez and Joel Nava): Before the Next Teardrop Falls
Freddy Fender: Mexican Rose
Joel Nava: Give Me All the Pieces; Ella
Rick Orozco: You Fell in Love But Not with Me; Living Without You's Been Good for Me
Flaco Jimenez: El Pesudo; Que Lo Sepan Todos; Que Problemas
Flaco Jimenez (with Freddy Fender, Rick Orozco, and Joel Nava): Volver Volver
La Diferenzia: Si Lo Quieres; Tu Eres; Alguien Especial; Linda Chaparrita

TAMMY WYNETTE / RICK TREVIÑO
Tammy Wynette: Your Good Girl's Gonna Go Bad; D·I·V·O·R·C·E; Singing My Song; That's the Way It Could Have Been; Till I Can Make It on My Own; Medley: Apartment #9/I Don't Want to Play House; What Do They Know; Stand by Your Man
Rick Treviño: I Wanna Girl in a Pickup Truck; Honky-Tonk Crowd; Looking for the Light; Just Enough Rope; Doctor Time; She Can't Say I Didn't Cry; Fingernails

MARK CHESNUTT / TRACY BYRD
Mark Chesnutt: Blame It on Texas; Big D; Just Wanted You to Know; Goodbye Comes Hard for Me; Gonna Get a Life; Sure Is Monday; Too Cold at Home
Tracy Byrd: First Step; Holdin' Heaven; Lifestyles of the Not So Rich & Famous; Keeper of the Stars; Medley: Lone Star Beer/Green Snakes; No Ordinary Man; Watermelon Crawl

SHAWN COLVIN / BILL MILLER
Shawn Colvin: Kill the Messenger; Heart of Saturday Night; Object of My Affection; Window to the World; One Cool Remove; Round of Blues
Bill Miller: River of Time; Tumbleweed; The Eagle Must Be Free; Let the River Flow; Turn Me Around

DAVID BALL / GARY P. NUNN WITH SPECIAL GUESTS JIM HENSON'S MUPPETS
David Ball: Pick Me Up on Your Way Down; What Do You Want with His Love?; Honky Tonk Healin'; Thinkin' Problem; When the Thought of You Catches Up with Me; Look What Followed Me Home; Wild Side of Life
Gary P. Nunn: Macho Man; Terlingua Sky; Corpus Christi; Roadtrip; London Homesick Blues

STEVIE RAY VAUGHAN: A RETROSPECTIVE
Pride and Joy; Texas Flood; Voodoo Chile (Slight Return); The House Is Rockin'; Tightrope; Leave My Girl Alone; Cold Shot; Cross Fire; Riviera Paradise; Tick Tock

LYLE LOVETT AND HIS LARGE BAND
Just the Morning; Penguins; L.A. to the Left; Good-Bye to Carolina; Ain't It Something?; Record Lady; That's Right (You're Not from Texas); Blues for Dixie; I Think You Know What I Mean; I've Got the Blues; Creeps Like Me; The Fat Girl; Old Friend; Church

SEASON 21 (1996)

ALISON KRAUSS / MERLE HAGGARD
Alison Krauss: Everytime You Say Goodbye; Remember Me Love in Your Prayer; Little Liza Jane; Baby Now That I've Found You; Ghost in This House; In the Palm of Your Hand; Oh Atlanta; I Will
Merle Haggard: Sin City Blues; No Time to Cry; They're Tearin' the Labor Camps Down; Farmer's Daughter; (Today) I Started Loving You Again; Silver Wings; Okie from Muskogee

JOHN PRINE / TODD SNIDER
John Prine: Picture Show; Ain't Hurtin' Nobody; Quit Hollerin' at Me; We Are the Lonely; Lake Marie
Todd Snider: Somebody's Coming; Talkin' Seattle Blues; Late Last Night; This Land Is Our Land; Alright Guy

ASLEEP AT THE WHEEL'S 25TH ANNIVERSARY
Asleep at the Wheel: Take Me Back to Tulsa; Miles and Miles of Texas; Bump Bounce Boogie; Liberty; Route 66; I'm an Old Cowhand from the Rio Grande; House of Blue Lights; Choo Choo Ch' Boogie
Asleep at the Wheel (with Wade Hayes, Tracy Byrd, Charlie Daniels, Delbert McClinton, Willie Nelson): Ida Red
Wade Hayes: Old Enough to Know Better
Tracy Byrd: Roly Poly
Charlie Daniels: Texas
Delbert McClinton: Lipstick, Powder and Paint
Willie Nelson: Still Water Runs (the) Deepest

B.B. KING
Let the Good Times Roll; Stormy Monday; Five Long Years; Playin' with My Friends; Moanin' Song; Night Life; A Whole Lot of Lovin'; Why I Sing the Blues; Rock Me, Baby; The Thrill Is Gone

PAM TILLIS / GUITAR PULL WITH WILLIE NELSON, MERLE HAGGARD, IRIS DeMENT, AND FREDDIE POWERS
Pam Tillis: Mi Vida Loca; Mandolin Rain; Tequila Mockingbird; You Can't Have a Good Time without Me; River and the Highway; Deep Down
Guitar Pull: Merle Haggard: Sin City Blues; Today I Started Loving You Again
Willie Nelson: Spirit; Waiting Forever for You
Freddie Powers: Tom Sawyer and Huckleberry Finn; The Drummer in Me
Iris DeMent: Sweet Is the Melody; Hobo Bill

LEE ROY PARNELL / A.J. CROCE
Lee Roy Parnell: A Little Bit of You; The House Is Rockin'; When a Woman Loves a Man; Milk Cow Blues; I'm Holding My Own; On the Road
A.J. Croce: Sign on the Line; How'd We Get So Good at Saying Good-Bye; That's Me in the Bar; He's Got a Way with Women; She's Waiting for Me; The Stuff You Got to Watch

THE ALLMAN BROTHERS BAND
Sailin' 'Cross the Devil's Sea; Ain't Wastin' Time No More; Ramblin' Man; Midnight Rider; Same Thing; Blue Sky; Back Where It All Begins; One Way Out

CLASSIC: ROGER MILLER / MARTY ROBBINS
Roger Miller: Me and Bobby McGee; Dang Me; Medley: You Can't Rollerskate in a Buffalo Herd/Chug-a-Lug; England Swings; Husbands and Wives; King of the Road; I Can't Go On This Way; Invitation to the Blues; Old Friends; Milk Cow Blues
Marty Robbins: Big Iron; Laredo; Buenos Dias Argentina; I Washed My Hands in Muddy Water; My Woman, My Woman, My Wife; You Gave Me a Mountain; All-Around Cowboy; El Paso

LISA LOEB / JIMMY LaFAVE
Lisa Loeb: Do You Sleep; Garden of Delights; Hurricane; Waiting for Wednesday; Furious Rose; Stay (I Missed You); Taffy
Jimmy LaFave: Buffalo Return to the Plains; When It Starts to Rain; Walk Away Renee; Sweetheart; This Land Is Your Land

LOS LOBOS / JOE ELY
Los Lobos: Kiko and the Lavender Moon; Manny's Bones; Just a Man; Maricela; This Bird's Gonna Fly; Mas y Mas
Joe Ely: Boxcars; Gallo De Cielo; Run, Preciosa; Letter to Laredo

FAITH HILL / TRISHA YEARWOOD
Faith Hill: Someone Else's Dream; It Matters to Me; Do Right Woman, Do Right Man; Wild One; I Can't Do That Anymore; Take Me As I Am; Let's Go to Vegas
Trisha Yearwood: XXX's & OOO's; You Can Sleep While I Drive; That's What I Like About You; The Song Remembers When; Wrong Side of Memphis; On a Bus to St. Cloud; You Don't Have to Move That Mountain

GATEMOUTH BROWN / KEB' MO'
Gatemouth Brown: Born in Louisiana; Early in the Morning; Honky-Tonk; Up Jumped the Devil
John D. Loudermilk: Tobacco Road
Gatemouth Brown (with John D. Loudermilk): Abilene
Keb' Mo': Victims of Comfort; Dirty Low Down and Bad; Tell Everybody I Know; Every Morning; Am I Wrong?; City Boy

SAGEBRUSH SYMPHONY
Orchestra (with J. Hanna): Backward Turn Backward
Michael Martin Murphey: Cowboy Logic; The Old Chisholm Trail; Red River Valley; Back in the Saddle Again
Herb Jeffries: I'm a Happy Cowboy
Sons of the San Joaquin: Medley: Tumbling Tumbleweeds/Cool Water; Timber Trail
Michael Martin Murphey: San Antonio Rose; Riders in the Sky; Wildfire; Happy Trails
Robert Mirabal: Chief Seattle Speech
Hank Thompson: Oklahoma Hills
Robert Mirabal and Michael Martin Murphey: Geronimo's Cadillac
Orchestra: Storms on the Prairie

SEASON 22 (1997)

WYNONNA
Somebody to Love; To Be Loved by You; What It Takes; Change the World; Rock Bottom; Only Love; Live with Jesus; Had a Dream; Mama He's Crazy; Give a Little Love; Grandpa; Girls with Guitars; No One Else on Earth

SONGWRITERS' SPECIAL

Kris Kristofferson: The Fighter; Sam's Song; Here Comes That Rainbow Again
Waylon Jennings: Out of Jail; I Do Believe; I Can Get Off on You
Willie Nelson (with Kris Kristofferson): We Don't Run
Kimmie Rhodes (with Willie Nelson): Just One Love
Billy Joe Shaver: You Just Can't Beat Jesus Christ; Live Forever
Willie Nelson: Sittin' Here in Limbo; I'm Not Trying to Forget You (Anymore)
Kimmie Rhodes (with Waylon Jennings): Lines
Willie Nelson (with Waylon Jennings, Kris Kristofferson, Billy Joe Shaver, Kimmie Rhodes): On the Road Again

CLASSIC: BLUEGRASS TRIBUTE TO BILL MONROE

Bill Monroe: Muleskinner Blues; Blue Moon of Kentucky; Bluegrass Breakdown; Uncle Pen; Good-Bye Old Pal; Kentucky Mandolin; My Sweet Blue-Eyed Darlin'; In the Pines; The Panhandle Country; The Old Crossroads; Medley: John Henry/Y'all Come; Watermelon on the Vine; The Old Brown County Barn
Bill Monroe (with Jim and Jesse): I'm on My Way Back to the Old Home
Bill Monroe (with Mac Wiseman): Travelin' This Lonesome Road
Bill Monroe (with Ralph Stanley): Can't You Hear Me Calling?
Bill Monroe (with Jim and Jesse, Ralph Stanley, Mac Wiseman): Medley: Swing Low Sweet Chariot/I'll Fly Away/I Saw the Light

A TRIBUTE TO WALTER HYATT

Uncle Walt's Band: Keep on Working
David Ball and Champ Hood: Going to New Orleans
Willis Alan Ramsey: Lonely in Love; As the Crow Flies
Jimmie Dale Gilmore: Georgia Rose
Marcia Ball: Are We There Yet Mama?
David Halley: Motor City Man
Walter Hyatt: King Tears; This Time, Lucille; In November
David Ball: Houston Town
Allison Moorer: Tell Me Baby
Junior Brown: Diggeroo
Lyle Lovett (with Shawn Colvin): Babes in the Woods
Lyle Lovett: I'll Come Knockin'
Lyle Lovett (with Shawn Colvin, Junior Brown, Jimmie Dale Gilmore, Willis Alan Ramsey, Marcia Ball, David Halley, Allison Moorer, David Ball, and Champ Hood): Aloha

"BEST OF AUSTIN" COUNTRY SHOWCASE

Libbi Bosworth: East Texas Pines; Don't Call Me Crazy
Libbi Bosworth and Dale Watson: After the Fire Is Gone
Dale Watson: Truckin' Man; Hair of the Dog
The Derailers: Jackpot; Lies, Lies, Lies; Just One More Time
Wayne Hancock: Thunderstorms and Neon Signs; Juke Joint Jumpin'
Mary Cutrufello: Johnson Motel; Love's to Blame
Don Walser: The Party Don't Start Till the Playboys Get Here; Country Gold; Rollin' Stone from Texas

MARY CHAPIN CARPENTER / BR5-49

Mary Chapin Carpenter: Keeper for Every Flame; Naked to the Eye; The End of My Pirate Days; Sudden Gift of Fate; Better to Dream of You; What if We Went to Italy; I Want to Be Your Girlfriend
BR5-49: I Ain't Never; Hometown Boogie; Little Ramona; Even If It's Wrong; My Name Is Mudd; Knoxville Girl; Gone, Gone, Gone

TRAVIS TRITT / WADE HAYES

Travis Tritt: The Restless Kind; More Than You'll Ever Know; Back Up Against the Wall; Tell Me I Was Dreaming; She's Going Home with Me; Anymore
Wade Hayes: Old Enough to Know Better; I'm Still Dancin' with You; On a Good Night; Medley: Tulare Dust/Tonight the Bottle Let Me Down; It's Over My Head; Don't Stop; This Is the Life for Me

ERIC JOHNSON / KENNY WAYNE SHEPHERD

Eric Johnson: Righteous; Rock Me Baby; Camel's Night Out; S R V; Cliffs of Dover; Zap
Kenny Wayne Shepherd: Ledbetter Heights; Born with a Broken Heart; Deja Voodoo; Down to Bone

LYLE LOVETT AND HIS LARGE BAND

Promises; That's Right (You're Not from Texas); Fiona; Don't Touch My Hat; Private Conversation; Who Loves You Better; Her First Mistake; I Can't Love You Anymore; It Ought to Be Easier; The Road to Ensenada; The Girl in the Corner

SON VOLT / GILLIAN WELCH AND DAVID RAWLINGS

Son Volt: Straightaways; Cemetery Savior; Tear-Stained Eye; Windfall; Ten-Second News; Loose String; Drown
Gillian Welch and David Rawlings: Tear My Stillhouse Down; Barroom Girls; Pass You By; Annabelle; Acony Bell; Caleb Meyer; Orphan Girl

ROBERT EARL KEEN / JACK INGRAM

Robert Earl Keen: Shades of Gray; Amarillo Highway; The Coming of the Son and Brother; Then Came Lo Mein; Undone; Over the Waterfall
Jack Ingram: That's Not Me; Ghost of a Man; Picture on My Wall; I Can't Leave You; Big Time; Beat Up Ford; Flutter

SHERYL CROW

Every Day Is a Winding Road
Sheryl Crow (with Shawn Colvin): Hard to Make a Stand
Sheryl Crow: Leaving Las Vegas; A Change; Run, Baby, Run; If It Makes You Happy; Redemption Day; Strong Enough; Sweet Rosalyn; I Shall Believe

BLUES NIGHT WITH DELBERT McCLINTON AND MISS LAVELLE WHITE

Delbert McClinton: Old Weakness; Monkey Around; Sending Me Angels; Leap of Faith
Delbert McClinton (with Lyle Lovett and Lee Roy Parnell): Too Much Stuff
Delbert McClinton: Somebody to Love You; Every Time I Roll the Dice
Miss Lavelle White: Voodoo Man; Mississippi, My Home; Wootie Boogie; Go to the Mirror; I Never Found a Man

SEASON 23 (1998)

JUNIOR BROWN / ROBBIE FULKS

Junior Brown: Broke Down South of Dallas; A Long Walk (Back to San Antone); Freeborn Man; My Wife Thinks You're Dead; I Hung It Up; I Want to Hear It from You; Walk, Don't Run
Robbie Fulks: She Took a Lot of Pills (and Died); Every Kind of Music But Country; Love Ain't Nothing; The Buck Starts Here; Let's Kill Saturday Night; Barely Human; Let's Live Together; Cigarette State

PATTY LOVELESS / COLLIN RAYE

Patty Loveless: Tear-Stained Letter; Here I Am; You Don't Seem to Miss Me; You Can Feel Bad; Lonely Too Long; Blame It on Your Heart; I Try to Think About Elvis
Collin Raye: That's My Story; Dreamin' Dreams with You; What If Jesus Comes Back Like That; Heart Full of Rain; And I Love You So; Fortunate Son; Love Me

MARCIA BALL, IRMA THOMAS, AND TRACY NELSON

Marcia Ball, Irma Thomas, and Tracy Nelson: Sing It; I Want to Do Everything for You; In Tears; Woman on the Move; People Will Be People; If I Know You; Shouldn't I Love Him; Lovemaker; Don't Mess with My Man; Yield Not to Temptation
Marcia Ball and Tracy Nelson: Heart to Heart
Irma Thomas and Tracy Nelson: You Don't Know Nothin' About Love

THE MANHATTAN TRANSFER WITH SPECIAL GUESTS RICKY SKAGGS AND ASLEEP AT THE WHEEL

Manhattan Transfer: Moten's Swing; Sing a Study in Brown; Route 66; I Know Why and So Do You; King Porter Stomp; Blee Blop Blues; Aren't You Glad You're You; Tuxedo Junction
Manhattan Transfer (with Asleep at the Wheel): A-Tisket, A-Tasket; Java Jive
Manhattan Transfer (with Ricky Skaggs): Air Mail Special; Uncle Pen
Manhattan Transfer (with Asleep at the Wheel and Ricky Skaggs): Choo Choo Ch' Boogie

THE INDIGO GIRLS WITH SPECIAL GUESTS VONDA SHEPARD, FREEDY JOHNSTON AND MARK EITZEL / KIM RICHEY

Indigo Girls: Shame on You; Get Out the Map
Freedy Johnston: Bad Reputation
Vonda Shepard: Baby Don't Break My Heart Slow
Mark Eitzel: Why Don't You Leave My Sister Alone?
Kim Richey: I Know; Fallin'; I'm Alright; Don't Let Me Down Easy; Those Words We Said; That's Exactly What I Mean

LORETTA LYNN

Hey, Loretta; Thank God I'm a Country Girl; When the Tingle Becomes a Chill; They Don't Make 'Em Like My Daddy (Anymore); You're Lookin' at Country; Love Is the Foundation; You Ain't Woman Enough; Your Squaw is on the Warpath; Here I Am Again; Don't Come Home a-Drinkin'; Somebody Somewhere; Medley: One's on the Way/The Pill; Message from Jesus; Medley: Walkin' After Midnight/I Fall to Pieces; Naked in the Rain; Long Way Baby; How Great Thou Art; Coal Miner's Daughter

NANCI GRIFFITH WITH THE CRICKETS

Nanci Griffith: Everything's Comin' Up Roses; These Days; Gulf Coast Highway; This Heart; Darcy Farrow
Nanci Griffith (with The Crickets): Do You Wanna Be Loved?; I Fought the Law
The Crickets: The Real Buddy Holly Story; Peggy Sue; That'll Be the Day
Nanci Griffith (with The Crickets): Rave On; Walk Right Back; Not My Way Home; The Morning Train; Well All Right; This Heart

HAL KETCHUM / TERRY ALLEN

Hal Ketchum: The Unforgiven; Awaiting Redemption; Tell Me; I Miss My Mary; For Tonight; The Way She Loves Me
Terry Allen: Amarillo Highway; The Great Joe Bob; The Beautiful Waitress; New Delhi Freight Train; Gone to Texas; Gimme a Ride to Heaven, Boy

CELEBRATION OF TOWNES VAN ZANDT

Guy Clark: To Live Is to Fly; Don't You Take It Too Bad
Peter Rowan: No Lonesome Tune
Steve Earle: Fort Worth Blues

Nanci Griffith: Tecumseh Valley
John T. Van Zandt: Highway Kind
Willie Nelson and Emmylou Harris: Pancho & Lefty
Emmylou Harris: If I Needed You
Rodney Crowell: Heavenly Houseboat Blues
Lyle Lovett: Lungs
Jack Clement: For the Sake of the Song
Guy Clark (with Emmylou Harris, Willie Nelson, Lyle Lovett, Nanci Griffith, Steve Earle, Rodney Crowell, Peter Rowan, Jack Clement and John T. Van Zandt): White Freight Liner Blues

BOZ SCAGGS / 8½ SOUVENIRS
Boz Scaggs: T-Bone Shuffle; It All Went Down the Drain; Lowdown; High Sierra; Runnin' Blues
8½ Souvenirs: Kazango; Souvonica; Off-White; Shut the Door; Wet and Dry; After You've Gone; Happy Feet; No Lo Visto

OLD 97'S / WHISKEYTOWN
Old 97's: Barrier Reef; West Texas Teardrops; Salome; Big Brown Eyes; The House That Used to Be; Streets of Where I'm From
Whiskeytown: Sixteen Days; Everything I Do; Dancing with the Women at the Bar; Houses on the Hill; Yesterday's News; Battle

CLAY WALKER / TRACE ADKINS
Clay Walker: Who Needs You Baby?; If I Could Make a Livin'; Hypnotize the Moon; Dreamin' with My Eyes Wide Open; Then What!; This Woman and This Man; The Hardest Thing; What's It to You!
Trace Adkins: Big Time; Girl in Texas; Lonely Won't Leave Me Alone; The Rest of Mine; I Left Something Turned on at Home; Every Light in the House; This Ain't No Thinkin' Thing

BUDDY GUY / STORYVILLE
Buddy Guy: Come See About Me; It Feels Like Rain; I Got a Problem; Goin' Down
Storyville: Good Day for the Blues; Don't Make Me Suffer; Two People; Wings Won't Let Me Fly

SEASON 24 (1999)

DEANA CARTER WITH SPECIAL GUEST MATRACA BERG
Deana Carter: You Still Shake Me; Angels Workin' Overtime; Absence of Heart; The Train Song; Brand New Key; We Danced Anyway; Did I Shave My Legs For This?
Deana Carter (with Matraca Berg): Ruby Brown; Dickson County; Strawberry Wine

Deana Carter (with Fred Carter): Everything's Gonna Be All Right

DIXIE CHICKS / CHARLIE ROBISON
Dixie Chicks: There's Your Trouble; Loving Arms; Love Me Like a Man; Roanoke; Wide Open Spaces; I Can Love You Better; Give It Up or Let Me Go
Charlie Robison: My Hometown; Arms of Love; Sunset Boulevard; You're Not the Best; Barlight

RUTH BROWN / LIONEL HAMPTON AND HIS ORCHESTRA
Ruth Brown: That Train Don't Stop Here Anymore; 5-10-15 Hours (of Your Love); Love Letters; If I Can't Sell It (I'll Keep Sittin' On It); Mama, He Treats Your Daughter Mean
Lionel Hampton: Hamp's Boogie Woogie; Soul Serenade; When I Fall in Love; Flying Home

BILLY BRAGG SINGS WOODY GUTHRIE / LUCINDA WILLIAMS
Billy Bragg: Way Over Yonder in the Minor Key; Walt Whitman's Niece; I Guess I Planted; Christ for President; Ingrid Bergman; My Flying Saucer
Lucinda Williams: Can't Let Go; Greenville; Still I Long for Your Kiss; Jackson; Joy

VINCE GILL / MARTINA McBRIDE
Vince Gill: One More Last Chance; If You Ever Have Forever in Mind; I'll Take Texas; Kindly Keep It Country; The Key to Life; I Will Always Love You; One Dance with You
Martina McBride: Happy Girl; Wild Angels; Wrong Again; Valentine; A Broken Wing; Independence Day

RAY PRICE / HANK THOMPSON WITH JUNIOR BROWN
Ray Price: San Antonio Rose; Medley: Crazy Arms/ Heartaches by the Number; Faded Love; Night Life; Crazy; For the Good Times; Mansion on the Hill
Ray Price (with Junior Brown): The Other Woman
Hank Thompson: Oklahoma Hills; Humpty Dumpty Heart; Blackboard of My Heart; Green Light; Wild Side of Life; The Older the Violin, the Sweeter the Music; I'll Still Be Here Tomorrow; Six Pack to Go
Hank Thompson (with Junior Brown): Sell Them Chickens

JONNY LANG / JIMMIE VAUGHAN
Jonny Lang: Still Rainin'; A Quitter Never Wins; I Am; Breakin' Me; Lie to Me
Jimmie Vaughan: Out There; I Like It Like That; Can't

Say No; Like a King; Sweet Soul Vibe

MEXICAN ROOTS MUSIC: A CELEBRATION
Los Super Seven (with Flaco Jimenez, Freddy Fender, Cesar Rosas, David Hidalgo, Ruben Ramos, Rick Treviño, Joe Ely): Canoero; Rio De Tenampa; Gallo De Cielo
Ruben Ramos: La Morena
Flaco Jimenez: Margarita; Un Beso al Viento
Freddy Fender: Un Lunes Por La Manana; Piensa En Mi
Rick Treviño Jr. (with Rick Treviño Sr.): Mi Ranchito
Campanas de America: Tita
Tish Hinojosa: Esperate

FASTBALL / MARY CUTRUFELLO
Fastball: Fire Escape; Which Way to the Top?; Out of My Head; The Way; Slow Drag; Are You Ready for the Fallout?; She Comes Round
Mary Cutrufello: Miss You No. 3; Goodnight Dark Angel; Sad, Sad World; Stupid Girl; Highway 59; Sunny Day

DAVE ALVIN / LOUDON WAINWRIGHT III
Dave Alvin: King of California; Border Radio; Dry River Blues; Out in California; Blackjack David; Marie, Marie
Loudon Wainwright III: Livin' Alone; Homeless; Tonya's Twirls; OGM; Bein' a Dad; A Father and a Son; Rufus Was (Is) a Tit Man

BRUCE HORNSBY / MONTE MONTGOMERY
Bruce Hornsby: Great Divide; King of the Hill; The End of the Innocence; Sugaree
Monte Montgomery: 1st and Repair; Set Your Soul Free; All I Can Do; When Will I; Sounds Too Wonderful

HOOTIE & THE BLOWFISH WITH NANCI GRIFFITH
Hootie & the Blowfish: Wishing; Time; Desert Mountain Showdown; Michelle Post; Let Her Cry; Hold My Hand; Only Lonely; Only Wanna be with You
Hootie & the Blowfish with Nanci Griffith: Gulf Coast Highway; Gravity of the Situation; Las Vegas Nights; The Earth Stopped Cold at Dawn

BOBBY BLUE BLAND / SUSAN TEDESCHI
Bobby Blue Bland: That's the Way Love Is; Further On Up the Road; I Pity the Fool; Soon as the Weather Breaks; Love of Mine; Share Your Love with Me; Get Your Money Where You Spend Your Time; 24 Hours a Day
Susan Tedeschi: Rock Me Right; Just Won't Burn; You Need to be with Me; It Hurt So Bad; Angel from Montgomery

INDEX

Acuff, Roy, 42
Adams, Al, 154
Adkins, Trace, 188
Alabama, 66, 71, 178
Albert, Christine, 121, 186
Allen, Terry, 107, 130, 181, 188
Allman, Greg, 49
Allman Brothers Band, 16, 43, 44, 49, 55, 187
Alvin, Dave, 105, 189
Amazing Rhythm Aces, 176
American Bandstand, 29
Amram, David, 161
Anderson, John, 179, 180, 186
Antone, Clifford, 25
Archenhold, Mike, 34, 35, 165, 169
Arhos, Bill, 5, 9, 10, 11, 15, 26-27, 34, 35, 44
Armadillo World Headquarters, 8, 22, 27, 90
Armstrong, Louis, 50
Arnold, Kristine, 127
Ashlock, Jesse, 37
Asleep at the Wheel, 10, 16, 17, 25, 29, 36, 37, 39, 40, 42, 43, 44, 59, 69, 78, 121, 161, 176, 177, 178, 182, 183, 185, 187, 188
Atkins, Chet, 9, 37, 42, 63, 67, 68, 69, 78, 142, 150, 177, 179, 182, 185, 186
Austin, Texas, 20-25
Austin City Limits, 5, 8-9, 10-11, 20
   a day in the life of, 164-171
   frequently asked questions about, 172-174
   history of, 12-17
   legends of, 46-57
   lone stars of, 122-131
   original stage of, 27
   rising stars of, 132-141
   singer-songwriters of, 100-109
   timeline for, 36-44
   unlimited, 26-35
Austin City Limits (University of Texas Press), 26
Axton, Hoyt, 178
Ayala, Ramon, 98

Bad Livers, 74
Badu, Erykah, 121, 126
Baez, Joan, 23, 50, 55, 186
Bailey, Edward, 35
Bailey, Razzy, 179
Balcones Fault, 161, 176
Ball, David, 17, 158, 159, 187, 188
Ball, Marcia, 16, 25, 40, 110, 117, 121, 142, 176, 177, 182, 184, 188
Bandy, Janet, 5
Bandy, Moe, 178, 183
Bare, Bobby, 177, 178
Barton, Lou Ann, 24, 90, 121, 184
Basie, Count, 46
Batson, Paula, 99
Baugh, Phil, 177
Beatles, 22, 23, 43

Beausoleil, 142, 146, 184
Beck, Roscoe, 142
Bell, Vince, 129
Bellamy Brothers, 179, 183
Benson, Ray, 25, 29, 39, 69
Berg, Matraca, 189
Berline, Byron, 17, 177
Bernstein, Leonard, 161
Berry, Chuck, 23, 47
"Best of Austin" Country Showcase, 188
Beto y Los Fairlanes, 153, 178
Betts, Dicky, 49
Bishop, Gary, 5
Bland, Bobby Blue, 42, 83, 90, 189
Blank, Les, 95
Block, Rory, 89, 186
Blondell, Jon, 24
Bluegrass, 12, 74
Bluegrass Special, 186
Blues, 80-91
Bogguss, Suzy, 42, 186
Bone, Ponty, 151, 182
Bosner, Paul, 5, 8-9, 15, 26, 69
Bowie, David, 132
Bowser, Erbie, 24
Bosworth, Libbi, 188
BR5-49, 140, 188
Bradford, Carmen, 121
Bragg, Billy, 55, 142, 148, 189
Brammer, Billy Lee, 21
Bresh, Thom, 182, 183
Bridger, Bobby, 161, 176, 177
Brody, Lane, 183
Brooks, Garth, 9, 16, 41, 42, 44, 66, 97, 105, 134, 135, 141, 175, 184
Brown, Clarence "Gatemouth," 16, 38, 81, 83, 90, 176, 177, 178, 187
Brown, Junior, 16, 43, 62, 63, 69, 123, 159, 186, 188, 189
Brown, Milton, 46, 126
Brown, Ruth, 55, 84, 117, 189
Brown, Sawyer, 181
Bruce, Ed, 179
Bruton, Stephen, 127
Buchanan, Roy, 41, 55, 158, 177
Buffalo, Norton, 135, 177
Buffett, Jimmy, 37, 132, 133, 176, 180
Bufwak, Mary A., 110
Bullock, Sandra, 99
Burns, Kenneth "Jethro," 38, 41, 74, 78, 161
Bush, Sam, 77, 154
Butthole Surfers, 25
Byrd, Tracy, 59, 78, 187
Byrds, 103, 127

Cajun music, 122
Caldwell, Susan, 34, 35, 114, 165, 166, 169, 171
Callari, Frank, 169, 170
Calvert, Craig, 10
Campbell, Glen, 28, 52, 181
Campi, Ray, 180
Canales, Laura, 121
Carey, Mariah, 110

Carlson, Paulette, 184
Carlton, Larry, 182
Carpenter, Mary Chapin, 16, 17, 31, 42, 100, 101, 110, 116, 175, 184, 185, 186, 188
Carrasco, Joe "King," 179
Carson, Johnny, 60
Carson, Kit, 185
Carter, Anita, 44, 184
Carter, A.P., 46
Carter, Carlene, 43, 113, 186
Carter, Deana, 69, 117, 135, 189
Carter, Helen, 44, 184
Carter, June, 40, 130, 182
Carter, Maybelle, 46, 110
Carter, Sara, 46
Carter Family, 40, 44, 182
Cash, Johnny, 16, 38, 40, 42, 43, 48, 55, 69, 86, 130, 182
Cash, Rosanne, 16, 17, 34, 38, 40, 43, 109, 113, 114, 180, 182, 183, 185, 186
Cashdollar, Cindy, 121
Caswell, Bill, 179
Cate Brothers, 177
Chalmers, Howard, 5, 26
Charles, Ray, 9, 10, 22, 26, 38, 39, 40, 50, 54, 55, 56, 58, 62, 178, 180
Chenier, C.J., 130, 142, 145
Chenier, Cleveland, 42
Chenier, Clifton, 36, 40, 50, 130, 142, 145, 161, 178
Chesnutt, Mark, 59, 187
Christian, Charlie, 90, 126
Chulas Fronteras, 95
Clapton, Eric, 48, 53, 84
Clark, Guy, 17, 107, 125, 129, 160, 176, 179, 184, 188
Clark, Roy, 38, 40, 83, 178
Clark, Susanna, 160
Clark, W.C., 24, 41, 44, 128, 184
Clement, Jack, 160, 188
Clements, Vassar, 17, 177, 184
Clinch Mountain Boys, 74, 178
Cline, Patsy, 46, 66, 108, 113
Cochran, Hank, 108, 178, 179
Cockburn, Bruce, 185
Coe, David Allen, 180
Cohen, Leonard, 15, 32, 33, 38, 41, 100, 155, 184, 186
Cohn, Mark, 185
Coleman, Keith, 37
Coleman, Ornette, 126
Collie, Mark, 184
Collins, Albert, 16, 42, 55, 82, 90, 126, 185
Collins Sisters, 180
Colter, Jessi, 37, 130
Colvin, Kay, 114
Colvin, Shawn, 16, 17, 23, 32, 42, 44, 105, 106, 114, 121, 140, 142, 158, 159, 185, 187, 188
Conjunto music, 92-99
Conlee, John, 180
Conley, Earl Thomas, 180, 181
Cooder, Ry, 10, 38, 96, 176
Cook, Joe, 34, 35, 54, 167
Cooper, Dana, 178

Corporation for Public Broadcasting, 8
Cosgrove, Pat, 35
Cotten, Elizabeth, 17, 39, 40, 81, 177
"Country Legends," 180
Country music, 58-79
Country Music Association, 31
Cowboy Junkies, 16, 115, 184
Cramer, Floyd, 44, 180
Cray, Robert, 84, 91, 185
Crenshaw, Marshall, 41
Crickets, 183, 188
Croce, A.J., 187
Crow, Alvin, 161, 176, 177
Crow, Sheryl, 13, 16, 43, 44, 104, 142, 188
Crowell, Rodney, 11, 17, 37, 38, 43, 59, 60, 107, 160, 179, 183, 188
Cullen, Sharon, 35
Cutrufello, Mary, 16, 110, 112, 188, 189

Dalhart, Vernon, 62
Dalton, Lacy J., 17, 40, 109, 135, 178, 182
Daniels, Charlie, 43, 176, 178, 183, 187
David Grisman Quintet, 37
Davies, Gail, 17, 40, 109, 178, 180, 182
Davis, John T., 5-6, 78, 99, 120, 136, 169
Davis, Miles, 46
Davis, Quint, 85
Dean, Jimmy, 28, 186
Dell, Michael, 20
Del Santo, Dan, 177
Dement, Iris, 186, 187
Denim, 176
Denver, John, 41, 44, 47, 175
Derailers, 188
Desert Rose Band, 183
Diamond Rio, 186
DiFranco, Ani, 110
The Dillards, 177
Dirty Dozen Brass Band, 142, 144, 186
Dixie Chicks, 9, 16, 41, 44, 69, 117, 121, 130, 189
Dixie Diesels, 23, 105
Domino, Fats, 9, 40, 85, 142, 182
Donahue, Tom, 43
Don Kirschner's Rock Concert, 29
Double Trouble, 25
Doucet, Michael, 146
Douglas, Jerry, 154
Dunn, Holly, 121, 183, 185
Dylan, Bob, 42, 101, 132, 160
Earle, Steve, 16, 17, 21, 58, 160, 182, 188
Eberhard, David, 5
Eddy, Duane, 41
Edwards, Don, 185
8 1/2 Souvenirs, 152, 188
Eitzel, Mark, 188
Ellington, Duke, 46
Ely, Joe, 23, 38, 59, 60, 98, 99, 123, 124, 126, 130, 178,

181, 185, 187, 189
Embry, Al, 85
Emery, Michael, 34, 35, 165, 169
Emery, Ralph, 60
Emilio, 99
emmajoe's, 23
Endres, Clifford, 26
Erickson, Roky, 21
Erwin, Emily, 41, 130
Estefan, Gloria, 92
Ewing, Skip, 184
Exile, 181

Fabulous Thunderbirds, 16, 25, 40, 44, 90, 139, 140, 182
Facemire, Glenda, 35
Farrar, Jay, 73
Fastball, 16, 25, 120, 128, 137, 189
Faulkner, William, 25
Fender, Freddy, 20, 36, 43, 93, 95, 97, 98, 99, 187, 189
Ferguson, Keith, 44
Fernandez, Vincente, 98
Fiebre, 98
Firefall, 176
Fitzgerald, Ella, 43, 46, 62, 90
Flatlanders, 124
Fleck, Bela, 74, 77, 154, 185
Fleming, Kye, 183
Flores, Rosie, 99, 120, 121, 183
Fogerty, John, 41
Foley, Red, 28
Foose, John, 85
Forbert, Steve, 186
Ford, Tennessee Ernie, 28
Forester Sisters, 183
Forte, Dan, 36
Foster and Lloyd, 183, 185
Foster, Radney, 186
Fountain, Pete, 142, 146, 179
Franklin, Aretha, 44, 117
Fraser, Randie, 35
Freeman, Denny, 184
Fricke, Janie, 178, 180
Frizzell, Lefty, 62, 108
Frizzell and West, 180
Fromholz, Steven, 10, 22, 23, 25, 107, 176, 177, 182
Fuentes, Ed, 35, 168
Fulks, Robbie, 69, 188
Furgeson, Joe Frank, 44

Galton, Danny, 38
Garza, Ricardo, 35
Gatlin, Larry, 177, 179, 181, 183
Gatton, Danny, 43, 47, 55, 158, 185
The Gay Place, 21
The Geezinslaws, 60, 179, 181, 183
George, Lowell, 149
Ghost, Grey, 24
Gibbs, Terri, 179
Gilkyson, Eliza, 121, 180
Gill, Janice, 127
Gill, Vince, 9, 31, 32, 34, 38, 42, 66, 134, 181, 185, 186, 189
Gilley, Mickey, 25, 58, 179
Gilmore, Jimmie Dale, 17, 21, 22-

23, 124, 128, 158, 159, 179, 183, 185, 188
Gimble, Johnny, 16, 37, 38, 42, 43, 78, 130, 146, 150, 161, 177, 182, 185, 186
Ginn, Bill, 142
Glaser, Tompall, 37
Godfrey, Arthur, 60
Gold, Julie, 42, 116, 185
Gonzalez, Freddie, 98
Goodman, Benny, 90
Goodman, Dan, 99
Goodman, Steve, 17, 34, 39, 55, 177, 181
Gordon, Robert, 38
Gorka, John, 186
Gosdin, Vern, 181
Gracey, Joe, 5, 26, 69, 161
Gray, Mark, 181
Great Plains, 186
Greenwood, Lee, 180
Greezy Wheels, 25, 161, 176, 182
Griffith, Nanci, 9, 11, 16, 17, 21, 23, 40, 42, 44, 107, 115, 116,
120, 121, 128, 129, 135, 136, 138, 147, 160, 181, 183, 185, 186, 188, 189
Grisman, David, 37, 38, 78, 161, 178
"Groover's Paradise," 21
Guerra, Carlos, 5
Guitar Pull, 187
Guthrie, Woody, 142, 148
Guy, Buddy, 53, 55, 185, 188

Haggard, Merle, 9, 13, 16, 17, 37, 56, 69, 74, 78, 79, 108, 109, 177, 179, 180, 181, 185, 186, 187
Hall, Tom T., 177
Halley, David, 179, 188
Hammond, John, 87, 185
Hampton, Lionel, 16, 142, 154, 189
Hancock, Butch, 105, 124, 179
Hancock, Wayne, 188
Hanna, Jeff, 77, 187
Hardesty, Herbert, 85
Hargrove, Linda, 177
Hargrove, Roy, 126
Harris, Emmylou, 9, 17, 20, 30, 37, 40, 66, 109, 120, 137, 160, 179, 182, 183, 185, 188
Harris, Gene, 35
Harris, Joe, 141
Hartford, John, 177
Harvey, Alex, 177
Hayes, Wade, 43, 187, 188
Hee-Haw, 28, 40, 66
Hendrix, Jimi, 63
Henley, Don, 167
Hernandez, Little Joe, 24
Hernandez, Nash, 24
Hester, Carolyn, 121
Hiatt, John, 102, 184, 186
Hickman, Sara, 116, 121, 184
Hicks, Dan, 42, 148, 185
Hidalgo, David, 94, 98, 99, 189
Highway 101, 182
Hill, Faith, 69, 72, 187
Hill, Lauryn, 44, 110, 117
Hillis, Craig, 5
Hinojosa, Tish, 94, 98, 99, 121,

184, 186, 188
Hole in the Wall, 120
Holiday, Billie, 46, 90, 110
Holly, Buddy, 22, 31, 41, 47, 105, 126
Holmes, Johnny, 22
Holmes, Vance, 35, 165
Homer and Jethro, 161
Hood, Barbara, 4
Hood, Champ, 158, 159, 188
Hootie & the Blowfish, 17, 154, 189
Hope, Bob, 29
Hopeful Gospel Quartet, 42, 150, 186
Hopkins, Lightnin', 15, 38, 39, 82, 177
Hornsby, Bruce, 6, 43, 100, 142, 164-169, 171, 186, 189
Horton, Johnny, 62
Hot Band, 37, 120
Hot Licks, 42, 148, 185
Hot Rize, 182
Hough, David, 31, 35, 166, 168
House, Son, 84
Houston, Sam, 122
Houston, Whitney, 121
Howard, Harlan, 106, 183
Huerta, Baldemar, 95
Hunley, Con, 135, 180
Hyatt, Walter, 11, 17, 36, 43, 158, 159, 161, 184, 187, 188

Ida, Queen, 110, 151, 182
Idlet, Chris (Ezra), 10
Indigo Girls, 17, 42, 116, 134, 185, 188
Ingram, Jack, 188
Inman, John, 25
Introcable, 98

Jaceldo, Caesar, 169
Jackson, Alan, 15, 16, 29, 66, 184, 186
Jackson, Janet, 121
Jaime y los Chamacos, 98
James, Elmore, 23
Jazzmanian Devil, 179
Jefferson, Blind Lemon, 88, 126
Jeffries, Herb, 187
Jennings, Waylon, 16, 17, 20, 22, 31, 37, 44, 107, 130, 181, 184, 187
Jim and Jesse, 182, 187
Jimenez, Don Santiago, 96
Jimenez, Flaco, 15, 16, 20, 41, 43, 92, 95, 96, 97, 98, 99, 130, 161, 176, 178, 187, 189
Jimenez, Santiago, 16, 96, 99, 130, 151, 182
Joe Ely Band, 130
John, Dr., 42, 142, 143, 185
Johnson, Clifton "Sleepy," 37
Johnson, Eric, 16, 25, 40, 138, 181, 184, 188
Johnson, Robert, 46, 84
Johnston, Freedy, 188
Jones, George, 16, 38, 55, 59, 61, 69, 73, 78, 178, 181, 184
Joplin, Janis, 22, 90, 121
Joplin, Scott, 126
Jordan, Esteban, 95, 99, 178
Jordan, Stanley, 50, 55, 183
Judds, 9, 39, 72, 130, 181

Keb' Mo', 16, 132, 134, 187
Keen, Robert Earl, 16, 69, 107, 128, 130, 137, 138, 183, 187, 188
Keillor, Garrison, 42, 78, 142, 150, 186
Keller, Van, 5
The Kendalls, 180
Kennedy, Mary Ann (Kennedy-Rose), 109, 182, 184
Kerouac, Jack, 161
Kershaw, Doug, 147, 178
Ketchum, Hal, 16, 42, 64, 185, 186, 188
Keillough & Eckley, 177
Killough, Rock, 108, 177
King, Albert, 42, 90
King, B.B., 9, 16, 39, 40, 41, 55, 80, 86, 90, 180, 187
King, Freddie, 90
King, Martin Luther, Jr., 143
King, Pee Wee, 180
Kiwi, 176
KLRU-TV, 5, 8
KLRU-TV's Studio 6-A, 13
Kottke, Leo, 149, 179, 183, 185
Krauss, Alison, 16, 33, 37, 39, 42, 74, 75, 110, 140, 185, 187
Kristofferson, Kris, 17, 38, 44, 52, 79, 107, 127, 179, 187
Kuipers, Dave, 35
KUTH, 10
Kymmel, Augie, 26-27

La Beef, Sleepy, 180
La Diferenzia, 43, 97, 187
LaFave, Jimmy, 12, 105, 187
Lane, Red, 108, 178, 179
Lang, Jonny, 16, 33, 38, 84, 89, 189
lang, k.d., 16, 36, 140, 183
Las Campanas de America, 98, 99
Lawrence, Tracy, 186
Leadbelly, 88
Lee, Brenda, 23, 182
Lee, Johnny, 179
Lehmusvirta, Linda, 35
Le Roi Brothers, 180
Lennon, John, 91
Lester, Lazy, 24
Lewis, Jerry Lee, 9, 39, 47, 49, 55, 58, 85, 117, 180
Leyendas y Raices, 98
Lickona, Terry, 10, 11, 34, 35, 38, 42, 46, 54, 56, 61, 66, 76, 79,
82, 85, 86, 96, 108, 117, 136, 141, 150, 154, 155, 158, 160, 164, 166, 167, 168, 169, 171, 175
Lilith Fair Festivals, 117
Lipscomb, Mance, 88
Little Feat, 149, 185
Little Joe y la Familia, 93, 98, 99, 178
Little Richard, 23, 47
Livingston, Bob, 25
Loeb, Lisa, 118, 121, 140, 187
"London Homesick Blues," 8, 9, 171, 176, 182, 183
Longoria, Valerio, 96
Los Lobos, 37, 39, 40, 41, 94, 98, 99, 184, 187
Los Super Seven, 97
Los Terribles del Norte, 98

Lost Gonzo Band, 25, 122, 173, 176, 177, 182
Loudermilk, John D., 187
Love, Courtney, 110
Loveless, Patty, 69, 73, 183, 186, 188
Lovett, Lyle, 9, 10-11, 17, 23, 34, 40, 42, 43, 91, 107, 128, 129,
158, 159, 160, 182, 184, 185, 187, 188
Lowe, Jim, 88
Lucero, Ray, 35
Lynch, Laura, 41
Lynn, Barbara, 121
Lynn, Loretta, 13, 16, 38, 39, 41, 50, 69, 71, 113, 116, 180, 188
Lynne, Shelby, 184

Macy, Robin Lynn, 41
Madonna, 121
Maines, Lloyd, 123, 130, 131
Maines, Natalie, 44, 130, 131
Maines Brothers Band, 130, 131, 181
Mandolin Special, 161, 178
Mandrell, Barbara, 121
Mandrell, Louise, 121, 181
Manhattan Transfer, 16, 17, 42, 44, 153, 161, 188
Manilow, Barry, 47
Maphis, Joe, 40, 180
Marcus, Greil, 84
Marley, Bob, 50
Martaus, Dan, 35
Martin, Dean, 50
Martin, Jimmy, 77, 184
Martin, Ray, 77
Martinez, Narciso, 96
Massey, Will T., 135, 185
Masters of Bluegrass, 185
Mattea, Kathy, 40, 44, 65, 182, 184, 186
Mavericks, 16, 29, 96, 140, 187
Mayall, John, 9, 90, 186
McAuliffe, Leon, 41, 69, 76
McBride, Laura Lee, 121
McBride, Martina, 64, 189
McBride and the Ride, 135, 184
McClain, Charly, 179
McClinton, Delbert, 16, 41, 91, 127, 176, 177, 180, 183, 186, 187, 188
McCoy, Chas., 177
McDaniel, Mel, 181
McEntire, Reba, 16, 40, 41, 55, 59, 64, 66, 121, 183
McEuen, John, 17, 75, 177
McGraw, Tim, 72
McGuinn, Roger, 103
McLachlan, Sarah, 117
McLean, Don, 41, 103, 179
McMurty, James, 184
Meador, Steve, 142
Mendoza, Lydia, 96, 117, 121
Menotti, Gary, 10, 11, 34, 35, 165-169, 171
Mexican Roots Music Celebration, 17, 98, 99, 189
Meyer, Edgar, 154
Meyers, Augie, 20, 97, 99
Michelangelo, 100
Midnight Special, 29
Miller, Bob, 187

Miller, Roger, 39, 42, 56, 70, 78, 180
Miller, Steve, 90
Miller, Wayne, 10
Milsap, Ronnie, 73, 182
Mims, Connie, 10
Mirabel, Robert, 187
Mitchell, Joni, 110, 117
Mitchell, Waddie, 185
Moffatt, Katy, 121
Monroe, Bill, 12, 15, 17, 33, 38, 43, 44, 50, 74, 75, 86, 178, 182, 187
Montgomery, John Michael, 186
Montgomery, Monte, 138, 189
Moore, Abra, 25
Moore, Tiny, 38, 40, 78, 161
Moorer, Allison, 16, 17, 140, 159
Moorhead, Robert, 35, 165, 169
Morgan, Emily, 122
Morgan, George, 71
Morgan, Lorrie, 71, 140, 184
Morisette, Alanis, 117
Morris, Gary, 180, 181, 184
Morris, Rebekah K., 4
Morthland, John, 23
Mother of Pearl, 177
Muir, Allan, 5
Mullican, Moon, 126
Muppets, 43, 187
Murphey, Michael Martin, 10, 24, 42, 43, 107, 122, 125, 156, 161, 177, 179, 180, 182, 184, 185
Musical Brownies, 46
Myers, Billy Lee, Jr., 31, 35
Mystery Train, 84

The Nashville Network, 29
"Nashville Sound," 9
"Nashville Super Pickers," 177
Nava, Joel, 43, 97, 187
Navaira, Emilio, 99
Nelson, Tracy, 25, 117, 176, 182, 188
Nelson, Willie, 8-9, 10, 11, 16, 17, 20, 23, 26, 27, 29, 30, 36, 37, 38, 39, 40, 42, 43, 44, 56, 57, 58, 62, 69, 76, 78, 107, 108, 109, 121, 137, 160, 176, 177, 178, 179, 180, 181, 187, 188
Nesmith, Michael, 185
Neville, Aaron, 44, 143
Neville Brothers, 10, 15, 20, 38, 55, 130, 134, 142, 143, 177, 181, 186
New Grass Revival, 77, 180, 183, 184
Newton, Juice, 181
Newton, Scott, 6, 24, 27, 30, 34, 35, 47, 49, 53, 55, 56, 61, 84, 86, 88, 89, 90, 101, 102, 122, 124, 128, 138, 140, 155, 158, 164
"A Nitty Gritty Christmas," 44
Nitty Gritty Dirt Band, 15, 41, 44, 75, 77, 176, 181, 183
Nunn, Gary P., 9, 10, 22, 25, 37, 43, 122, 173, 180, 182, 183, 187

Oak Ridge Boys, 70, 181
O'Connell, Chris, 121
O'Connell, Maura, 185

O'Connor, Mark, 154
O'Daniel, W. Lee "Pappy," 126
O'Kanes, 182
Oermann, Robert K., 110
Olden, Walter, 35, 165
Old 97's, 16, 69, 188
Olney, Dan, 179
Omar and the Howlers, 87, 182
One Knite, 23
Orbison, Roy, 9, 15, 39, 40, 41, 46, 55, 85, 105, 179
Original Texas Playboys, 13, 15, 17, 37, 40, 69, 76, 78
Orozco, Rick, 43, 97, 187
Oslin, K.T., 68, 183, 185
Ostermayer, Paul, 142
Ostroushko, Peter, 182
Owens, Buck, 15, 28, 40, 41, 43, 44, 55, 66, 183
Ozark Jubilee, 28
Ozuna, Sunny, 24, 98

Panhandle Mystery Band, 130
Pankey, Todd, 35, 165, 169
Park, Sung, 165, 166, 167, 168
Parker, Charlie, 46
Parker, Junior, 90
Parnell, Lee Roy, 91, 126, 186, 187
Parton, Dolly, 117, 121
Passenger, 38, 142, 179
Patoski, Joe Nick, 22
Paycheck, Johnny, 68, 178
Payne, Jody, 8
PBS, 8-9
Perez, Selena Quintanilla, 43, 92, 121
Perez, Tony, 183
Perkins, Carl, 15, 23, 38, 40, 44, 47, 85, 178
Peterson, Dick, 27, 35
Peterson, Jeff, 35, 165-169, 171
Phillips, "Little Esther," 121
Phillips, Sam, 50
Pierce, Jo Carol, 20
Powers, Freddie, 109, 180, 181, 187
A Prairie Home Companion, 150
Presley, Elvis, 23, 37, 46, 47, 50
Price, Ray, 22, 33, 62, 63, 66, 69, 178, 189
Price, Richard, 166
Pride, Charley, 72, 179
Prine, John, 10, 17, 101, 177, 179, 181, 183, 185, 187
"Progressive country," 9
Pure Prairie League, 9, 38, 66, 140, 177

Rabbitt, Eddie, 44, 181
Raitt, Bonnie, 16, 32, 39, 41, 110, 112, 127, 127, 180
Ramey, Gene, 24
Ramirez, Augustin, 98
Ramos, Ruben, 24, 98, 99, 189
Ramsey, Willis Alan, 10, 129, 159, 177, 188
Ranger Doug, 73
Rank and File, 180
Raven, Eddy, 181
Rawlings, David, 140, 188
Ray, Amy, 116
Ray, Paul, 90
Raye, Collin, 188
Redbone, Leon, 177

Red Hot Louisiana Band, 36
"Redneck Rockers," 8
Reed, Jerry, 68, 179
Reid, Mike, 183, 185
Reinhardt, Django, 20, 58, 152
Restless Heart, 182
Rhodes, Kimmie, 187
Richard, Zachary, 142, 144, 186
Richey, Kim, 188
Riders in the Sky, 42, 73, 178, 182, 185
Riot Grrrls, 110
Robb, Doug, 35, 169
Robbins, H., 177
Robbins, Marty, 15, 38, 39, 55, 68, 178
Roberts, Jason, 43
Robey, Don, 90
Robison, Charlie, 130, 189
Rockin' Sidney, 181
Rodgers, Jimmie, 58, 105
Rodman, Judy, 182
Rodriguez, Johnny, 99, 177, 178, 180
Rogers, Kenny, 37
Rogers, Mary Beth, 35
Rolling Stone, 24, 142
Rolling Stone Encyclopedia of Rock & Roll, 80
Rosas, Cesar, 94, 99, 189
Rose, Pam, 109, 182
Rowan, Peter, 160, 188
Royal, Darrell K., 9, 108
Russell, Leon, 40, 49, 182
Russell, Shake, 178

Sagebrush Symphony, 43, 156, 187
Sahm, Doug, 20, 21, 24, 43, 97, 176
Saliers, Emily, 116
"Salute to the Cowboy," 185
Sanders, Don, 129
Santa Ana, General, 122
Sawyer Brown, 39
Scafe, Bruce, 5, 8, 26
Scaggs, Boz, 84, 90, 188
Schlitz, Don, 183
Schneider, John, 181
Schuyler, Knoblock and Bickhardt, 183
Scruggs, Earl, 37, 74, 75, 176
Scruggs, Randy, 184
Seidel, Martie, 41, 130
Selby, Bob, 35, 165, 166
Selena Quintanilla Perez, 43, 92, 121
Sessions at West 54th, 29
Setzer, Brian, 41
Sex Pistols, 25
Sexton, Dusty, 35, 169
Shafer, Whitey, 108, 178, 179, 181
Shamblin, Eldon, 44
Shaver, Billy Joe, 178, 179, 181, 187
Shaw, Robert, 24, 40, 177
Shenandoah, 184
Shepard, Vonda, 140, 188
Shepherd, Kenny Wayne, 16, 33, 37, 135, 188
Sheppard, T.G., 179
Shines, Johnny, 84
Shocked, Michelle, 118, 121, 184

Sinatra, Frank, 46, 63
Sir Douglas Quintet, 24, 179
Skaggs, Ricky, 17, 37, 43, 44, 74, 161, 179, 181, 183, 186, 188
Skiles, Robert "Dude," 153
Slaughter, Marion Try, 62
Slim, Memphis, 90
Smith, Darden, 183, 186
Snider, Todd, 187
Songwriters' Specials, 17, 38, 56, 108-109, 178, 179, 182, 183, 185, 186, 187
Sons of the Pioneers, 180
Son Volt, 69, 73, 140, 188
Soul Train, 29
Soundstage, 29
South by Southwest Music and Media Conference (SXSW), 25
Southern Pacific, 181
Sparks, Larry, 43, 186
Spivey, Victoria, 121
Squeezebox Special, 182
Stampley, Joe, 178
Stanley, Ralph, 43, 74, 75, 178, 182, 186
Stehli, Angela, 184
Steinbeck, John, 127
Stevenson, B. W., 8, 26, 41, 107, 176
Stewart, Gary, 178
Stewart, Redd, 63
Stone, Doug, 185
Stone, Sly, 90
Storyteller series, 29
Storyville, 140, 188
Strachwitz, Chris, 95
Strait, George, 14, 16, 23, 39, 42, 58, 59, 97, 140, 180, 182, 183
Strehli, Angela, 24, 90, 121
Streisand, Barbra, 121
Strength in Numbers, 154, 184
Strickland, Al, 40
Stuart, Marty, 28, 37, 75, 182, 184
Sturr, Jimmy, 44
Subdudes, 139, 140, 185
Sun, Joe, 178
Sweethearts of the Rodeo, 127, 130, 182, 184
SXSW (South by Southwest Music and Media Conference), 25
Sykes, Keith, 179
Sylvia, 181

Taj Mahal, 10, 38, 186
Taylor, Eric, 129
Taylor, Jesse, 130
Teagarden, Jack, 126
Tedeschi, Susan, 16, 89, 117, 189
Tejano music, 92-99
Tejano Music Special, 187
Texas Playboys, 13, 15, 17, 37, 44, 69, 161
Texas Showcase, 183
Texas Tornados, 20, 24, 92, 96, 97, 99, 184
Tex-Mex, 20
Thirteenth Floor Elevators, 21
Thomas, B.J., 180
Thomas, Irma, 117, 142, 188
Thompson, Butch, 182

Thompson, Hank, 38, 62, 64, 178, 179, 189
Thornton, Big Mama, 50, 90, 121
Thorogood, George, 151, 179
Threadgill, Kenneth, 22
Throckmorton, Sonny, 108, 178, 179
Tillis, Mel, 38, 65, 126, 130, 178, 181
Tillis, Pam, 126, 130, 185, 187
Tillman, Floyd, 62, 69, 78, 108, 178, 179
Timbuk 3, 25, 120, 137, 140, 184
Timmons, Margo, 115
Tolleson, Mike, 5, 8
Tompall and the Glaser Brothers, 179
Too Slim, 73
Travis, Merle, 20, 39, 67, 69, 177
Travis, Randy, 40, 67, 182
Travolta, John, 25
Treviño, Lee, 28, 97, 98, 99, 137, 187
Treviño, Rick, 16, 187, 189
Triple Threat Review, 24
Tritt, Travis, 42, 67, 185, 188
Tubb, Ernest, 15, 39, 62, 63, 177
Tucker, Tanya, 110, 121, 181
Twain, Mark, 46, 55
Twain, Shania, 110, 117
Two Jaws, 73
Tyson, Tiffany, 35

Uncle Tupelo, 73
Uncle Walt's Band, 129, 158, 159, 178, 187
Union Station, 75
University of Texas, 5
Unplugged, 29
Urban Cowboy, 25

Valentine, Kathy, 121
Van Shelton, Ricky, 183, 184
Van Zandt, John T., 160, 188
Van Zandt, Townes, 10, 11, 15, 17, 36, 37, 44, 59, 80, 107, 129, 160, 161, 176, 179, 188
Vaughan, Charles, 5
Vaughan, Jimmie, 16, 24, 41, 42, 53, 88, 90, 128, 130, 139, 186, 189
Vaughan, Sarah, 90
Vaughan, Stevie Ray, 12, 15, 16, 20, 22, 23, 24, 25, 39, 41, 43, 48, 53, 55, 88, 90, 130, 155, 158, 175, 184
Vaughn, Kenny, 170
Vee, Bobby, 41
Vega, Suzanne, 43, 119, 186
VH-1 divas, 110
Vulcan Gas Company, 22

Wagoneers, 183
Wainwright, Loudon, III, 102, 183, 189
Waits, Tom, 10, 15, 38, 40, 142, 147, 177
Walker, Cindy, 121
Walker, Clay, 59, 188
Walker, Jerry Jeff, 8, 10, 16, 21, 25, 38, 40, 105, 106, 107, 122, 161, 173, 176, 178, 182, 183

Walker, T-Bone, 90
Wallace, Sippie, 121
Walser, Don, 43, 134, 188
Ward, Ed, 24
Warden, Monte, 186
Wariner, Steve, 134, 180, 182, 184
Waters, Muddy, 46
Watkins, Mitch, 142
Watson, Dale, 188
Watson, Doc, 10, 40, 74, 177
Watson, Gene, 183
Watson, Merle, 40
Welch, Gillian, 16, 140
Wells, Jack, 35
Wells, Kevin, 185
Wells, Kitty, 113, 180
West, Dottie, 42, 66, 180
Wewer, Jimmy, 35
Wheatfield, 10, 176
Whiskeytown, 16, 69, 74, 140, 188
Whites, 180, 183
White, Miss Lavelle, 188
White, Tony Joe, 178
Whitley, Keith, 41, 55, 64, 184
Wier, Rusty, 24, 161, 176, 182
Williams, Don, 65, 178, 179
Williams, Hank, 22, 23, 46, 100
Williams, Hank, Jr., 38, 65, 178
Williams, Linda, 150
Williams, Lucinda, 6, 23, 117, 119, 121, 164-166, 169-171, 184, 185, 189
Williams, Robin, 34, 150
Willis, Kelly, 16, 121, 184, 186
Wills, Bob, 13, 15, 17, 31, 36, 37, 40, 44, 46, 50, 59, 69, 76, 78, 126, 177, 181
"Will the Circle Be Unbroken," 184
Wilson, Cassandra, 117
Wilson, Kim, 24, 139, 184
Wilson, Ron, 82
Wilson, Teddy, 90, 126
Winchester, Jesse, 177
Winter, Johnny, 90
Winthrop, John, 80
Wiseman, Mac, 182, 187
Wolf, Kate, 40, 55, 121
Women in song, 110-121
Women Songwriters' Special, 109, 185
Woody Paul, 73
Wright, Johnny, 180
Wright, Mark, 183
Wright, Stephanie, 35
Wynette, Tammy, 14, 15, 39, 44, 50, 66, 113, 180, 181, 187
Wynonna, 110, 111, 121, 187

Ybarra, Eva, 121
Yearwood, Trisha, 16, 42, 69, 137, 185, 187
Yoakam, Dwight, 15, 16, 41, 51, 96, 120, 134, 182, 183
Young, Faron, 43, 180
Young, Neil, 40, 43, 53, 55, 101, 160, 181

Zuniga, Miles, 137
Zydeco, 122

B.W. Stevenson • Bobby Bridger • Wheatfield • Balcones Fault • Marcia Ball / Greezy Wheels • The Charlie Daniels Ba
Revue • Jimmy Buffett / Rusty Wier • Gatemouth Brown / Delbert McClinton • Firefall / Denim • Guy Clark / Steve Fromho
John Prine • Bob Wills' Original Texas Playboys / Ernest Tubb and the Texas Troubadors • Chet Atkins / Merle Travis • Do
t the Wheel / Bobby Bridger • Vassar Clements / Gatemouth Brown • Merle Haggard and The Strangers • Killough & Eckle
Dan Del Santo / Taj Mahal • The Neville Brothers / Robert Shaw / Lightnin' Hopkins • Nashville Super Pickers / Tom T. Hall •
Marcia Ball • Hoyt Axton • Little Joe y La Familia / Esteban Jordan • Doug Kershaw / Clifton Chenier • Roy Clark and G
Don Gant, Rock Killough, Sonny Throckmorton, and Whitey Shafer • Ray Charles and His Orchestra • Ralph Stanley and The
Texas Swing Pioneers • Johnny Paycheck / Billy Joe Shaver • Flaco Jimenez / Beto y Los Fairlanes • Moe Bandy and Joe Sta
• George Jones with Hank Thompson • Ray Price and The Cherokee Cowboys / Asleep at the Wheel • Johnny Rodriguez /
Bluegrass Boys / Riders in the Sky • Tony Joe White / Gary Stewart • Songwriters' Encore with Willie Nelson, Floyd Tillman, I
Murphey / Ed Bruce • Leo Kottke / Passenger • Joe "King" Carrasco / The Sir Douglas Quintet • Emmylou Harris / Rodn
Haggard and The Strangers • The Bellamy Brothers / John Anderson • Larry Gatlin / Ricky Skaggs • Tompall and the Glaser
Thorogood and the Destroyers / Dave Olney and the X-Rays • Mickey Gilley / T.G. Sheppard • Don Williams / West Texas S
Showcase with Rodney Crowell, John Prine, Billy Joe Shaver, Guy Clark, Keith Sykes, Rosanne Cash, and Bill Caswell • B.B. Kin
Rank and File / Delbert McClinton • Tammy Wynette / John Conlee • Roger Miller / Earl Thomas Conley • Loretta Lynn • R
• The Whites / New Grass Revival • Jimmy Buffett • Johnny Rodriguez / David Allen Coe • Dottie West / Floyd Cramer • Bo
Country Legends • Stevie Ray Vaughan and Double Trouble / The Fabulous Thunderbirds • Oak Ridge Boys / Bob Willis' Orig
Billy Joe Shaver • Eddie Rabbitt / Tammy Wynette • Ricky Skaggs / The Judds • Glen Campbell / Eddy Raven • Joe El
Powers with Willie Nelson and Merle Haggard / Whitey Shafer • Earl Thomas Conley / Vince Gill • Gary Morris / Sylvia •
Merle Haggard and The Strangers with special guest Freddie Powers • Rockin' Sidney / The Neville Brothers • Roger McGu
The Virginia Boys, Mac Wiseman, Ralph Stanley and The Clinch Mountain Boys, Bill Monroe and The Bluegrass Boys • Son
Limits Reunion Special with Steve Fromholz, Asleep At the Wheel, Tracy Nelson, St. Greezy's Wheel, Marcia Ball, Rusty W
Sweethearts of the Rodeo • Leon Russell / Steve Earle • Fats Domino • Chet Atkins & Friends with Larry Carlton, Thom Bre
Carter Family • Squeezebox Special with Queen Ida, Santiago Jimenez Jr., and Ponty Bone • The Fabulous Thunderbirds / C
O'Kanes / Highway 101 • The Forester Sisters / Thom Bresh and Lane Brody • Rosanne Cash / Desert Rose Band • Reba M
& Lloyd • Jerry Jeff Walker / Loudon Wainwright III • Leo Kottke / Schuyler, Knoblock and Bickhardt • Ricky Van Shelton /
/ The Wagoneers • George Strait • K.T. Oslin / Rodney Crowell • The Charlie Daniels Band / Gary P. Nunn • Stanley Jor
Loveless • Songwriter's Special with Harlan Howard, Don Schlitz, Mike Reid & Others • Buck Owens / The Geezinslaws • T
Ewing • Timbuk 3 / Eric Johnson • John Hiatt and The Goners / Los Lobos • George Jones / Carl Perkins • Marcia Ball / I
Vaughan & Double Trouble / W.C. Clark Blues Revue with Stevie Ray Vaughan, Jimmie Vaughan, Kim Wilson, Lou Ann Barton,
Band, John Denver, Randy Scruggs and The Core Pickers, The Carter Sisters, New Grass Revival, Michael Martin Murphey, P
Lucinda Williams / Guy Clark • Garth Brooks / Shenandoah • James McMurtry / Sweethearts of the Rodeo • Lorrie Morgar
/ Mark Collie • Cowboy Junkies / Walter Hyatt • Texas Tornados / McBride and the Ride • Merle Haggard / Masters of Bluegra
• Little Feat • Joe Ely / Foster and Lloyd • "A Salute to the Cowboy" with Michael Martin Murphey, Riders in the Sky, Wadd
Julie Gold • Los Lobos / C.J. Chenier • Dan Hicks and the Hot Licks Revisited plus the Acoustic Warriors • Vince Gill / Alis
and the Flecktones • Trisha Yearwood / Hal Ketchum • Rosanne Cash with special guests Bruce Cockburn and Lucinda W
Emmylou Harris and the Nash Ramblers • Marc Cohn / Leo Kottke • Asleep at the Wheel / Riders in the Sky • Pam Tillis /
Keillor and the Hopeful Gospel Quartet with Chet Atkins and Johnny Gimble • Tracy Lawrence / Suzy Bogguss • Kathy Matt
Willis • Zachary Richard / Dirty Dozen Brass Band • Bruce Hornsby / John Mayall and the Bluesbreakers • John Anderso
Nelson, Lyle Lovett, and Rodney Crowell • Joan Baez / Rory Block • Diamond Rio / John Michael Montgomery • Suzanne
Gill / Junior Brown • Nanci Griffith / Iris DeMent • Bluegrass Special with Ricky Skaggs, Ralph Stanley, and Larry Sparks
Music Special with Freddy Fender, Flaco Jiminez, La Diferenzia, Rick Orozco, and Joel Nava • Tammy Wynette / Rick Trevino
Stevie Ray Vaughan: A Retrospective • Lyle Lovett and His Large Band • Alison Krauss and Union Station / Merle Haggard a
Tracy Byrd, Wade Hayes, Delbert McClinton, and Charlie Daniels • B.B. King • Pam Tillis / Guitar Pull with Willie Nelson, Merle
• Lisa Loeb / Jimmy LaFave • Los Lobos / Joe Ely • Faith Hill / Trisha Yearwood • Gatemouth Brown / Keb' Mo' • "Sagebru
Nelson, Waylon Jennings, Kris Kristofferson, Kimmie Rhodes, and Billy Joe Shaver • Bluegrass Tribute to Bill Monroe • A Tr
Junior Brown, David Halley and Allison Moorer • "Best of Austin" Country Showcase with Libbi Bosworth, Dale Watson, The
Johnson / Kenny Wayne Shepherd • Lyle Lovett and His Large Band • Son Volt / Gillian Welch and David Rawlings • Robert
Patty Loveless / Collin Raye • Marcia Ball, Irma Thomas, and Tracy Nelson • The Manhattan Transfer with special guests Rick
• Loretta Lynn • Nanci Griffith with the Crickets • Hal Ketchum / Terry Allen • Celebration of Townes Van Zandt with Guy
8½ Souvenirs • Old 97's / Whiskeytown • Clay Walker / Trace Adkins • Buddy Guy / Storyville • Deana Carter with spec
Guthrie / Lucinda Williams • Vince Gill! / Martina McBride • Ray Price / Hank Thompson with Junior Brown • Jonny Lang
Tish Hinojosa, Joe Ely, and Campanas de America • Fastball / Mary Cutrufello • Dave Alvin / Loudon Wainwright III • Bru